MW00790846

Josephine McCallum

~ *too soon forgotten* ~

Gordon Galloway

DEERFIELD PUBLISHING
1994

Also by Gordon Galloway

SCARS OF A SOLDIER
HILLBILLY POET
THE BULLDOG
RIVERS CHANGING

Library of Congress Catalog Card Number: 2004090088
Copyright © 2004 by Gordon Galloway
All rights reserved
Printed in
The United States of America
Published by Deerfield Publishing Inc.
1613 130th Avenue
Morley, MI 49336
ISBN 0-9644077-4-4

JACKSON PRISON

Southern Michigan Prison in the 80's.

John Penrod photo.

Table of Contents

The Rest of the Story

Books by Gordon Galloway
with a 2003 Update to Each Story

FORWARD

GORDON GALLOWAY

I have had a great deal of official documentation and background information to write this book, however, considering all the people involved in this story, I was surprised at how few there were that were willing to discuss the subject matter. I had the distinct impression I was creating muddy waters. I can accept however, the fact that the female corrections officer I interviewed refused to be named or have her story published. I do commend her for helping me understand what a female corrections officer had to deal with in those days.

It was very difficult for Michael McCallum to rake up all the past. He still hasn't fully reconciled his mother's death. I do appreciate that he opened the door for all of us to better understand what he went through.

Hopefully after this book is published there will be others that are willing to bring their stories forward. We will continue to listen.

Throughout this story the reader may detect statements that contradict the observations of others. It is human nature for people to observe events and remember them differently. In most cases I didn't feel these differences significantly altered the story, but I thought it was important to include them just the same.

For the last 5 years I have done my best to put this story back together. I do hope it gives some peace of mind to Bill and Mike McCallum.

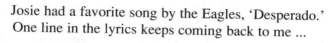

Josie had a favorite song by the Eagles, 'Desperado.'
One line in the lyrics keeps coming back to me ...

"your prison is walking this world all alone."

From Bill McCallum

J suspect that at one time or another most everyone, with a few idle moments to spare, reflect back on the substance of their life. For most, a quick inventory of accomplishments or property would bring forth enough warm fuzzies of fulfillment to make ones existence seem worthwhile. I chuckle to myself; Old Bill McCallum will have to think up something else for gratification.

Financially I'm really on shaky ground; no job, barely able to keep up with the house payments, and overweight and old enough not to be on anyone's short list for employment.

Accomplishments? Hmm… none that would rate first or second page news in any paper.

No, I'm not despondent, nor am I optimistic. Guess I'm just a sailboat in the sea with neither breeze nor storm to move me on. The experts say I have AAD. That's the acronym for adult attention deficiency. It seems to fit and may explain why for most of my life I've been the rolling stone that gathers no moss. And, now that the stone has stopped rolling, I feel vulnerable and exposed to the stream of life flowing over me.

Deep thoughts that yield little fruit, Ha.

There are two people that do make life significant for me. They are like giant pillars that are always exposed and what happens in their lives becomes an integral part of mine.

My mother is in her nineties now. She had been living alone, in her home until she broke her hip. Even though she made an excellent recovery, Ma stays in an assisted living unit now. She is a very determined, independent lady that is very set in her ways and quite hard of hearing.

Michael my son is 25 now. He aspires to be involved with the movies and is pursuing a filmmaking career. I also think he is a fine actor judging from the community plays in which he's had parts. I know that field may be difficult for him to succeed in. Hopefully he inherited his grandmother's determination, or better yet his mothers.

Mike certainly looks like his mother. When I look at him I think of her, and that brings back warm thoughts, then sadness and many times anger. It has been 16 years and that mix of emotions is still there: probably always will be. Mike and I don't talk about her. I think it would be better if we did, at least for me. For him the hurt is buried very deep. Warm and sensitive, he is a son any father could be proud of and the apple of his grandmother's eye. To his mother, Josephine, he was a treasure.

Josephine was the other pillar in my life, the one that's missing. She was only there a short time, but her influence was so profound. With her there was finally meaningful love and purpose in my life. I savor my memories of her. "Why couldn't it have lasted longer?" I ask myself. And what, if anything, could I have done differently to keep her from harms way? Of course, I always have some guilt feelings too, for not providing her with everything she deserved. Far too often, we realize that life can end unexpectedly, and leave us with so many things undone.

Newspaper headlines scream at us on a daily basis; Murder, Rape, Robbery, Corruption. The follow up article summarizes what we need to know about this headline; at least what the reporter thinks we need to know, or what they think we care about knowing. Sometimes, they refrain from telling things that may not sit well with people in power, even when those details are pretty easy to ferret out.

For myself, for Michael, but mostly for Josephine, we need to tell the story behind the headlines.

McCALLUM THE REBEL

It seems that all the ingredients needed were there. From a healthy young boy to a responsible, successful adult an easy path it should have been. I certainly did travel down a more devious road though. Probably a shrink, could direct lots of blame; an over controlling mother, a laid back father, the early onset of an attention disorder. Who knows, all the culprits that might have driven me in the wrong direction? I prefer to summarize it like this. Whatever challenged me and gave me satisfaction became my goal. Popularity was the icing on the cake.

First off, I have had one great love affair that has spanned my existence. That has been my attraction to automobiles. It started when my dad took me over to Uncle Don Bonifas' garage. My uncle and another man by the name of Whitey Davis had a body shop in Lansing. Uncle Don had a great talent for restoring wrecked cars and in his possession was a 1937 Hollywood Graham. This was an absolutely gorgeous car. It was a white, four-door convertible with the wheels and bumpers looking like they had been plated with gold. We took a ride around the town and I was smitten with its beauty. That was the first milestone in my life. As we tell this story you will discover many more auto-markers. My life is full of them.

Mother came from a well-to-do family. I guess I shouldn't really imply that they were rich, it's just that her folks, William and Selma Noffke, had a large farm on Saginaw Highway near Grand

Ledge. They sailed through the depression with few problems. Most everyone else I knew really had a rough time during those years.

As a young lady my mother drove her own car to Kalamazoo to attend college and was talented enough to also actually teach some art classes. Remember now, this was the late 20's. Very few women drove cars, let alone all the way to Kalamazoo. She was a determined and very directed young lady.

My father graduated from Syracuse as a chemical engineer and was working at Parson's Chemical Works when I was born. Later that company gained the reputation as one of the state's worst polluters. I think that there were a lot of other things in my father's background that I never found out about. Apparently when the depression hit he was running a flower shop in Detroit. He had no experience in flowers and just walked away from the business when hard times hit. Before that, he said something about running a speedboat back and forth from Canada hauling "cocktails" in to supplement his income. He must have been hauling alcohol in during prohibition. Dad was pretty closed mouth about a lot of things.

My mother was a secretary at Michigan Miller's Insurance in Lansing when Dad met her. He was in his late 40's and she her late 20's, so there was quite an age difference. In those days when women married they usually settled into being a housewife. I'm not sure my mother wanted to end her successful independent life style, but my father was quite insistent. When I came along six years later, it became clear that her status in the future would be judged by my achievements. My mother and father were very intelligent people and from all indications that mating had produced quite a bright child. My mother was determined to mold me into a person that would forever yield her self-satisfaction, an eternal shining star in her life.

My musical potential became evident when I was very young. At 6 years of age I was playing Chopin by memory. While the other kids were outdoors having fun, I was practicing on the piano; three hours a day. My classical music teacher was Vera Brown Lewis.

Mother envisioned another Liberace in me. She even had a little white suit for me to wear during the many recitals. Eventually I even had some training in jazz from Bob Sargent, a very well known popular musician. Ma sent me to school looking like little Lord Fauntleroy; sweaters, dressy slacks and big horn-rimmed glasses. To carry my books I had this leather case with a strap. I was the only child in our family so mother could concentrate on my upbringing. Through grade school I could probably have been classified by the community as a model child. That started to change in junior high. It's not that my classmates made fun of my straight-laced appearance, but rather, I could see that other kids were having lots of fun doing things that I wasn't doing. I felt left out and wanted to be a part of this fun even if it wasn't in my mother's plan. I started gradually working my way into the mainstream.

First to gain some social acceptance, I changed my eating habits. The wholesome lunches my mother sent along I ate on the way to school. I couldn't waste them; her words, "Think of the starving people in Europe" stuck in my mind. Then at lunchtime I scarfed down potato chips and pop like the other kids. My mother didn't allow soft drinks and junk food at home. Anyway, the change in my diet put me on the road to having a weight problem.

A real rift between my mother and I occurred over Zipper, a miniature Toy Manchester that Dad had given me as a surprise. I really loved that dog. I walked him, kept him clean, all the things I was supposed to do however, after only a few months I came home from school and found him gone. My mother said that a lonely old man had come to the door and she felt so sorry for him, so she gave him the dog. I was really ticked off. In later years I found out that the dog went to the humane society.

The pressure to become another Liberace on the piano let up when through testing in junior high my mother discovered my musical talent could be applied to the clarinet and saxophone. As a member of the band I could expand my social horizons while pursuing my excellence in academics. In other words keep nice and busy.

What really gave me satisfaction was that I soon discovered that I could say and do things, which would make other kids, laugh. And through little comical successes, I was becoming addicted to the attention. The class clown glove fit perfectly.

The first warning sign that caught my mother's eye was the day I came home from high school wearing a tan barracuda jacket. James Dean had gained popularity and the tan jacket was the rage at school. Dean played the hood roles and obviously I was in a gang, or so she thought. Mother started calling the school periodically to see how I was doing, if I was in any trouble. The teachers and principal probably wondered why she was calling. Thus far I hadn't been a problem. That would change however, and McCallum would soon be the new buzzword for trouble.

Although I wasn't old enough to have a car yet, I was learning plenty about them in my spare time. I would ride my bike down to Rod McLean's garage and watch what was going on. It was a fun place to be.

Rod McLean is a one-of-a-kind type person. Some people only see the gruff side of his personality, but I know the man inside of that crusty exterior. I think he could sense that I was hanging around because I was really interested in automobiles. For that reason he allowed me to stay. Rod was an expert mechanic. I focused my intellect, absorbing what he told me like a sponge and through those observations I gained a basic knowledge of auto mechanics.

As I understand it, Rod McLean was on his way to becoming an all-American college football player when some type of accident or sickness left him paralyzed from the waist down. Most people would probably have said, "To hell with it and gave up, but Rod became as good a mechanic as he had been a football player. He was one of the first very well known NASCAR mechanics. Lee Petty, Richard Petty's father was one of his clients. All the name drivers of that time knew Rod.

Rod McLean is one of the most avid University of Michigan football fans that I have ever known. His little garage is not far from the capitol building in Lansing. On the outside it says "The best damn garage in town." On the inside everything is maize and blue, the University colors. He has lots of pennants on his wall and many mementos of games and many references to the famous coach Bo Shembechler. He even named his dog Bo.

Rod used to push himself around the garage on a half office chair. Watching him was like observing a famous maestro at work. The handicap of not being able to use his legs was just not a significant part of the picture.

At West Junior High School I played some football. We were city champions that year. As a freshman at Sexton I made the second string team, however my clowning around was getting me days off from school more and more often. Football went by the wayside so that I could concentrate on my band activities. My talents with the clarinet and saxophone put me into first chair, and into trouble.

The only problem with band, was that the music director, Duane Corbett, didn't seem to appreciate my clowning around. Consequently he soon became my target. I don't remember exactly how it came into my possession, but I had the most realistic looking plastic dog shit that you have ever seen. The logical place to put it seemed to be right where Mr. Corbett stood during practices. He was kind of a prim and proper individual, so the sight of this pile didn't make him happy. Though the band was all boys, the orchestra was mixed. He asked the girls to leave the room. After the door closed behind the last one Old Duane said, "I'll tell you what. You cussed animals. Whoever did this should be shot! Whoever did this, clean it up. Now I'll leave the room and nothing more will be said."

Of course I'm setting there with a red face about ready to explode with laughter. My buddies were kinda glancing in my direction and it was rather obvious who the guilty party was. Not one to let a prime opportunity slip by I went to the front of the room, picked up my shit masterpiece and slipped it into my pocket. Everybody roared. It was a few days before I was allowed back into music practice. After that I don't think Corbett ever used my first name again. It was always that cussed McCallum.

Mr. Kimble was our homeroom teacher. He chain-smoked Camel cigarettes. Quite often you could see him start to get shaky and he would slip out of our room to the teachers lounge for some quick puffs. After class one day I managed to slip in and doctor up his smokes with a little powder charge designed especially for cigarettes. I just kinda poked it down inside of each one.

The next day in old homeroom 301 we were delighted to see Kimble start to shake. He made sure that each of us looked busy, "I'll be back in 5 minutes." We were about to come unglued.

From the teachers lounge we heard a telltale pop. Kimble was back with us in a matter of seconds. His thick mustache looked disturbed with a crescent shaped bald spot near the center of his mouth.

"God damn it! Who did this? Speak up!" He threw the stub of shredded cigarette on the floor.

Well, there were several of us involved, but I probably looked the guiltiest. My reputation for pranks was growing rapidly so I was the obvious choice to go see the assistant principal, Mr. Shaft. What a name. Cassius Shaft was a god-like little Napoleonic runt who took discipline to new levels. He patrolled the halls admonishing students to "spit out that gum; straighten up, that will get you demerits and a black mark on your records you'll never get a job— blah, blah." I became a regular to get the "shaft".

With a sneering look, he was right in my face. "Well what's your poison today asshole?"

"I'm getting framed for something," was my reply.

"Yah, right let's go up and see what you did this time."

As we topped the stairs I could see our homeroom door open and there was another 'pop' from the teacher's lounge. My initial sentence was two weeks off from school.

Word has it, that after I left Kimble said to the class, "Your fat buddy is never coming back to this school." Then he grabbed a fresh pack out of his drawer. Those were loaded too, though you couldn't even tell the package had been tampered with. When one of these blew, and removed a little more mustache, he raised enough hell to get me kicked out for a month.

I was holding a B or so average even though I was missing a lot of school. To be out for a few days or weeks I'd be well behind the class when I returned, but I had the talent to catch up quickly.

Some of the things I got disciplined for I was not even involved with. The combination of my established reputation plus my mother calling all the time to find out what I was up to made me vulnerable to everything bad that happened.

Twice I entered and placed high in the state finals with the clarinet. The opportunity to go to Interlochen music camp even came up, but I didn't go. Just didn't think it would be a cool thing to do. Even though I was a fine musician my days of being a regular band member were numbered. I was too much of an instigator to be part of Corbett's band.

Two final events sealed my departure. The first was when the big concert bass drum got filled with water. What a mess that turned out to be. I was hysterical over it. Corbett was not. I visited the other assistant principal, Miss Laurie. She was an older lady that had never been married. I liked her as she always treated me fairly. She was distressed because my mother was calling all the time.

"Well what did you do this time?"

I explained about the bass drum and at the same time couldn't keep from laughing about it. If she thought it was funny she must have laughed after I left for she gave me more time off.

The final straw was the incident that took place in front of Corbett's house. Dick Hall, Jim Porter, Austin Stephens and I were out cruising around. We had just stopped at Sully's, which was the local hangout and then thought we'd pay our respects to Corbett at home. It was innocent enough. In front of his house we offered a 'sha-coo' noise in unison. A 'sha-coo' noise is made by grabbing your throat and loudly yelling while moving your hand and lower jaw up and down. What caused the problem was when I tossed the glass milk bottle, and it bounced and found its way through his front window. Because it had to be my idea, I was expelled for the remainder of my sophomore year from Sexton High School. The others involved didn't get punished.

Looking back on all these things I can imagine the embarrassment I created for my mother. She was a regular church member and the whole congregation was aware of my activities. Some of the folks thought my antics were rather funny, especially the water in the drum deal. But, for a boy with so much potential I was quickly becoming a big disappointment to her.

Well, I transferred to Eastern High School. The assistant Eastern Principal, Don Johnson, called me in to his office. He said that they were aware of my problems at Sexton and would be keeping their collective eyes on me. I respected his honesty and cooled the jokes, for a while.

Mr. Denby was the band director at Eastern. He recognized my talent and was more than willing to groom me for the state band competition against Sexton. I of course, was just interested in what fun the whole thing could provide for me. When they had the state competition an ex girl friend by the name of Kathy Sisco chased me all over the concert tryout area. There was no trouble about that, however it was obvious that I was not really seriously focused on music. It was fun though to march past Corbett in my Eastern uniform. I knew that would make the vein in his forehead stick out.

My stay at Eastern High School was quite successful. I did not get in any significant trouble, kept up my academics and participated in band. With that under my belt, it was a mutual decision that I should give Sexton another try. That fall would start my junior year. I decided to go out for football.

In those years football practice could start quite early in the summer, but first I needed a physical checkup to be eligible. Mother said she had a physical set up at Saint Lawrence Hospital in Lansing. Dad quietly went along with us. Probably I should have suspected something was amiss here, but I didn't, and it was only after we got off on the 5th floor that I became aware of something fishy going on. I was forcibly restrained and taken in for mental observation. There had to be some reason for my lack of direction. Mother was going to do her best to find out what it was.

The 5th floor of Saint Lawrence was the mental ward, what a zoo. Dr. Assline (that's the way I remember them pronouncing it) was in charge of this little empire. There was enough going on around here to warrant me sleeping with one eye open for three days. They finally put me in a room alone, and I met an intern named Larry. Larry was nice to me and explained all about the mental ward.

Dr. Assline ran the floor like a dictator. You could almost see the staff snap to attention when he went by. There was no way out for the patients unless you were escorted with someone who had a key to the elevator. Assline determined how long you stayed and what testing was done to you. Glassy-eyed, drooling patients, shock treatments, drug therapy; whatever was going on around me vacated the class clown from within me in a hurry. I played it cool, answered the questions and cooperated.

There was one very good side to all of this. I ended up dating and loving a very beautiful young blonde nurse from Milwaukee, Wisconsin. Her name was Sue Bender. After I was there a few days Sue came in and asked what I was there for. She had studied my chart, finding no history of mental problems. "Guess I just pissed off my folks was my humble response." After that she came in quite often and we became good friends. She thought I was very normal and couldn't come to grips with why I was there. For that matter neither could I.

Sue came in for the late afternoon and evening shift. After we became acquainted she periodically helped me escape for part of the evening. As the employees could not smoke on the floor, when it was late I would position myself close to the elevator and when she would go down for a cigarette, I'd hop on and be free for a while. We'd drive around; maybe go over to Sully's for awhile. Eventually we even drank some beer and parked. Before she went home she'd tuck me in back at the hospital. It was to her credit that I kept my sanity.

After a month or so of observation and isolation from the public, it was Dr. Assline's professional opinion that I was lazy and unmotivated. That was the report sent to my parents and the school. I don't know what it cost my parents for that learned opinion. I did see Sue off and on for a few months after that.

Next, I found myself on a bus headed for Culver Military Academy in Indiana. If I couldn't be controlled at home this was the obvious solution. At a potty stop I managed to "jump bus". I hitchhiked my way back to Lansing and for a while hung out with some friends. Eventually I found my way back to Ma's great cooking, though she bitched about having me back under foot again.

I was 16 now and ready for my first automobile. I had done odd jobs and accumulated enough money to buy Dad's old 1950 Buick. He let me have if for only fifty dollars, so you might just as well say he gave it to me.

The Buick got a new look. I removed all the chrome and lowered it, which gave it a much cleaner more streamlined appearance. It had a Dyna-Flo transmission that was indestructible. One of my prime attention getting maneuvers was to glide up to a stoplight at 20mph, then just before stopping I would throw it into reverse. The tires would scream and a cloud of rubber smoke would envelop the car. The driver stopped in the next lane would be rather startled, to say the least. Then in neutral, I'd set there seriously looking straight ahead, and never bat an eye. The guys riding with me always liked that one. The other popular thing was to turn the key off at about 40mph then just glide past someone and turn the key back on. It sounded like a howitzer going off.

As I said previously for my junior year I was back in Sexton. They were going to give me another chance. That would be short lived.

The idea for the alcohol still was started in Rod McLean's garage. He had just finished showing me a car he had modified for some shiner down in Carolina. It had tanks installed in the roof to haul moonshine. I asked him what moonshine was. "You're kidding?" "It's white lightening Willy—good as airplane gas," and he laughed.

Believe it or not, I got the basic plan on how to make moonshine from an episode of the Andy Griffith TV show. They featured some hillbillies who had constructed an illegal still. The ingredients seemed to be mash, copper tubes and some heat.

With some interested partners and a little more research we set up our operation in Dad's garage. Within a couple weeks we had a few ounces of 200 proof materials to flavor our sodas. Others were interested in the high quality stuff we put out. Good businessmen are ready when the opportunity for making money presents itself. We were ready. It's just that being back in school; we had little time to devote to our project. The key would be to somehow move the operation to school. Would this be possible? Where there is a way, great minds will find it, besides Dad was getting nosy.

Fortunately or unfortunately, depending on how you look at it, we constructed a new production facility right inside my school locker. Of course all of this had to be done when the halls were empty. We were like a bunch of prisoners planning a break in instead of a break out.

The copper lines and burner could easily be connected behind a false back. The bookshelf above held this in place and a vent hole out in the top of the locker allowed air movement out to the cold air vent in the ceiling above. A small gas bottle serviced our heat source. We just did what seemed necessary. The transfer of our manufacturing process right to the consumer seemed like a smart business move and we were already calculating our profits.

It was Thursday and tomorrow was booze day. Things had been operating smoothly for almost a month. As I came down the hall that morning my mind was filled with expansion plans. There were five of us involved and there was an old garage available on Willow Street where we could set up an even bigger operation.

Sometime the night before or early that morning we thought a janitor had bumped my locker while cleaning. Tubes inside had been jostled and there were unhealthy fumes building up inside. About the time I rounded the corner headed towards my locker there was an explosion that blew my locker door open. "Oh shit," I uttered. Principal Rosenraad stood by the door. About 20 people milled around as he looked at the familiar locker number. "McCallum!"

He looked up and there I was...at least for a moment before I started running for an exit.

I heard Assistant Principal Shaft yell, "There he is! Don't ever come back, you SOB or I'll get you for a felony." So ended my high school days.

I think the administration was embarrassed by the existence of the still, because much later I got a copy of my record and "poor citizenship" or something like that was the given reason for my expulsion.

Of course it wasn't long before word got back to mother. She wanted me out of the house immediately. This had been threatened before if I didn't straighten up. Now she meant it. Dad was non-committal as usual. He asked if I needed some money. I thanked him and said I had a little. He slipped me some anyway.

GOOD TIME BILL

I remember the caption someone wrote under my last annual picture at Sexton, "Lead Foot". When I was a freshman, there was a Driver's Ed. '59 Olds obstructing a driveway and the teacher said, "That car must be moved. Can any of you boys do that?" "Sure," I replied.

It was a manual with the shift lever on the steering column. I had never driven one before, but figured it wouldn't be a problem. I got her in gear and laid rubber right out in front of all those kids. Hence the name, Lead Foot.

Well, I had lead-footed my way right out of high school. It was also obvious, that for a while at least, I wasn't going to be welcome around home. Was I down in the dumps? No, probably I felt more like Briar Rabbit, who had been pleading not to be thrown in the briar patch, but really wanting to be there.

At first I stayed in a boarding house. The rooms were so clean and neat it reminded me of home. It didn't take long to find another place to stay that had a more social atmosphere.

Dad said that I needed some direction in my life. If I were going to find higher paying jobs I would need to complete the GED. It would give me the equivalent credit of a high school education. That sounded like a good idea In short order I had passed the GED test with a very high score. Not to stop there, I enrolled in Lansing Community College. The community college would give me some basics if I wanted to further my education.

I was still dating a girl at Sexton during this time frame. It gave me all sorts of warm feelings to glide right up in front of the school to pick her up for lunch or after school, and have all my peers see how well I was doing. Here they were still piddling around in high school while I was a big college stud. I am sure that the assistant principal would have liked to run me out of there, but there was nothing he could do.

The old Buick finally ran into hard times, so to speak. Some buddies and I were out tearing around in a field one night and got her hung up on a rock. The field is right where the big Lansing Mall is now located. Mac's All-Car Towing finally arrived and by then it was pouring down rain. He pulled us off the rock and suggested I scrap the car. Instead I started it and drove it home. The oil pan had been dented upward significantly and from then on it would really be two quarts short of oil while it showed being full.

I decided it was time to sell the Buick and move up to something classier. Working in a grocery store I had saved up enough money for a down payment and I figured Dad would co-sign for the rest. My plan was to get in style, so with $500 down I drove the 1960 red MG home for Dad to see. He said that under no circumstances would he co-sign for that car. Disappointed I drove back to the dealership. On the way I put the old girl through her paces and the damn muffler fell off. I wired it back up, then drove the car in to get my $500 deposit back. The guy said, "You ruined that car, I'm keeping your deposit."

"Well, I'll just cancel the check," I said and, I did.

The next thing that happens is the dealer is having me charged with larceny by conversion: whatever that means. I ended up going to court, but the judge threw the whole thing out. A few years later that dealer got some jail time for selling stolen cars from Indiana.

My next car was a 1957 Chevrolet. It was a piece of junk, but I needed wheels. I didn't have much to put down on her, however the salesman said I could make payments. This guy was your typical, penciled on mustache, slick salesman. I guess he could see this sucker coming down the road. "Come on in, son. We'll fix you right up," with his slimy hand on my shoulder.

Dad also recognized this car as a piece of junk. He took it back and told the salesman that he had signed an underage boy to a contract. The man took the car back and refunded the money. Dad kept the money. He said I owed it to him. Probably he was just trying to keep me from running right out to get another junker. I resorted to friends and other means of transportation to get around.

After a while I was allowed to move back home, but my mother was determined that as far as automobiles, my wings would be clipped. I wanted to again have my own car like the other 17-year-olds I knew. I bought a junker with $500 I had saved. It wasn't in my possession long enough to remember what kind it was. When I was working my mother had a wrecker tow it off.

Dad took my side this time. "The boy earned the money himself, let him have it."

She probably figured I didn't deserve any favors. Each time I reclaimed my car and paid the towing she would have it towed again. Finally I didn't have money to get it out of hock anymore.

Occasionally, late at night, I would borrow my dad's '56 Cadillac. Unknown to him I had installed two four barreled carburetors and dual exhaust with dual cutouts. While Dad was sleeping I would push the car out of the garage and start it up once I got her down the street. At Mac's garage I would remove the cutouts from the exhaust pipes, allowing for a sweet powerful sound and then replace the air cleaner lids with low chrome pots. From there it would be to Washington Ave.; commonly referred to as the 'GUT' for an evening of cruising, dragging and generally raising hell.

It was at about this time that I also put some of my auto mechanic skills to work to develop a little handy dandy tool that would eliminate the key to start an automobile engine. There was a world of fine used automobiles out there on car lots, just setting around on weekends. Why not occasionally borrow one for a day? Sure seemed harmless enough to me.

Well my friends were certainly impressed when I rolled into Sully's with some new looking wheels. Word had gotten around that I was forced to sell my '57. They sure thought it was nice that I had a friend willing to loan me such nice wheels. They were even more impressed when on another occasion I rolled in with an even different beauty.

I've talked a lot about this place called Sully's; let me elaborate some. Sully's was the place to be on weekends. It was a drive-in located in Lansing on the corner of Saginaw and Waverly, where Wendy's is now. On a typical Saturday night cars might be seen lined up on Saginaw across from the Waverly golf course, just waiting to cruise through Sully's. This would start around 7 p.m. and continue for a good part of the evening. Sully's was the place to show off your car, your girlfriend or just a place to check in so your friends could see you 'were happening'. If we were lucky enough to get a parking spot we'd order some food and just hang out as long as we could. Sully's didn't serve beer so we'd just dump the coke out of their cups and replace it with a little of our own Pabst Blue Ribbon.

One night we were sipping away at our beer, getting just a little loud. Sully's owner, Doug Rice, had sent repeated orders over the loud speaker at our spot for us to leave. We ignored the warnings until I turned around to see at my window, a really huge guy with a menacing look on his face. I was at a loss for words and so rattled I knocked the tray right away from the car window. This big fella was Doug's cook/bouncer. He didn't have to say anything, we just left. By the way, the man's name was Dave Chamberlin, nicknamed Tiny. He stood just a few inches less than seven feet tall, and must have weighed close to 400 pounds. In time, Tiny and I became great friends. I'll tell you more about that later.

My studies at Lansing Community College were not going that well. I couldn't concentrate on school. Plus, it was getting in the way of my social activities. Perhaps my mother was right and it was time to give the military a try. I talked with the Army National Guard in Lansing and soon I was scheduled to go for a physical. It seemed like the perfect excuse for a party.

We had tubs of beer and lots of food, all for a slight cover charge. What a wild night it was. I paid for it with a nice hangover the next morning. The bus ride to Detroit seemed to take forever as we stopped several times to pick up more recruits. When we finally arrived in Detroit, I stumbled getting off the bus and sprained my ankle. That nullified the physical.

Soon my physical was rescheduled. Several people suggested another going away party. It seemed like a good idea to me. August was hot; a good beer-drinking month and vacations would soon end. What better time to throw a good end of the summer/going away party bash? Word got around fast and even though I didn't know half the people there, gate receipts were very respectable. These going away parties seemed to be a good way to make some extra cash.

I passed the next physical and attended a couple of National Guard meetings with the 119th Field Artillery located in Lansing on Marshall Street. Before I was fully instated with the Guard I decided that the Air Force was more my type of service and transferred over. I was set up for an Air Force physical and of course another going away party took place. McCallum's going away get-together's were a real joke, but certainly a good excuse to party. The last party was the biggest and best. We held it at Inn America in East Lansing and pocketed $400 in profits.

Unfortunately, I did not pass the Air Force physical because of a foot problem. I was classified 4F. The Army didn't catch it in their physical, but I guess the Air Force was a little more thorough. As a young boy I rode my bike into a wire Dad had stretched to a pipe in his flower patch. It cut the tendons to a couple of toes and my foot movement wasn't normal. Guess they figured it would hinder marching or something and threw me out. Well, at least the Army wanted me, but that service time is a story better left to be told sometime in the future.

The early 60's were a time of non-direction for me, except for the fact that I was turning into a party animal. Having a good time was my way of life, supplemented by a little work.

Even though I was still under 21 years of age, a well-done fake ID had provided me entrance to the bars for several years. Although I did like to consume alcohol, I usually appeared more under the influence than I actually was. What the bar atmosphere provided was the medium to be the clown again. That was a comfortable, fun role for me to play.

By this time, I had developed into quite a husky young lad who looked older than his years. Probably I weighed in at around 210 pounds. Invariably if you hang around bars long enough some dude with a snoot full will try to pick a fight with you. I liked to have fun and probably my big mouth had offended someone in the past, but I didn't go out looking for trouble and so far had been lucky in avoiding confrontations. That changed one night up at a bar near Prudenville.

Prudenville is located Southeast of Houghton Lake in the center of Michigan's Lower Peninsula. There is a nightspot up in those parts called the Music Box. The Music Box was a fun place to socialize with the natives. On more than one occasion we'd pack up the car and head there to raise a little hell. On this one evening we left the Music Box, or closed it, and were over at this other bar finishing off the evening. I don't remember the name of the place, just a bar with a jukebox. One of the guys, Orson, was done for the evening. He was out asleep in the car.

Orson was always a good guy to have along for fun and protection. He was big, intimidating, and most folks didn't try to mess with us as long as he was there.

We were sitting at the bar sipping some draft beer. It was time to drain the 'weasel' so I left my stool for the bathroom. Returning, I sat back down, picked up my mug and this guy beside me turns around and knocks the beer right out of my hand. It didn't seem accidental.

"What the hell ya doin'?", I asked.

The place quieted right down and I heard a voice from the crowd say, "Guess he don't know who Green is."

"Whoop-de-fucking-do; Green huh?", I said

This arm came around like a ball bat. I went off my stool into one table, which broke, and ended up sliding with another table before ending up on the floor. My nose was bleeding. One of the lens from my glasses was missing and Mr. Green was challenging me to step outside.

It seemed like my choices right then were limited. I gathered myself up, wiped the blood away from my nose and followed him toward the rear door. I was hoping my buddies would be following right along to help keep this thing from getting out of hand.

I had no more than stepped through the back door when this Green guy decked me again. The locals were now streaming out the back door to get in a good observation position for the evening's entertainment. I didn't see any familiar faces. Now this guy has me up against the building whaling me good. Finally I see one of my "so called" buddies stick his head out the back door, sizing up the fact that I'm getting the shit beat out of me, and with this big frown on his face says, "Oh, oh!" Then he went back in.

Mr. Green is now trying to pull my coat up around my head so I can't fight back. I come to the stark realization that if I don't do something this guy is gonna kill me. Adrenaline can do great things. I kind of went wild, ripping the coat apart and came around with a big one right in the guy's stomach. He was surprised. While he was trying to catch his breath I put everything into a punch that landed just below his nose. That put him right into a grill of a near-by car. Now I'm down on him. Grabbing his neck from both sides I start slamming his head up and down on the ground saying "So you're Wally Green huh? So you're Wally Green huh?!"

I cool down some and see he's out. The locals are quiet. When I stand up, it's no secret that I'm a mess. Not just the blood from my nose, but also a nice cut on my forehead.

Reaching down I flipped the limp body over and took out his billfold. "Who is this fucking guy Green?" I found out all I needed to know when the wallet unfolded exposing a big badge. The wallet and his gun I threw on a nearby roof, out of his reach, then walked down the street and through an alley to our car. Old Orson, the horse, was passed out in the back seat. I shook him awake and told him to get in the front seat. With Orson's hat on I slid into the driver's seat. With blood all over my face, I could barely see to drive, but managed to start out of town about the time the ambulance arrived.

We were almost to Alma before Orson comes to and asks me what happened. When I finish giving him the blow-by-blow details he says, "Didn't you get the guys gun?"

"No, no, hell no Orson. That guy almost killed me! And Bob wouldn't even help."

We heard that the newspaper stated that Mr. Green had been assaulted by four men and ended up with broken ribs and a broken arm. Some of the locals must have worked him over after we left, because I didn't do all that damage. I'm not sure whether old Green was a cop or what, but I did hear he was the town bully. There were no repercussions from the incident for me. Needless to say we didn't go back to that establishment, but we still frequented the Music Box.

For a while I worked part-time for the State Highway Department. I remember hanging on to a jack hammer until I thought my teeth would shake out, but it did net me enough money to buy a sharp looking 1957 Chevrolet hardtop. It was a beauty. In time it also gained me several points on my drivers license, as I really liked to drag race. I also did some legal racing over at US 131 dragway near Grand Rapids. There I painted the name "Watusi Ranger" on the side. That wasn't an original naming. I had seen it painted on a new silver GTO at the Ontonagon drag-way and thought it was such a cool name I would just borrow it for these races.

It was during deer hunting season when I next headed up towards the Music Box in Houghton Lake. Some friends were supposedly already up there, so I was by myself in the '57 Chevy and running on fumes. My luck finally ran out. I found myself out of gas out in the boonies, freezing my ass off trying to thumb a ride. What a dumb way to spend Saturday night.

It wasn't long before a car stopped. The driver motioned me to get in. As the door slammed shut this guy buried his foot in the accelerator. The smell of booze was over powering and I knew I shouldn't be there. In a matter of what seemed like seconds, I looked over and watched the speedometer needle moving past 100. My ride didn't last long. He missed the first curve we came to and we went sailing end over end out in this cornfield. When I came to my senses, I spotted the driver setting under a tree moaning. We were both lucky to be alive after being thrown out. Probably he was drunk enough not to feel much that had happened anyway.

I gathered myself up and started walking down the road eventually catching a ride to a gas station. Once I got some petrol in the '57 I was again headed north. Around Clare my conscience decided that I should phone in the accident. My God, I was paranoid back then. I had this great fear I would lose my license.

After taking a few summer classes I again started back full-time at Lansing Community College. Had I turned over a new leaf? Not really. I did have an interest in advertising and decided to pursue that course in school. Still my main interests were cars, racing and having a good time in the bars.

Parking for the students at the college was sparse, however the tickets for being parked illegally were only two dollars, so I just parked where I wanted to and tossed the tickets in the glove box. Mid way through my second year of college, my '57 was pulled over by a local cop when he becomes a spectator to one of my spur of the moment drag races. Before he wrote the ticket he had dispatch run my drivers license.

"Son, you're not going anyplace but to jail. You have 110 outstanding parking tickets and there's a warrant for your arrest."

My car was towed away and I was given free transportation to the lockup.

With my one allowed call I dialed home, praying my dad would answer. Mother said, "Hello."

"Hi, Mom. Can I talk to Dad?"

"Where are you?"

"Just hanging out at a friend's house."

She knew something was up. "Why do you want to talk to your father?"

Quickly searching for an answer, I came up with the wrong one, "I just needed to see if he'd loan me a couple bucks."

She hung up.

After spending 17 days in the jug I learned that to get out it would cost me $50 plus the tickets: $270 total. I called a friend in Mason. He went over to my home to get the title to my '57. Ma was more than happy to give it to him. Automobiles might have been the love of my life, but I think she thought they were the key to my demise. Well my buddy sold the beloved '57, paid my fine and, although I didn't know it at the time, lined his pocket with an extra hundred dollars.

After I earned a few credits at Lansing Community College I started picking up some basic courses at Michigan State University while continuing at the community college. I really had a great time at the MSU student union and at Coral Gables, the big university hangout.

During spring break I traveled down to Ft. Lauderdale for some sun and ended up staying for several months. I got a job with the Hughes radio network selling advertising. I liked the work and was good at it, but the job was temporary, so when the work and money ran out I came back up north to school.

One summer I did a very dumb thing. I was taking a few credits in summer school and during that timeframe my folks were spending some time at a cottage on Crystal Lake. After picking up our mail I spotted a government tax check made out to William McCallum. It was my Dad's check, but because our names were the same I thought that I'd just cash that rascal and have a good time with my friends. This I did. At one point I bought a round for the bar at the Coral Gables. I was the most popular and funny guy in the place that night. I even loaned my buddy Jan Barnes some cash to get his car reupholstered.

When my dad found out I had used his tax rebate check for my needs he hit the ceiling. Money was the fuse that lit my dad's fire. He went ballistic. My car, my bank account—even my life seemed to be at stake. Later he calmed down, but my mother made Jan pay back every dime I had lent him. For the record, I never did anything like that again.

Early in the summer of 1963 I was involved in another accident. It happened out by the Lansing Airport. There were four of us in Doug Van DeCarrs Gran Prix—he was showing off when he lost it on a curve, and rolled the beautiful car over. When I came to, I was by myself underneath the car. Maybe I had looked dead because everyone else had left the scene.

I gathered myself up and tucked my right hand under the other arm to slow the bleeding. I walked almost to Waverly Road before a man gave me a ride. When he saw how much I had bled he suggested I get out at the Willow and Waverly intersection. Probably he didn't want the inside of his car spotted with blood. From there I made my way down to Sully's. My good friend Mary Fisher happened to be there and she drove me down to Saint Lawrence Hospital in her almost new 88 Oldsmobile convertible. What a sweetheart that girl was.

My hand was really messed up from the accident and the healing process was slow. That summer I was unemployed, just banging around in a big white cast. I especially remember the day the cast was removed. I took the bus to the doctor's office and they had it partially sawed off when everyone ran into the lobby to watch TV. JFK had been assassinated.

The next summer I moved down to the Ann Arbor area with the hopes of getting enrolled in a brand new course they were starting for University of Michigan students interested in an advertising career. I shared a house with four single nurses. My buddies thought I was in hog heaven, which wasn't the case. Working nights I rarely saw the nurses. Neither was I able to get myself enrolled in the advertising course.

Well, I wasn't going to any school now, just finding whatever work I could.

Finally I lucked out and got a job selling advertising for WVIC radio station. WVIC was originally a Christian music station then it switched to rock under the ownership of Bob Sherman. In those days salesmen didn't make much per hour, instead they received goods and services from the advertising accounts they sold. Less money changed hands and although I didn't have a lot in my pocket I could eat free at several nice restaurants, had good clothes and free oil changes and in some instances free gas. I really liked Sherman. He had an excellent radio voice and was one of the first to do screaming commercials. I learned a lot and found out that I did have a gift for selling advertising.

Through the middle 60's I made other trips to Florida around spring break. Ft. Lauderdale was the party place to be. Believe it or not, once while I was there I even participated in a tryout for the Olympic pistol team.

There was some kind of advertisement in the paper and I knew a gentleman who was planning to participate. He didn't make the first cut so he jokingly suggested I tryout. Well we met at a Steak 'N Shake where he loaned me his weapon. At the tryouts I held my own for most of the day, but eventually, as always, I lost my concentration. Maybe it was just the hundred guns going off that interrupted my recovery from the hangover I was nursing.

Back up in Michigan, even though I wasn't attending college anymore, I still hung around with the MSU college crowd. I even won a drinking contest at Coral Gables. It involved downing, as many 16 oz. Budweiser's as possible in three minutes. Each beer had to be followed with a boiled egg. Seems like I drank 7 beers winning the privilege of having my name put on a papier-mâché duck displayed there. Just to show off some more, I followed all that with a pizza. When we left my buddy drove around the block while I puked my guts out through an open door.

In late 1968 I took my good friend Mike Hurl's brand new Malibu over to the Campus Car Wash on Grand River. To impress the workers there, I laid a little rubber as I passed through the exit door, almost running down this tall beauty outside. I apologized profusely and offered to buy her a cup of coffee. She seemed to take the whole thing pretty well and we had a nice visit. Her name was Carol. She was very intelligent and had a good sense of humor, the problem being that she was dating a good friend of mine, Tom Mikko.

Not long after the car wash incident I ran into Carol with Tom at a party. While Tom was off talking to others I spent some quality time visiting with her, or better said flirting with her. Tom was kinda like a bee in a flower patch among girls at a party, so my approach was to really give this girl lots of attention. Not too long after that Tom made the mistake of taking a little trip to Florida and I laid down a dazzling array of bullshit on Carol. We got serious. She moved back to Rochester, New York and shortly after that I followed and we were married.

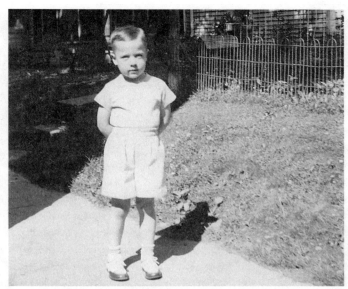

Young Bill - the pianist.

Science student McCallum (1956).

Second row clarinets (Bill 4th from front).

College student with hair - Bill.

First '57 Chevy.

JUST MARRIED

When Carol finished the spring term at MSU she returned to Rochester for the summer. A couple of months later I followed her out and we moved into her folk's home. Although we dated less than a year we seemed quite compatible.

I'm sure that Carol's father, Henry Ireland, was not dazzled when she brought his future son-in-law home. That morning when Henry first met me, I drove up in my 1962 Corvair convertible with the smashed in nose and the "Let's Ball" sticker on the back. Not known as a swanky dresser, with a full beard my attire might have been a Hawaiian shirt with an orange tie topped off with tattered jeans and sandals.

Carol's father was a perfectionist in his dress. He always wore a spiffy suit, white shirt and dark tie. If he didn't particularly like Carol's choice for a mate, he didn't show it and treated me respectfully. I would have liked to be able to read his mind though, it probably would have been entertaining.

Henry Ireland was an engineer of some sort with the Kodak Film Company. As I understand it, his father had been on a first name basis with George Eastman, the company founder. That certainly didn't hinder his status at Kodak, however Henry was a very hard working individual.

To me, the Irelands seemed quite wealthy. Their home was located right on Lake Ontario in Greece, New York. When Carol first took me to her parent's home I was duly impressed with not only the location, but also the size of the home. The front faced the lake, so when we came around to the lakeside I was even more impressed. Before me was a breath taking view of Lake Ontario and a perfectly manicured yard. Everything was beautiful, clean and spotless, just like Henry.

Carol's mother was as sweet a woman as I've ever known. Byrl was a gorgeous lady, with the personality to match. She had the soul of an artist, with a great sense of humor and treated me graciously.

The Irelands put on a grand wedding for us, with a beautiful reception. Our wedding took place at Colgate Divinity Chapel in Rochester. It was a beautiful church located on the highest hill in the area. We honeymooned in the Poconos; all top-drawer stuff paid for by Henry.

After Carol got her degree from MSU we settled into a small home in the Rochester area. Carol's father picked out a house for us to rent and we signed the agreement on a weekend. Little did we know, that the large bushes in the back yard hid a set of railroad tracks that were very well used during the week. When the trains went by the house shook like a bowl of jelly.

I went to work for WSAY radio selling advertising. WSAY was a little storefront dump that broadcast religion and watered down elevator music. It's difficult to sell advertising for a station that's not listened to much. After a few months, I left and went to work for Pacesetter Motors, in the parts department. The man that owned the place was a big guy with the sissy name of Corky, but he raced MGs. I really liked the excitement of being around the race environment again.

Even with Henry's generous help the pay at Pacesetters was not enough to maintain our better standard of living, so he gave me the chance to go to work for Kodak. He also made their old home available for us on 1050 Winona Blvd. It was a much bigger house in a middle class neighborhood, and unlike the previous house, it didn't have a railroad track behind it. Things were really coming together for us. I looked forward to being another successful branch of the family at Kodak.

Even though my background in advertising was limited, I really hoped I could expand in that role at Kodak, if Henry would give me the opportunity. What Henry had in mind for me was not exactly a position of prestige. I found myself in a dark room where huge rolls of material for film backing were cut. My shift changed each week from days to nights to swing, but because you worked in the dark it was always momentarily confusing as to what time of day it was when you came out and went home. I perceived that Henry was testing my mettle, and I was more than willing to prove myself to him.

I would say that old Henry was a perfectionist in more than just his dress. When I finished mowing my lawn, shortly thereafter he would come over and do it again. He demanded and received a lot of respect from others. If there was a family dinner at some restaurant, people just seemed to melt out of the way as we were ushered to our table.

I worked my butt off at Kodak to impress Carol's father. It was, however, the most miserable job I've ever had. Rolls of web film backing paper turned at high speed and were cut into strips for 26-type film. It was so dark you could barely see your hands. The room I worked in seemed small and I was bent over a lot working around these fast-moving machines. Nevertheless, as miserable as it was, I met all production goals and was actually improving.

Once a year they cleaned my work place, moved out the film and turned on the lights. The floor corners were six inches thick with film dust. No wonder my allergies were acting up. Silver nitrate was in the dust, with no breathing protection furnished. In later years I wondered how many people had died of lung cancer from working there.

What finally brought me to my senses was on a break when I talked to this other employee. He said, "Oh, you're working the web rolls huh? Lost a finger yet?" He held up his hands and I could see fingers missing. Proudly he said, "They gave me office work now."

Here I had been doing everything next to those fast moving machines with my hands, and in the dark too. From then on I used a stick to move things. I didn't need a promotion to the office that bad. Unfortunately my production plummeted.

After about a year and a half, I could see my efforts to pay my Kodak dues with Carol's father weren't getting any place, no matter how hard I worked. I was exhausted by the swing shift and finally one night I fell and hurt my shoulder. It was at that point I decided it was time to find other work. I wanted to get back into advertising, so I left Kodak. Maybe that was Henry's plan anyway, but he wasn't bashful about showing his disapproval.

For a period of time I worked for radio station WBBF, then switched to WHFM. A lot of their advertising clients were auto dealers, so to attract more listeners and lure more dealership advertising I formulated a station sponsored 5 car racing team; WHFM Performance Group. It all started out with five of my friends who had some hot cars. I would set up challenges at local drag strips and then get some businesses to contribute a case of oil or something to the winning team. That idea seemed to grow quite rapidly. Once the racing team name was attached to the radio station it gave extra exposure to the businesses contributing to the events and did draw new listeners, which also attracted more advertising.

Although I didn't own a race car, I really didn't need one. I referred to the team as my team. I was the "Colonel Parker" of racing, basking in the notoriety it was giving me. My paychecks were now looking respectable, but I was also spending less time at home, always hanging out after work with the racers and groupies.

I think the Irelands were a bit mystified as to why I hadn't tried to tough it out at Kodak. Had they been aware of my previous track record of switching jobs it probably wouldn't have been such a surprise at all.

While I was at Kodak I tried going to school at a brand new area college, Rochester Institute of Technology. To impress Carol and the Irelands I even attended Syracuse. All these efforts at education were half hearted and ended up just as they did in Michigan. I had the intelligence to succeed, but not the concentration or drive to stick with it. Looking back on my attempts at education, AADS (Adult Attention Defect Syndrome) probably contributed to my failures.

My success at selling radio ads had improved, but was sporadic. As a racecar team handler my reputation was growing rapidly. The pinnacle of my career as a promoter was the year I orchestrated a large car show for a General Motors dealer. The goal was to bring in the public to see the new GM models. To do this I organized a hot rod show around the new car showing. The turnout was fantastic. I called the show Thunder in Upstate. It was billed as the largest new car show in the U.S., and I won an award for it.

I can't remember if any of the Irelands came to my show. They could sense though, that I was savoring my success, and seemed to do everything possible to give me the benefit of their doubts. In fact, some of the happiest weekends I can remember were at the Irelands' home. Despite what they might have been thinking, they treated me with respect and we enjoyed each other.

I liked Carol's brother, Tom. His wife was also named Carol, and they seemed to be at the Irelands all the time. I admired Tom because he seemed to be doing his own thing despite his father's insistence of overseeing everything. Tom and Carol had a daughter, Michelle, who referred to me as Uncle Boom. In Michelle's presence I had kidded Carol about having some boom-a-loom later. Michelle was only about six years old, but she picked right up on that. At the family get-together's, I always took time to visit with her, so we had a good bond. Twenty-eight years later she even invited me to her wedding.

Carol became pregnant. Everybody was happy. My folks thought the world of her and flew out for a short stay with us. On the surface everything was picture perfect, but underneath cracks were forming.

With my success at the Thunder car show and the continued exposure of our racing team, there came a lucrative job offer from a competing radio station, WCMF. I jumped ship bringing the racing team to that station with me. I was really a big shot now and there was even more opportunity to travel to car shows, racing events and just hang out for a couple beers with my racing buddies. Working for the station, there were also lots of free lunches, drinks and show tickets to take advantage of.

Carol had always been very close to her parents. Her mother, Byrl, and her were constant companions; talking on the phone daily. At first, Carol was very patient with my increased absence from home; she just spent more time with her parents. Eventually, though, she started hinting that I spend less time with my racing

buddies and more with her. I brushed off her concerns. I was top
dog in the racing world, and I had responsibilities there.

Complete Area Racing (C.A.R.) was a newsletter I came up with
as a scam to get on the infields during racing events. I'd have a
camera and track operators always want publicity anyway, so I was
right there where everything was happening. It turned out to be a
pretty well accepted little racing newspaper. Another guy and I
co-owned it. We had subscriptions, advertising, and the whole bit.

At the height of my success, in 1973, my son Scott was born. He
was the first grandson in the family and the star attraction. I was on
top of the world. In 1974 my world started to unravel.

I was out in my father-in-laws' boat when we got a call relayed
through the ship to shore radio from my mother. Her message was
simply, "Your Dad died-come home." There were no cell phones in
those days, but once we got to shore I called home. There was no
answer. I was devastated.

Flying is not something I like, so we drove home as fast as we
could. The funeral took place the day after our arrival. He looked
so natural in the casket. I almost could imagine him breathing.

Dad's father was a Civil War veteran, who had lived to be 90
years old. My dad was 79 when he passed away. He had felt bad in
the morning and went in for an EKG. My mother was concerned,
but he said, "Hell, don't you worry I'm going to live to be a hundred." He handed mother his wallet and joked, "We'll go out for
supper." That was unusual as they rarely ate out. Later that evening
he started coughing up blood. They thought it was indigestion, but
they should have known something major was wrong. It wasn't
until the next morning that he went to the hospital for a check up.
I guess a vein or something had ruptured in his chest. He died in the
hospital. In my years growing up I don't remember a lot of physical contact, hugging etc. with my dad, but he always treated me
well and I did love and respect him very much. When I was quite
young he had started work for the Michigan Highway Department
and eventually was honored for his design work for the expressway
layout up to the Mackinaw Bridge. Instead of keeping the north and
south bound lanes exactly parallel he allowed them to separate to

preserve the natural scenic beauty. He used to laugh when he told me, "I'm so important they named the bridge after me; Big Mac".

By the time I arrived home mother had collected all of Dad's clothes and donated them to the Salvation Army. Everything was over too fast. There was no closure for me.

The last contact with my dad had been an argument, orchestrated by Ma. We both yelled at each other about something stupid. I called him when we reached Rochester and apologized, but even though we made up, the incident will always bother me.

My grandmother died soon afterwards. She was 87 years old; a round, happy little lady. Growing up I had spent many hours with her. She had a great personality and was a real kid's type of grandmother. She was also the cohesion in my mother's family. Once she was gone the daughters were continually at odds with each other, until all Ma's sisters were gone.

Having been in New York for almost six years, I felt that I had really missed something not being around my father and grandmother for their last years. After the funeral, I also had some time to hang out with my old buddies. They were mostly divorced or separated now, picking up their old habits of partying and carousing. It seemed like they were having a fun time, and I missed their companionship.

Back in New York, my car racing program hit a brick wall. The gas crunch of those years didn't help and once I lost my celebrity status, my interest in advertising waned. My shoulder still hurt from my fall at Kodak, so I got the wild idea to sue Kodak for damages. That paved the way for my exit from the family. Kodak had been the Ireland family's bread and butter for years, and the lawsuit was a great embarrassment to Henry.

It was Carol's opinion along with the rest that I was biting the tit from which I had been nursed. It was pointed out that this was an ungrateful thing for me to do after all the money Henry had spent to make things comfortable for Carol and me. Of course they were absolutely right, but I didn't budge on my lawsuit. Although I did love Carol and my new son very much, the atmosphere was uncomfortable enough that I decided to move back to Michigan.

Before I could act on that plan, with Henry's blessing, Carol filed for a no fault divorce. I headed back to Michigan in Carol's old yellow '68 Impala with a bottle of Southern Comfort as a companion. My lawsuit against Kodak dragged on and I had to make several trips back and forth, sometimes only to learn the case had been postponed. The final settlement was about eight hundred dollars, hardly worth what I had lost. When I was in New York I briefly saw my son Scott, but I was not instrumental in raising him; probably to his benefit.

Bill and Carol.

Bill and
son Scott.

Bill's first radio station sponsored race car (WAXC). His engine blew on the start.

Bill McCallum driving '69 Camaro for Stoldi Blair Engineering.

WCMF Super Group. Bill one-half owner of car in foreground.

Bill's "Boss Pinto" 427 HiPo/4spd.

AWAKENING

Once I was settled back in Michigan, I hooked up with my old drinking buddies and tried to make up for lost time. Of course, many things had changed in our lives since our more youthful days. Everyone had their side of a divorce story to bitch about, and then there was talk of the success or failure of mutual friends. Once all these subjects were covered, the bar talk would drift to women, sports and sometimes politics.

My old radio station WVIC in Lansing rehired me. The sales manager was Joe Buyes. He was always looking for gimmicks to sell more time. His favorite saying was "Get out there and sell some spats". He gave me the opportunity to prove myself again. While I was employed at WVIC I staged what was billed as "The Worlds Largest Indoor Free Car Show." It was to kick off the opening of the Meridian Mall, and I named it "Thunder in Mid State", trying to capitalize on my reputation with Thunder in Upstate from my New York days.

The car show was a rousing success with hundreds of cars on display. About every car club of distinction was represented there: racing, custom, hot rods and supposedly the largest collection of Chrysler Hemi's ever assembled in one place. The Hemi was a big 426 cu. in. Plymouth hemispherical head engine that was very popular and installed in several Chrysler models. Chrysler engineering came out with these monsters in the 60's and 70's to compete with the big Chevrolet engines of that era.

In that time frame vans were becoming popular, so the grand prize we gave away was a Chevrolet van called the Coke Denim Machine. The inside was all upholstered in denim and it had a fancy paint job. "Thunder in Mid State" was a wild, crowd-pleasing show that won an award for originality.

Basking in the glow of my success with Thunder in Mid State, I started to drink and carouse more. Soon my radio ad sales fell off. Too much of my work was in trade for goods and services anyway. I needed hard cash to survive.

I moved to another radio station, WIBM. The sales manager, Dan Hagsforth, put me over in the Battle Creek area to develop what he called "new territory". Actually, I think he wanted me to do poorly there as he was afraid of my car show successes. I put on some small shows, but now the shows were becoming boring and I turned in another lack luster performance.

Before I married Carol I did menial jobs for Martha Dixon of cooking show fame on Channel 6 TV. That ended when I smashed up their news vehicle. Now brandishing my most mature line of bullshit, I landed a sales position with them. I convinced the sales manager, Mel Stebbins, that I was better than sliced bread, so he gave me a chance. It was a great start with great ideas and fine people to work with, but then with zero follow through, in short order I fell on my face.

Next I was selling cars for Max Curtis Ford. Part of the job was having a nice new car to drive, so with that adding to my image I acquired a good sales position at Channel 10. Poor performance dictated another lost job. It seemed to be habit forming.

I really loved selling radio and TV advertising, but I just wasn't quick enough to make money without having to concentrate. Looking back on those years it seems obvious now that my attention deficiency was probably largely in control of my inability to concentrate on anything. My friends were kidding me about it, and I laughed it off, but inside I was wondering what was going on with me.

The Point After, was a disco located where the Lansing Center is now. That became a regular meeting place and watering hole when all my friends got off work. We laughed, drank beer and made noise, but our social connection was just not the same as it had been in the past, even though we drank more in an attempt to reconnect to it. Perhaps it was because we were each carrying the extra baggage of loneliness and guilt that goes along with split up families. My extra load was also not being able to hold a job. One night I staggered out into the 'Point' parking lot and caught a guy breaking into my car. All of life's frustrations inside me formed into a force of rage and I tore into this guy unmercifully. An officer arrived and tried to restrain me. I threw him off. Then I remember the helicopter cop shining a light down on me and abruptly I just dropped my hands down for them to cuff me. A police friend of mine convinced the cops to release me and then he took me home.

After the parking lot incident the drinking and nightlife began getting me down. The social life of being a barfly was losing its luster, plus, 2 weeks later my Impala was stolen and I never saw it again. I stopped hanging out at 'The Point After' and instead spent my extra time at Roger Stamboli's restaurant. He was a good buddy of mine.

Roger was one of the funniest fellows I'd ever met. He was a bachelor and had this neat playboy pad with a pool and one of the first projection TVs. Several of my friends would also stop around at his restaurant to heal up from the previous nights drinking, shoot the shit and then likely try to hustle the waitresses. They were being quite successful at getting dates with the girls except for this new waitress, Josie. She was a cool one, but not date hungry like the rest.

I was mesmerized with this young lady's stunning looks. Josie had long gorgeous auburn brown hair that she wore tucked up on her head for work. Her eyes were a noticeable green and she had a beautiful smile. One evening I was about to start on a salad that another waitress had brought me when Josie stopped by my table, "Don't eat that, it'll kill ya. Wait a minute; they're making up a fresh batch in the back. I'll bring you out a bowl." I was flattered that she even noticed me.

I hung around enough that she would exchange a few words with me when she waited on the table or walked by. Eventually I invited her to sit down to visit during one of her breaks. She accepted. Yes, it was obvious that she was really young, but she was so intelligent and mature to talk with. The age difference didn't seem to be a factor.

Our brief get-together's went on for several weeks. Being with her just to visit was the highlight of my day. I really wanted to ask her out and have more time with her—away from the restaurant and all the people. Here I was, 34 years old and scared to ask this beautiful girl out. Maybe I was in fear that she would turn me down, and that refusal would end up in no more time with her, even in the restaurant. There was also the chance that she was just friendly for the sake of being friendly. If I showed signs of seriousness she might be turned off, especially by my age. It seemed there was considerable risk to my next move—whatever that was going to be.

I decided before I did anything drastic, like ask her out, I'd follow her home to see where she lived. Even though that seemed like one course of action, I wasn't at all sure where that would get me.

In the parking lot, I waited for her to come out at the end of her shift. My "wheels" in those days was a jet black 1968 Oldsmobile Cutlass, with a manual shift kit. It had a 400 cu. inch engine that allowed me to smoke 'em regularly at the stoplights.

Josie came out and climbed into her Pinto. When I looked up, after snuffing my cigarette out, whoosh she was gone. I wasn't ready for that kind of departure.

The next day I was more prepared. With a yelp of the tires she was off and I was in careful, calculated pursuit. At the Saginaw and Waverly intersection traffic light, I sat second in line while she disappeared in the distance. This was disgusting: smoked again by a Pinto. Over 400hp out maneuvered by 60hp. That girl drove like a mad woman and I was going to have to rethink my following strategy. Certainly I had no intention of giving up.

Well another day and here we go again. I'm barely within view of her car, but finally lose it in traffic. I make a circle around the block where she disappeared and joyfully spot her Pinto in the alley. I parked on the street and ran up the alley, almost colliding with her.

"What are you doing out here?" she asked.

"Er—just looking for an apartment to rent."

"Well my Dad's got one to rent. He works 3 to 11 at Oldsmobile. Why don't you stop back later and talk with him."

"Ok, I'll do that."

That was a damned poor excuse. I wasn't looking for an apartment because I was living at home and couldn't afford one. I couldn't lose anything by going back to meet the old man—or could I? She was really young and I was a hell of a lot older. If he sensed that I was interested in his daughter, not an apartment, how would he take that?

After mustering up all my courage, I came back later that same afternoon and knocked on Josie's door. After only the third rap the door abruptly swings open and this big dark dirty looking old man says in a loud gruff voice, "What the hell do you want?"

I stammered, "Josie."

"Why?"

"I don't know."

He slammed the door in my face.

I walked mournfully down the alley like some beaten critter. I'd never gotten around to ask him about the apartment that I really didn't want. So much for my chances with that girl.

Before I got past the rear of the house the back door opened and there stood Josie laughing.

"What's the matter—scared?"

"Damn straight I am!"

We laughed and laughed over the situation. Later, I found out there was no apartment to rent anyway. She just wanted to see how interested I was. I blurted out, "I really wanted to ask you out!"

"Cool," she replied.

On our first date I took her to Mountain Jacks to eat. She could probably sense that this place was a little beyond my means so she just ordered a snack off the menu and after that and coffee we left. When we got in the car she said, "You didn't have to impress me by bringing me here, honey, you did that when we met."

And then she started laughing, "God that was stupid sounding wasn't it?"

Damn was I hooked; really hooked. She knew it and I knew it. Like a schoolboy with his first love, from then on my whole world revolved around her. As distant as she had first seemed in the restaurant, now when she climbed in my car, she moved over right next to me.

Ma had taught me good manners, and around Josie I was always there to open the car door for her, pull out her chair in a restaurant and do all those other gentlemanly things she wasn't used to. Youngest in a family of three brothers, she was used to waiting on others. She really liked the attention I was showering on her and I was elated that someone so young and beautiful could care for me.

I knew that there would eventually have to be another meeting with her father and that I didn't look forward to.

"Dad this is my friend, Bill McCallum."

This time he didn't growl. Just said hello and shook my hand. I didn't want him to hate me for hitting on his young daughter so to keep his mind off the situation I started pumping him about his experiences in the war. She had told me earlier that Frank loved yakking about the big one—WWII.

Fortunately the highlight of Frank's life was WWII. He was a cook in one of General Patton's support groups and was also responsible for driving one of the unit's water trucks. His only experience with Patton was when the General told him to, "Keep that fucking water truck out of my tanks way or I'll have them run over it."

Sometimes when Frank laughed he would accidentally spit little bits of chewing tobacco right in your face.

He liked to tell about the time he took some nurse and a bottle of wine into a mountain cave. He said that as they went farther into the cave there seemed to be an unusual amount of rocks to walk on. Finally he flicked on his Zippo lighter and as far as he could see the floor was littered with German potato masher hand grenades. There had been wire mesh holding them in storage near the cave walls, but repeated bombing had loosened the screen allowing the grenades to spill over the floor. Yep, he said, "I could have bought the farm that time." Guess that was his one near death experience in the war.

Frank talked about finding a bunch of dead horses in another cave. He also found some that were alive but half-starved. They were tied in the back of the cave. He untied them and allowed them to escape. I'd just sit and listen as Frank rambled on. We'd joke around a little and I seemed to be getting on his good side. He actually had a good sense of humor in the beginning.

In all of my visits with Josie I had learned little snippets about the family, but rarely did she get into the more serious aspect of the family personality. I did find out that Josie's mother had become seriously ill with cancer and her father, Frank, pulled her out of high school to care for her. Her mother passed away in 1975, but even before, Frank insisted Josie stay out of school to take care of the house for him. He thought that high school wasn't that vital for a woman, as long as she could cook and clean she could get along.

Early on I met her older brother, Jim. We seemed to hit it off OK and he didn't show any resentment for me dating Josie. He and his wife Jane lived upstairs for a while, and then moved away.

John was the brother that was closest to Josie growing up. He and Josie would stick together against the other brothers and he seemed more responsive to Josie. John was a very handsome man and the women hung all over him. Unfortunately John drank and smoked pot a lot.

Barry was a half brother—the boy Josie's mother had before she married Frank. He was close to my age and went to Eastern High School in Lansing. He was an outstanding student and athlete—even President of the Student Council.

Josie never talked much about her mother, but she went out of her way to please her father. I'm sure Frank thought a lot of Josie, but you wouldn't know it by the way he treated her. On the surface it appeared that she was there to keep the house clean, wash the clothes and get some of the meals. She kept the house spotless and I remember once when she'd just finished mopping the floors, Frank called in a couple of his dogs, then crushed up some Oreo cookies all over the clean floor for the dogs. He was at times rude and emotionally cruel towards her. I would grind my teeth over the way he and the brothers treated her, but I did my best to stay on the good side of Frank because I knew Josie loved him very much.

Josie and I just couldn't spend enough time together. It seemed that we had a limitless amount of things to talk about, plus she liked rock and roll music and cars just as I did. We didn't go on formal dates to dances, the movies or with other couples. We just seemed perfectly content to talk, listen to the radio or tapes and yes we did find time to park, hold hands and smooch. It was several months before we went further than that.

After a couple of weeks going together I spent the night at her place and slept on the couch. As we saw each other even more frequently I would spend more nights there, but now she would be in the top bed of the bunk bed and I would nap on the floor in her room. Her bottom bunk was covered with books. We would talk until one of us fell asleep, then the other would turn off the light.

Dave Chamberlain (Tiny), the huge bouncer from Sully's, and I became good friends. Occasionally when Josie and I wanted to spend some time by ourselves away from Frank's house, we'd go over and stay with Tiny. Tiny would have the bedroom, Josie the couch: and due to lack of space I'd again be on the floor.

One morning when Tiny got up to get ready for work, he came through the living room in the dark and stepped on my hand. I yelled, jumped up and Tiny stumbled into the hallway. He only had a towel around his waist, so when he jumped back the towel fell off and there was Tiny buck naked in front of Josie, totally red all over. For a moment he just stood there staring at her, then he scrambled around grabbing a couch pillow to cover his front. I thought Josie would die laughing.

Shortly after I started going with Josie, I convinced her to study for and complete the GED for her high school equivalency. My dad had given me that good advice, so I in turn passed it on to her. Josie was a very intelligent individual and I didn't want her to have a life just cleaning and waiting on others. She did as I suggested, passing with high scores.

More and more I was closing myself off from my friends. It was just Josie and I together during our hours away from work. She did suggest that she would like to frequent a bar and do a little drinking just to experience the other side of life. Though she was under-age I figured she would have to fill that square sooner or later. Frank ran a pretty permissive household, so that it wasn't that Josie had never had alcohol before, it was just that she hadn't frequent-ed bars.

Donnie Albert was an old childhood friend of mine who was a local star musician and owned a bar, The Hidden Camel. I agreed to meet Josie there at a certain time, but I was late. When I finally arrived one of the guys had bought her some drinks and she was feeling no pain. She was belligerent about why I was late and began dishing out a tongue-lashing and couldn't tolerate my excuse. This was not the Josie I knew, so I said the hell with it and left. I found out later that someone had bought her a few more drinks and she threw up all over the table.

The next morning I stopped over to see how she was doing. By then she had given me a key to the house, so I didn't wake her Dad up coming in. I woke her up but she was real groggy and her color was the mottled white of spoiled veal. She could barely hold her head up. Josie was supposed to be at the Landmark for work at 1:30pm. I told her she better forget about work and recover. That was not an option in her mind. If she didn't work there would be no money. Frank never would give her anything. If she borrowed money from him she would have to pay back extra for interest.

An old hangover remedy came to mind. It was a concoction of eggs, tabasco sauce, lemonade and olive oil. Unfortunately I forgot to put the olive oil in and that must have been the key ingredient, for the rest caused her to throw up all over the living room floor. Josie did manage to show up for work though. I felt that she had achieved a good exposure to the drinker's world.

It was a surprise to both of us when Josie learned she was pregnant. Yes, we had progressed from the hand holding and kiss-ing stage to a more intimate relationship. It seemed like a natural progression of the love between us, and it was beautiful. We knew we were in love; marriage was something we both wanted, so this only moved our plans up some. Personally, I was very happy to have a child coming. For a long time I had thought about how nice it would be to have a family again; especially after botching up things the first time. We made plans for an April 15th wedding. As it was income tax day she knew I wouldn't forget.

With my advertising career by the wayside, I was now working for the Lansing Police Department in a new program funded by a government CETA grant. This program involved putting representatives of the police department on bicycle patrol in high-risk areas, with the hope that this presence might curtail some crime. It might also allow for the recovery of stolen bicycles, and lead to some arrests.

At 34 I was the oldest individual pedaling around the city on patrol. I did love the work with total respect for my boss, Louie Mills. He was a 36-year veteran of the police force, with the distinction of never having to draw his pistol during all his years of service. After working for him for awhile I could understand why he was so well liked and respected. Our liaison with the Lansing Police Department was Officer Tom Wilson. He was also a great guy with a fine sense of humor.

Josie and I wanted a nice wedding. From what Josie said her father had helped out a lot when the brothers were married, but he wasn't offering anything for his only daughter's marriage. I thought that was rather mean.

More and more Josie opened up about unpleasant family things. Frank used to rent space for a beauty shop in the lower level of his house and at the age of 9 or so he had Josie working down there as a part-time receptionist. Of course she didn't make much, but the patrons thought it was a novel idea. She said that Frank took most of her earnings for the 'family'.

When I started work at the police department they of course did a background check on me and when I told them I was marrying Josie Welbes, they raised their eyebrows, "Frank Welbes's daughter?" I knew something was up. Questions led me to the fact that in the past they had numerous complaints of Frank beating his boys. As far as I know he never laid a hand on Josie, but apparently when the boys got out of line his frustration led to beating the hell out of them, and the neighbors or somebody regularly complained. I found out later from Josie, that John was the one that got beat on the most.

With meager funds we put on one fine wedding. I sold my car to pay for a nice wedding dress for Josie and I arranged for the use of a small banquet room at Longs Convention Center on Cedar Street.

Unknown to Jo, I called in some favors from old clients and friends from the radio days. A good friend of mine, Fred Guetschow, was the owner of Consumer Foods. He said, "Don't worry about it Bill, I'll take good care of you and your bride." Wow, did he. Probably there was $1,500 worth of food and he only charged me a little over two hundred. Guests marveled over the spread he provided. For the reception I hired a small band, but only had them play ten or fifteen numbers before we switched over to records. It was a smooth transition with hardly anyone noticing. There was a bar, but the guests paid for their own drinks. We even rented a tuxedo for Frank and he looked great.

The wedding was held at Trinity Lutheran Church in Lansing and with a captive audience, the minister lectured on morality. I'm standing there with a pregnant young girl—just sweating like a sinner and he goes on for 30 minutes. Anyway Jo looked gorgeous and it was a wonderful celebration; one that we couldn't afford, but one that did demonstrate how much we were in love. The families might not have been enthralled with the union, but our friends had a great time and many thought it was a neat relationship even with the big age difference. On our wedding day, April 15, 1978, Josie was 19 and I was 34. Her brother John was best man and his wife maid of honor.

Frank did allow us to rent a new Ford Thunderbird in his name for the honeymoon. We drove it to Upper Michigan and toured the whole peninsula. It was a great time punctuated by one close call. Driving up to look off Castle Rock I almost didn't see the chain closing off the access road. When I stopped it was almost touching the windshield of the new Ford. Frank almost had a heart attack when we told him about that.

A great wedding and honeymoon and we were totally in love. Our first child was on the way and we didn't have much, but we were ready to tackle the real world, or so we thought.

Josephine at
Lansing Eastern
High School.

Wedding Day.

Duane and Joyce (his girlfriend).

Duane and the Bride.

Honeymoon in the U.P.

ROCKY ROAD

We began our marriage living upstairs in Frank's home; the house where Josie was brought up. I was back at the bike patrol for the city of Lansing and she was back to work for the Landmark Restaurant. It was time to work and save some money. We still had to pay Frank rent. He collected like Ebenezer Scrooge.

There was one little problem that had to be fixed straight out. Her father and brothers showed Jo very little respect for maintaining the household after her mother died. That was not just my observation, it was also the way Josie felt. As we were living in her father's house, I really didn't think it was prudent for me to try and straighten him out, but the brothers were a different story. We hadn't been home from our honeymoon for more than a couple days when Josie's brother John pops in. "Hey I've been waiting for you guys to get home. Here are my dirty clothes." I handed John the phone book. "Here, you can find the number to the cleaners. Josie's not doing your laundry anymore."

"Well if that's the way it's gonna be," He said.

I was surprised at how good-natured he was about it.

Word got around and I had a call from brother Jim.

"What ya pulling over there?"

"Well John seemed to take it pretty well. Josie's not doing the brother's laundry anymore. She's got a husband to take care of."

"We'll see for how long." Then he hung up.

I didn't want housekeeping to be the whole focus of Josie's life.

She was too intelligent for that. I had encouraged her to get her GED —maybe someday when we could afford it, she could enroll in college.

We both did our best to treat Frank well. Josie doted on him, but for some reason he seemed to always keep her at a distance. Maybe it was different when I wasn't around, I'm not sure. She wanted to please him so much, to make him like her. Josie kept his part of the house clean as well as ours. When the beauty or barbershop downstairs was rented, she would collect the rent and put it in an envelope for him. It seemed like his normal response for all she did was, "Get me something to eat", or "get me a Coke."

It seemed that the best way for me to keep on his good side was to do little chores for him. I tried to keep the yard taken care of, fixed his car a couple of times and picked up stuff from the store when he needed it.

I was really enjoying my patrol job. Just recently I nabbed this 20 year old that had three outstanding felony warrants. I saw him go by with this brand new looking racing bike that seemed out of place in this poor neighborhood. We were on Baker Street and when he saw me coming he jumped off the bike and let it bounce down the side of a neighborhood store. It was an expensive 1500 molycrome endurance bike; certainly it didn't belong to this dude. I stopped him at the store door and requested some ID. He took off running, but he was on foot now and I had my bike, so in short order I had him and his identification. When I radioed his information in I was alerted to his warrant status.

The neighborhood where Josie was brought up had been racially mixed for some time. A couple doors down were the Crumps. They were a black family, whose children grew up and went to school with Josie. Rubin, their father, worked at Motor Wheel Corporation.

Another close neighbor was Duane Leland. Although Duane wasn't a blood relative, everyone considered that he was part of the family, and called him Uncle Duane. He was about the same age as Frank and worked at Oldsmobile. The story goes that Duane's parents had abandoned him during the depression and Josie's grandmother ended up raising him as a member of her family.

Everyone loved Duane. He was not only fun to be with, he was generous and always provided loads of food for the family get-together's. Duane was in WWII too. He fought in the Pacific and I saw a picture of him in uniform. He never talked much about it, and when I asked him for details, he'd just say, "We fought the Japs, that was it." On the other hand Frank talked about his experiences all the time.

It was just a 50's type neighborhood and I enjoyed being a part of it. In the summertime everyone hung out on their front porch and visited while the kids ran between the houses, through sprinklers and all the things kids do in the summer. Occasionally Rubin Crump would tell me stories about how rough old Frank was on the boys.

Once, brother John stole Duane's car and drove it to Detroit; blowing the engine. John was only about eleven or twelve years old. He had tried to take a bunch of Duane's food along too, but the grocery sacks had ripped leaving food spread over the front lawn. Rubin giggled, then said, "When we heard where he was Duane and I went down and brought him home otherwise Frank probably would have killed him."

Duane helped Josie and I out more than once. He knew we were pretty hard up so I'd do some job for him and he'd give us a hundred dollars or so. Sometimes I didn't do anything and he was still offering us money. "Take it. It's just a loan," he'd say.

Joyce was Uncle Duane's girl friend. They were never married, but she was there all the time. If we came to the door unexpectedly you could hear the rustle of clothes and things. By the time the door opened they were presentable. I think at one time she was a boarder with Jo's grandparents and just ended up staying on.

One summer Duane rented a cabin up on Drummond Island and invited me along to go fishing. We took this rowboat and a 12 pack of beer out into the big lake; too far out for me. I'm not one to be a long ways from shore in big open water, so when this freighter went by I was petrified. The waves generated by its wake just about capsized us, but Duane loved it. He said, "Let's do it again." Being around the man was a real joy.

During these years, even though I was not particularly close to Jo's brothers, we did tolerate each other. Jim even asked me to ride with him one evening in his patrol car. It seemed like a nice gesture from him. It wasn't a particularly exciting evening but then we got word that there was a break in at the high school. Jim deputized me as we drove toward the school. When Jim entered the parking lot he didn't see the cement barriers and drove right over them.

"I'm going in to check things out. You stay here," he said. Jim showed me how to work the radio and handed me a shotgun.

I stood there under the light holding the empty shotgun. 'This is not smart.' I thought. In the light I was a perfect target. I walked over to the bushes and melted into the shadows by the building. It wasn't long before this guy slips out the school window close to me and I have him on the ground. I didn't know how to get Jim's attention so I moved the culprit over to the car and turned Jim's siren on and off. Jim heard the siren and came running out. His pistol fell from the holster breaking the sight off. It was a weird evening and my last on patrol.

It seemed like Jim always had something to prove, especially concerning his shooting ability. We competed with tin plates and cans as targets, and I'll have to say, I was a very good shot. At one of Duane's barbeques Jim had a pellet gun. We sat at a picnic table and Jim spotted a pigeon on the roof. Right there in town the deputy sheriff takes aim and hits the pigeon. "That's the way a real man shoots," he said. I hate shooting creatures for no reason at all and it sickened me watching this pigeon flopping around on the roof.

Jim hands me the gun and in the process the sight gets moved a little. I thought at first, that the sight twist was accidental. After straightening the sight I took aim and nailed the bird in the head, putting it out of its misery. Probably there was some luck to the shot, but Jim didn't know what to say. "How'd you do that?"

"You ought to tighten that sight you moved around with your thumb."

Jim climbed in his car and drove around for a couple hours then returned. It was hard to know how to take the guy. One time he

could be like Andy Griffith, the comic guy, and the next like Ted
Bundy the killer.

Our son Michael was born on September 25th. Josie was in labor
for 23 hours and pretty wrung out. They let me hold him. After
wiggling and crying a little, he settled right down in my arms. I laid
him next to her and we both cried we were so happy. Another automobile marked that event too. I had left our '55 Chevy station
wagon parked by the maternity entrance. As I was putting on a
gown and mask for the delivery a security guard informed me that
my car had rolled down the driveway, over the curb and had ended
up in a fence.

Later that day, Jo's family came to visit. They lined up at the
nursery to look at Mike. Barry's wife Carol said, "Oh he's not
deformed at all. Looks pretty normal." That was typical Carol. My
mother had never really approved of me marrying Jo, but when she
saw him, Michael became the star attraction in her life too.

When we got Michael home, things were really not that pleasant. He was sick for almost three months. The poor little fella had
the croup, hardly ever sleeping. Of course when he didn't sleep,
neither did we. We finally started taking turns on a shift basis so we
could get rest. In December, they cut off the CETA funds for my
job with the Lansing Police. Fortunately Jo's hospitalization and
the medicines for Michael were covered.

Out of a job again, I got part-time work weekends at a car dealership in Haslett. Finally I started delivering papers for the Detroit
News. It didn't pay much, but I thought there might be potential.

Frank's house was not in very good shape, plus it was obvious
that in that neighborhood the property values were not increasing.
Josie convinced her father that maybe he would be wise to fix the
place up to code and sell while he could, then find a nicer place.

Frank ran into this real estate lady, whom he described as being,
"very nice." And, over a cup of coffee she sold him this huge three-
story farmhouse near a subdivision on Waverly. Frank envisioned
turning the place into a boarding house with a monthly income of
$2,000. The nice realtor avoided mentioning to Frank, that the area
wasn't zoned for that.

Frank said that if we took care of the lawn we could stay in the new place too. I don't think he wanted to lose Josie, his house-keeper, but then it seemed like a good deal for us. The lawn was huge, but I kept it up and tried fixing things in the house, starting with the kitchen. Frank lived downstairs, but would eat some meals with us. Eventually Frank suggested that it would be fairer if we paid $200 a month plus the yard work. He found out that he couldn't legally rent out the upstairs because of zoning restrictions, but he did rent the mother-in-law type house out back to our friend Tiny. It was a good deal for Tiny at first, but Frank soon started upping the rent on him until he moved. That's how Frank operated.

The house on Waverly was obviously not turning out to be a good deal for Frank or us. Several things needed repair, especially the roof. Poorly insulated, it was also very expensive to heat. Frank would say, "You guys talked me into this!" In reality Josie only suggested he sell the other place; he picked out this monstrosity. That was only a part of the problem though.

I don't think life was pleasant for Frank. Everything in his life revolved around work at Oldsmobile and his war experiences. He had no hobbies. At Oldsmobile his job was repairing bumpers. He used to brag about being able to polish the bad spots out of the bumpers in two or three hours and sit on his ass for the rest of the shift; a good Union job. From people he worked with I heard he did a substandard job, but because of his seniority he was protected, plus he never missed a day of work.

When Frank came home from work he'd throw down his lunch bucket and watch TV with his two dogs Earl and Sarge. The dogs were spoiled and over-fed. When Frank was home they had the run of the house and made a mess shedding and slobbering on every-thing. He'd feed them on clean floors that Josie had polished, and then bitch cause the house wasn't clean. I love animals but it was bothering both of us and occasionally we'd ask him to control them. Finally, one day in a fit of rage he had them both put to sleep. After that he said, "I hope you're both happy—you killed my dogs." I never did understand that one. I think toward the end of his life, he was mentally unstable.

Frank also hoarded money. We didn't know this until he accused us of taking some of it. Apparently he had stacks of 20's and 50-dollar bills hidden in this flimsy cabinet. John also accused us of taking it, but I'm sure that was just to cover his tracks. John had a real reputation for stealing anyway—starting with Duane's car.

It was close to Christmas when the final confrontation with Frank took place. We all were sitting in this huge old kitchen and Frank was bitching about all the things that needed fixing—hinting that I wasn't doing my part. I said, "You've got money, you get them fixed." Little Mike was about 2 years old then, and for some reason he started screaming. Frank backhanded him right across the kitchen floor. I was livid. He could beat his boys, but not mine. I came over the counter and nailed him against the refrigerator. He took a swing but I was faster and punched him a good one. Frank ran to the basement door and said, "You S.O.B. I'll have them (meaning Jim and John) kick your ass." He headed down the stairs closing the door behind him. In hot pursuit I splintered the old oak door with a kick. Josie was now holding Michael, both of them crying. I tried to comfort my family and cool my temper.

That day I had to take a job application test with the State. I would keep Josie informed when I was out job hunting—leaving phone numbers to reach me. Late in the day she was on the phone crying. Frank had called John and Jim. All our belongings had been thrown out in the front yard, baby clothes and everything. Jim was even there in his Eaton County deputy's uniform. I knew I was wrong to slug Frank, but I wasn't going to let him start manhandling my kid as he had his.

It was three days before Christmas and we had little money and no place to stay. After all the unpaid loans from my parents, my mother was cool to the idea of offering us any help. There was nowhere to turn and we were desperate.

The only way Social Services would help was if Josie was on her own with Michael. As a last resort Josie applied for ADC as a separated wife. We got shelter for her and Michael in a low income-housing complex at the north end of De Witt and I stayed at my mothers.

The De Witt apartment was rather small and shabby, but it was something. The ADC check was about $215 a month, which gave us something to get on our feet. I would be there late in the day and tuck them in at night, then leave to sleep at Ma's. I'd be back to check on them around 6am, then look for more work the rest of the day. Josie was worried that somebody would be watching us so I did not sleep overnight.

This arrangement worked fine until the Shawnborns moved in.

The Shawborns were an extended family of gypsies. How many there were or when they actually started taking up residence there I'm not sure, but they were well established before we were aware of their presence. Josie had an upstairs apartment and mentioned a couple of times of a lot of noise around the lower level. Her first exposure to them was when she carried Michael downstairs and there were two men standing near the foot of the stairs. One of the men said something to her and when she ignored him he spit on her. When she went out to get in her car, three of the tires were flat. When she came back to return to her apartment they were still by the stairs. This time the other guy spat on Michael.

She got a hold of me on the phone, saying for some reason there were three flat tires on her car. There was no mention of being spat-on, probably because she didn't want to upset me right off the bat. When I arrived I could see Josie's tires had been slashed.

I had two tires, but her spare needed air too. Fortunately I brought a little hand pump along. I just finished changing the last tire and I noticed a group of dark skinned men were standing around me. A couple of them were fairly old, but the one closest to me was about 20 years old with this bandage in a figure eight around his shoulder. He must have had some kind of injury.

As I became aware of their presence I also sensed that the smart-assed remarks coming from the group were aimed at me. I was still knelt down when I felt this wetness on my neck. I kinda wiped at the spot and looked up at the young one with the bandage. He said, "What you lookin' at mother-fucker?"

I don't think they thought a guy that weighed almost 200 pounds could move that quickly. I turned that young fellow around, smashed him into the wall and forced his elbows together behind his back. Ouch, that had to hurt as I thought I could hear his collarbone crack.

From the corner of my eye I could see this sixty-year-old guy swinging something at me. It looked like part of an aluminum-hunting bow. That guy I caught right in the stomach with my foot. I picked up the metal pump and caught another across the face. One guy slipped into the near apartment momentarily and was on his way back out, probably with something to hit me with. He met the door head on thanks to my footwork.

About this time I heard Josie scream. Near the stairway one of the gypsy women was trying to hassle her. Josie held Michael around the waist with one arm and was punching the lady in the face with the other fist. The rest of these dudes were standing there with their eyes wide open not believing that they were seeing this little girl with the child punching hell out of one of their women.

I motioned for Josie to take her car and leave. When she was safely underway I climbed in the old Chevrolet. A car was parked blocking my way in front, but with a little start I bumped it right out of the way. Meanwhile they smashed my back window.

We called the police and came back the next morning when we were sure they had arrived. Josie's apartment window was broken. Everything was calm with all the gypsies. They were just standing in the road minding their own business. One was bouncing a basketball. We told the police what happened. One of the family said, "We don't know what happened. He's a liar."

While the police were talking to the group Josie and I went up to the apartment. It had been broken into and her things were scattered around in disarray. I said, "You need to move out of here. Let's pack." Stubborn Josie would have none of it. "I'm not leaving, we've paid our rent! If I move out where will I go?"

I couldn't imagine her staying there again with those people around. While we were arguing the police left. I started carrying things down and the gypsies began harassing us again; this time throwing stuff. I go back upstairs and call the police. We wait, but no police. I call again. The lady dispatcher says, "We've had a lot of trouble with those people and my husband is a policeman. I'm not going to send him out there in harms way." Holy God, I didn't believe what I was hearing. "Come on Jo let's go." We threw her stuff in the car. I made sure Jo was in before I floored it. This guy was running along the driver side and got my door partially open. Quick as a wink I had my foot on the door and cleaned him off of his feet dumping him into the rough pavement.

As I drove off I could see that these folks could view the police coming for a half mile before they got there. Later I called a State Police friend of mine and told him the story. The next day when we drove in, our neighbors were ready to come out and bug us again. What they didn't see was the State Police cruiser coming in from the back way. The troopers arrested a whole bunch of them and one was on their most wanted list for attacking a policeman in Wisconsin or Michigan with an axe.

Later I heard that a judge allowed them to post bail. They left town immediately and disappeared.

We cleaned up the apartment and despite our supposed separation I stayed there nights, even though all the gypsies had left. Again, the local police let us know we were on our own if anything happened.

Those people had been terrorizing the whole complex, not just us. The old folks there were scared stiff. Josie and I were treated like heroes.

That summer we moved from De Witt to an old farmhouse down by Potterville. Although not everything that happened there was good, Mike and I remember it as the place where as a family we had our best times. If Josie were here I know she'd say the same thing.

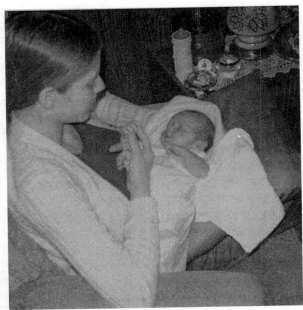

Jo and Mike.

Michael's proud parents.

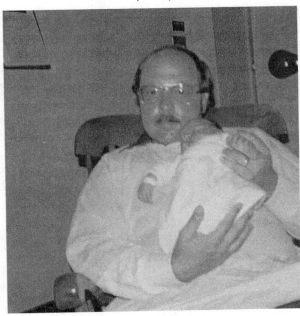

Bill and Mike.

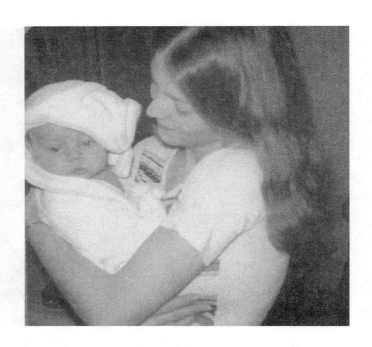

Bath in the kitchen sink.

Dave Chamberlain "Tiny" and Michael.

THE FARM

Let me tell you about another member of our family, who had been with us since we lived with Josie's father in Lansing. Princess was the smallest of 13 gorgeous puppies born to Shenandoah Valley Red an AKC registered Irish setter. Her owner rented a tiny house behind Franks and one by one we saw the puppies being sold. The only pup no one wanted was the one we called Princess. Her official name was Lady Redford. While we tried to scrape up the money to buy her, Josie kept an eye on her to make sure she was still there and healthy. One day Jo came in crying, "Princess is sick. She's all bloated up and laying on her side." We ran out and picked her up. She was as big as a beach ball. The owner let us take her to the vet, at our expense. The vet said that she had overeaten, probably had eaten all the other dogs feed along with her own. The owner felt a little guilty about having us pay the vet bill for his dog, so he just said, "You can have her."

Princess went with us to the farm on Kinsell Highway by Potterville. She enjoyed the freedom of running around in the fields and big yard just as much as we enjoyed being out in the country.

'House for rent in the country,' said the newspaper ad. The farm belonged to Don Hume, a neat old gentleman in his 70's. He had grown up on the place, but finally retired, rented the land out and moved into Lansing with his wife. Don seemed to take a liking to our young family right away. He said he'd rent it to us for only $150 a month. That sure seemed reasonable to me.

After we rented the house Mr. Hume still came out visiting on a regular basis. He would trim the apple trees or just putter around with some job to keep busy. I think he didn't have enough to do in town and missed the farm. Of course, my impression was that his wife was a little domineering, so maybe the farm was a getaway.

It was a nice old farmhouse with a dairy barn not far away, and a dilapidated corncrib in between. What really made the place attractive was the big oak tree right in the front yard. It shaded the house and most of the yard.

My mother was kind enough to assist us financially for the move to Potterville. I was expanding the newspaper delivery route but still we qualified for food stamps and were dirt poor.

As little as we had these were such happy times. The three of us would sneak out to the barn and hide in the hay from Princess. She always found Jo and Mike first because they couldn't keep from giggling. We were all really like a bunch of kids running around that farm.

Like Frank's big house on Waverly, this house was not insulated. Basically there was just siding with wallboards and paper in the inside. You could sit on the couch smoking and watch the smoke drift right out through the cracks by the windows. There was a big old fuel oil tank outside which I couldn't afford to fill, so I'd just bring five gallons home each night and pour it through a funnel into the tank. Some nights it would be so cold that I was shaking, spilling it as I tried to hit the funnel.

In the dead of winter I thought we were lucky to have the house temperature in the fifties. At night we'd all huddle up under a blanket on the floor to watch TV. Of course every night of the week the newspapers had to be delivered, so while Jo and Mike were sleeping I'd be out on the road dropping off papers.

As the route expanded I recruited other workers to deliver to a certain area and I would leave a quantity of papers at a drop off point for them. We delivered to private residences, newspaper coin boxes and businesses. In many instances there were several areas we drove through where there were no drop offs at all. Probably the reason the routes became available to us in the first place was that they had proved unprofitable for someone else. We worked diligently to develop the dead areas and our business was becoming more profitable all the time. As soon as the cash became available I put a good pair of snow tires on the old '72 Chevy. Being reliable was the most important part of our business.

Jo would handle all the newspaper bookwork and make the collections from the paper coin boxes. In fact, I actually had the business registered in her name. With my lack of concentration this seemed like a smart thing to do.

We were no longer on welfare now, and it was tough to make ends meet. We did scrape up enough money for Josie to take a few basic courses at Lansing Community College. Although our schedule was hectic, we spent a lot of quality time with our son. Josie was just fascinated with Michael. During those early years it seems like every time I turned around she was taking another photograph of him.

Not too long after we moved to the farm Jo's brother Jim and a deputy named Carpenter showed up on our doorstep. It looked like an official visit as they both were in their Eaton County Sheriff Department uniforms and they had arrived in their patrol cars. Josie went to the door to see what they wanted. I could hear Jim say, "Where's your husband?" When I heard that, I glided down to the basement. I could still hear them talking, something about an arrest warrant for me. Josie told him I wasn't there, but that wasn't good enough for Jim, he wanted to look around inside. After searching the ground floor he went upstairs. The other deputy waited on the porch.

While Jim was upstairs Josie came by the basement stairway and we made plans to meet later on another road bordering the farm. Neither of us could figure why Jim was here with an arrest warrant, but we decided it would be better to deal with the problem in our own good time.

Between the house basement and the barn there was a false wall and entrance to the root cellar. I moved the canvas covering the entrance and had to crouch down to fit inside. It wasn't any place I wanted to be, however it was one way to be out of sight.

With a flashlight in my mouth I made my way through the cobwebs and spiders and slipped out the root cellar door to the barn. I peeked out a crack and saw a deputy walking into the garage to look for me. I could hear our car door slam shut so he must have been looking in the car too. From there I slipped through the adjacent cornfield and waited near the road.

It seemed like a couple hours before Josie came roaring down the road in our old 1972 Bel Air. She spotted me, slid to a stop and motioned me to jump in the back. She said, "I think they're still around and probably following me." Michael was strapped in the front seat and I lay on the back floor. There were no seats in the back because that's where I hauled my papers. Josie said, "Here they come!" The tires spun in the dirt and we were off. She had been right about them being near by, waiting out of sight to see if I'd show up. I'd like to have been driving, but in this instance I just hunkered down in the back while Josie poured the coal to the old Bel Air.

It was like a scene out of "Dukes of Hazzard". The cops were behind with their lights on and we were literally flying over these country roads.

"How fast you goin'?" I yelled from my prone position.

"Hell, I don't know," was the reply.

From Nixon Road to the Vermontville Highway, we were now in Ingham County. They followed us for another mile then turned around just past Waverly. We kept going and ended up over at Tiny's place for the night. Apparently Jim had found out that I was in arrears for a child support payment in Clinton County. That would have been while we were separated and Josie stayed in De Witt. He pulled my name off some state bulletin and I heard he bragged to somebody that he was going to bring me in on the fender of his car, just like a trophy deer.

We decided it was best to go up to St. Johns and for me to turn myself in. That afternoon we sat in the Clinton County courtroom while the Judge went through the other cases. Jo's brother Jim also slipped in and sat in the back of the courtroom. He was in full uniform.

In each of the cases prior to mine, several thousand dollars were involved in missed child support payments. When the judge was given my paperwork, he looked rather puzzled.

"Are these figures right?" He asked. "Where are the other zero's? There must be some mistake."

I responded, "Well sir, the Eaton County Sheriffs Deputies were at my door with an arrest warrant yesterday."

"I've got real problems with that," he said.

"Who would issue an arrest warrant for $150?"

Jim slipped out of the courtroom and soon the Eaton County patrol car was leaving.

"Well what can you arrange for this late payment?" asked the judge.

"I've got my checkbook right here your honor. I'll write a check today."

Summers on the farm were the best. Our picnics and activities seemed to happen around the big tree in the front yard. Josie's friend, Jane Carpenter, whom she had known since high school, and her husband Mark came out often. They had two girls for Mike to play with and Jo's other friend Tina had a boy a year older than Mike. I had pretty much drifted away from my old buddies as my life centered on the family and the newspaper route.

I have told you about the incident with Jim trying to arrest me—that was nothing compared to what happened with her brother John. At midday I was still upstairs in bed trying to get some sleep.

Downstairs I heard this loud crash and arguing. John and Josie were in a heated argument about something. When I went downstairs I saw Josie's china cabinet laying face down on the floor with broken crystal keepsakes inside.

John had been delivering newspapers for us for a couple months, but things weren't working out. Along with his pay Jo had been giving him money for lunches and gas—John wanted more. I think he had a drug habit to support along with his drinking. I'm not sure what precipitated the argument, but when I came downstairs John headed out the door to his car. Josie was crying and followed him out. I was trying to get myself in tune with the situation and followed Josie out. Michael was sitting on the porch crying.

John climbed into his Pinto and proceeded to spin around in our yard. The porch steps faced the barn and Michael was on the bottom step. John was now coming right toward the porch. I grabbed Michael and literally threw him up on the porch while John knocked the bottom step off and stopped. I felt like a raging bull staring at a red cape. I was trying to get a hold of John. Meanwhile Josie is screaming, "Don't hurt him, don't hurt him!"

John spun around again, knocking Josie down. I thought he had run over her. I hit the driver's side of the windshield with my fist; hard enough to drive it inside. John tore out in the road and stopped. Now he's yelling, trying to coerce me into coming out to fight him while Josie's on the ground hurting and crying. I take her into the house to call an ambulance. She doesn't want me to call one. Her jeans are torn, her leg bloody. I'm not sure how bad she's hurt. John meanwhile is squealing his tires up and down the road, and then pulls back up in the driveway. I'm out the front door like a shot, quicker than he expected. I grab his door and get it open as he's taking off again. Holding on tight and digging my heels in, the top hinge on the door breaks and the door drags on the ground as he speeds down the road.

From Kinsell Highway John must have taken M-100 to US-27, for when the state police caught him he was heading north towards Lansing in the southbound traffic lane. I'm not sure exactly how it happened, but I heard somehow the state police found out that John's brother Jim worked for the Eaton County Sheriff Department, so John was released to Jim's custody. Charges were never filed and John got off scot-free.

John's wife Corey went to the hospital to see Josie. She said, "Jo, this is awful, you have to forgive John." Josie was still in semi-shock. She asked Corey to get her purse, which was under the bed. She wanted a cigarette to settle down. Josie started to light up, but the nurse said, "No smoking in here."

When I came back in to see Josie, she reminded me that our rent money was in her purse. Just checking to make sure, we discovered the money was missing. The only visitor Josie had was Corey.

As brother and sister, Josie and John were very close. Josie said he acted screwy that day and I had never witnessed such violent behavior from him either. If he were on drugs it would explain his actions. We all were lucky though as he could have easily killed Josie or for that matter, Michael, if I had not been there to move him out of the way. Our relationship with Josie's family was already strained and that incident made things even worse. We turned more to ourselves and didn't see her family at all.

We tried to keep our lawn looking nice in the summer. Usually Josie and I would trade off on the mower when the grass needed cutting. One warm afternoon Michael and I sat on the porch while Josie took her turn behind the mower. Jo had just made a swipe past us when she suddenly abandoned the mower and jumped up on the porch. She really looked frightened. When I walked over I could see a large King snake lying in the grass in front of the mower. She was screaming, "Just get rid of it!" Being Mr. Macho, I just picked it up and threw it over in the garden. She wasn't in the mood to continue so with a half ass grin on my face I took over.

A half-hour or so after Josie's snake incident. I found another one. Probably it was the same one who had decided to return to the yard. I was mowing with shorts on, but didn't discover our slithery friend until the lawn mower had chewed him up and spit him or parts of him all over my legs and shoes. Josie thought that was hilarious. "Well how do you like your snake skin shoes?" she asked.

Our pet family gradually expanded. Joining our Irish setter, Princess, was Molly a female black Lab. Then one day we were headed to my mothers and saw this little black cat running down the highway centerline. Josie and Michael were insistent that we pick her up. That was Toby. She became a good mouser and was aggressive in removing snakes from our yard. She too became a full-fledged family member.

Christmases on the farm were very memorable. We all were so close—lots of hugging and kissing. There weren't a lot of expensive presents, but we had each other and Josie's homemade cookies. Man, they were good.

One winter day we had quite an ice storm. I lay on the living room couch trying to catch up on my rest while Josie and Mike went into town. Later in the afternoon I looked out the front window and saw them both trudging up the driveway. Our '74 Malibu Chevrolet was not in sight.

Josie said the corner was so slippery she had missed the turn and ended up out in a field. Pissed off and tired, I didn't even ask if they were both OK. I was just interested in the condition of the car. I put on my snowsuit and boots—grumbling about her driving ability as I headed out the door. I cut across our yard to the road. The ice was crunchy beneath my feet in the yard, but once I plodded out in the road my feet went out from under me and I was sliding down the hill on my back. Rolling over on my hands and knees I was back up again and then instantly down again. As I carefully picked myself up one more time, I glanced towards the house and saw two red laughing faces framed in the front window. I used the culvert for the rest of my walk to the corner. Driving the car in a circle I got it out of the field and onto the road. I still needed to get 5 bags of water softener salt in town to put in the trunk to get home. Josie never forgot that little incident and regularly brought it up in years to come.

Even though relations with Josie's brothers and Dad were not good, she would still always remember their birthdays with a card and gradually we started attending the family holiday gatherings again. Usually they were at one of the brothers' or Duane's house. I'm not sure why we attended; as once we were there no one had much to say to us. Each time when we started to go home everyone would say, "Are you guys rushing off already?" And then we'd say to ourselves, as we drove away, "They didn't act like we were really there until we got ready to leave." It was always the same, but still it was Jo's wish that we still go.

Michael started school while we were at the farm. I'd get home early in the morning and be there with Josie until he climbed on the bus, then head for the bed. Josie would collect the monies from the paper route, attend one of her classes at the community college then we'd all be together again when Michael came home, until bedtime. I would get another hour of sleep, and then head out to pickup and deliver the papers. A strange schedule, but one that did put

Josie and I with our son while he was growing up. I learned to survive really well on four or five hours sleep. As always, in my spare time, I would be fixing up old cars to sell for a little extra cash.

As good as things were for us on the farm, one little problem did come up. And, it gradually grew into major proportions. We had these neighbors down the road that were really strange. Mike remembers them as the big fat witchy woman with the skinny husband. I guess the problem started when the husband made a feeble little pass at Josie down at the local grocery store. Really, I can't remember what the guy actually said to her, but Josie had the knack of being able to come up with the perfect rebuttal comment on the spur of the moment. Josie's remark was demeaning enough to completely embarrass the guy. Other people in the store heard her comments and started laughing. He just left his shopping cart and stomped out of the store.

I wasn't aware of the store incident Josie had with our neighbor, until there seemed to be a lot of trash appearing in our yard. We traced its origin to the neighbor. This seemed rather strange to me until Josie mentioned the fact that she'd thoroughly embarrassed the guy in the store. I tried to settle the trash in our yard problem, but not always being Mr. Smooth, their unhappiness with us got to the point that when they went by our house they would drive off the road to scare our dog Molly. One day she didn't move out of the way fast enough. Their car hit and killed her. Jo was devastated.

When I arrived at our neighbor's door to discuss Molly's death, the husband met me with a ball bat. He was kind of twirling it in his hand. The bat slipped from his grip and fell to the ground. Fortunately I was quicker than he was in retrieving it. After smashing in his front window I slung the bat out in the field. Also I mentioned to him what would happen if he ever showed up on our property again. The rest of the summer was quiet. Hopefully the problem with these people was over.

We still had two dogs left, Princess the Irish setter and LW which was Molly's daughter. Molly possessed a great personality, however she did enjoy an occasional toss in the hay, so to speak.

Molly mated with a champion Weimaraner named Buck. The resulting eight puppies looked like shaved Irish setters. We managed to give them all away except the one female, which Mike claimed. Later he told us the initials stood for Little Woman. Fortunately the puppies were all weaned before Molly was run down.

It was early that fall and we had been away from home all day. When we walked into the house it was obvious from the mess that something was wrong. We found Princess in our bedroom and she was all swelled up. The veterinarian said that it must have been a slow acting, corrosive poison that caused her great pain and bleeding. We weren't there to help her when the suffering started. She had panicked and ran all over the house ending up convulsing in our bed. We were all in tears.

For some reason I suspected the neighbors might be responsible. The man's father lived down the road and I calmly spoke with him about their son. The father admitted that his son poisoned Princess's feed. Later that evening, with a piece of pipe I broke the windows out of the guy's new Ford truck and stomped on the hood. I'm afraid of what I might have done if he'd ever stepped out of the house. That was the last contact we ever had with those people. The truck damage was never reported.

Other than the conflict with the neighbors and Josie's brothers, our time on the farm gave us our best family memories. Both Mike and I feel that way. Unfortunately all good things come to an end sooner or later. Don Hume the owner of the farm didn't want to rent the house anymore. He liked us and wanted us to buy it, but we couldn't come up with the money. Also, Josie's father's health was deteriorating too and she wanted to be near and care for him, so we moved back into Lansing. Dark clouds were forming on the horizon and soon our lives would be changed forever.

. . . MICHAEL . . .

I really enjoyed living on the farm. My memories of that time are very warm and comfortable. Times there were tough monetarily, but as a family we were very close and away from the rest of the world.

The house wasn't well heated so there were many nights when we'd be all huddled on the couch watching TV. Winters were especially rough there, but I'd to outside and make snowmen or run around the house with one of our dogs.

One memory in particular, that still brings a smile to my face, was one ice cold evening when my father got upset and stormed out of the house to go get his cigarettes from the car; not realizing he was only wearing his socks and underwear. The door shut and he didn't have his keys. He tried to open the door and my mother and I stood there in the window and laughed our asses off. She rolled on the floor laughing and I with her. Neither of us would let him in so after walking in the knee-high snow he sat in the car trying to keep warm. After what we felt was a fair punishment time, we let him back in the house. He came in with a sheepish grin on his face, knowing that we had gotten the better of him.

Even though Mom and Dad both worked a lot then, they were always around. It's really hard to roll up all my memories and experiences from the time on the farm into one thing. I remember in vivid detail the big tree out front that I'd play under. There was also an old hay silo that I would always be in with our dog Princess and one of Molly's pups, that I had named "Little Woman", we all just called her LW. There are pictures of me at this time and I look at them and see a child who's very happy with not a care in the world.

I can recall the time when our dog Molly was hit by a car. The wife of our neighbor down the road, who I remember as very heavy set and having a witch-like quality, swerved over just off the road and hit her. I was playing in the yard and saw it happen. When you're young and you lose a pet that's close to you, it can affect you deeply. The same neighbors then poisoned our beloved dog Princess.

Princess was one of those pets in your family that is closer to you than most of your relatives. She was very protective of me and loyal as any dog we've had since. We had her from the time I was born.

I remember coming home from school and seeing her bloated. My father was upset at her discomfort and took her to the vet. My parents were both heartbroken at having to put her down. The vet said that she had been poisoned and for us it was all too clear who did that. So my father reacting in the best way that he knew how, went down the road to their house and beat the hell out of the husband's new truck with a baseball bat. We never had any more trouble from them after that.

Another incident that hangs with me is one night when my Uncle John stopped over. It was right around Christmas and I was getting ready for bed. There was a loud knocking on the door and there stood my Uncle John, who was drunk.

Ever since I can remember my mother's side of the family had issues. My Uncle John was the youngest brother and he had a sense of humor, but he also had substance abuse problems. This night in particular he was stumbling around and speaking loudly. My father tried to talk to him and mother went and got him a cup of coffee. John threw the coffee cup down on the floor. Pieces of the broken cup went everywhere and I felt a shard of it hit my cheek. John then stormed out of the house. My mother was upset and my father was livid. We then heard what sounded like glass breaking outside.

My mother would sell crystal through catalogs to make extra money and her crystal was stored in the garage. Mother ran out of the house and towards our garage to see Uncle John smashing the crystal on the ground. Mom tried to stop him and calm him down, but he pushed her away and got into his car. I stood on the porch watching all this happen; dressed in my blue zip-up pajamas with the little feet attached to them.

John got into his car and spun the tires. He then hit my mom with the car and ran over her. He was drunk or high, and out of control. The car was now heading directly towards me on the porch. Father grabbed me and threw me back up into the doorway off of the porch. He then ran towards the screaming car and started to punch it.

My father is a man of principle with a witty sense of humor, but beneath lies a burning temper. Especially in a moment like that with his family in danger, the rage came out and there was no hesitation on his part to defend us. My father's adrenaline must have been pumping because he punched the moving car and broke out the driver's side window and unhinged part of the driver's side door. John then drove to the end of the driveway, got out and yelled at my father. Finally he drove off into the night.

Dad quickly ran to my mother and then called an ambulance. I remember riding in it with her to the hospital. I'm not sure if John meant to hit her or not but the result was the same. She had deep bruises and burn marks on her legs from the squealing car tires running over them. It was a while before we talked to John again and even longer before she forgave him. But, my mother was a forgiving person and still saw him as her brother and not the drunk out-of-control loser he was. Father, however, wasn't so forgiving.

The Christmas' there I remember very vividly. Mother would go into high-gear around Thanksgiving time, putting Christmas decorations up and around the house. My parents didn't have a lot of money at that time but they would do everything in their power to make sure I had plenty of gifts under the tree. I don't think my parents had the best Christmas' growing up, especially Mother, and now with a child of their own they were going to make sure that I had the best Christmas' possible.

Decorating the tree was always a big sacred ceremony in my eyes. The three of us would decorate the tree with old ornaments that had belonged to mother's mother and her grandmother. She and I would gently and strategically put them in the right place on the tree and then we would stand back and admire it, adjusting the ornaments until they were just so.

My mother *loved* Christmas. She loved Christmas more than any other time of year and any one who knew her would say that. I look back on some of those Christmas' as being the best of my life. I still decorate our tree every year with some of those same ornaments. I know she would love that.

Michael and LW by barn.

Michael with LW and Bill with Princess.

Christmas
at Duane's.

FRIENDS - NEIGHBORS - FAMILY

We now rented a house on South Francis Street in Lansing. Josie's Dad, Frank, lived down the road by Hunter Park Pool and Duane lived close on North Francis Street Josie reassumed her role as the family's caregiver, looking after her father as she had her mother. She also continued to collect the money and handled the books for the newspaper route.

The newspaper delivery business was really doing quite well. While most people delivered papers just to get by, we treated it like a business and expanded into one of the largest routes in the area. Unfortunately we did have some problems along the way. Our immediate supervisor at the News had been Ed Stonebraker. He was a one armed man that reminded me of Ernest Borgnine. I liked Ed and he treated us fairly. His replacement was Bill Stilli. Bill's secretary was basically in charge of the routes and her boyfriend delivered too. The secretary and boyfriend wanted to go on a vacation for a couple of weeks so he asked us to deliver his papers while they were gone. Picking up another persons route is a difficult undertaking, and this one was a major route too, so it took us almost five days before things were going smoothly.

When the couple returned from their vacation, I approached the man, asking for a little over three hundred dollars for our work. His reply was, "I don't owe you shit!" I had been working all night, was tired and certainly not prepared for that statement. Before he could step back I grabbed and hauled him right over the top of the desk.

"I want my money. Write a check or I'll kick your scruffy ass." He wrote the check out. But, all of a sudden I didn't trust him. I grabbed his wallet from his pants pocket. "Think I'd rather have cash." He had $300 in his wallet so I just said, "You can tear up the check". I took the cash and threw the wallet on the desk.

The next problem involved the boss. He was good looking and funny, but not what I would consider real smart. Somewhere along the line he made a pass at Josie. She rebuffed his advances, but soon he started taking some of our routes away. At first Jo didn't say anything about it to me, but finally explained the problem and her frustration with the guy. My reaction was to go in and kick his ass, but Josie cautioned against that because we needed the work. She said, "Why don't you take over the routes now and I'll look for some other work." That did seem like a very good idea. Most of the papers were being delivered by people we'd hired for the various routes, so I could just make sure everyone arrived at the drop site to get the papers and then go back to bed and run the collection the next day. I had already been collecting from the stores, so now I just had to get the boxes too. I also put my name on all the paperwork in place of Josie's.

After a couple weeks I went into the main office to settle up for the month. Stilli said, "What are you doing here?"

"I'm taking over for my wife."

"You can't do that," he said.

"Yes I can and by the way, I don't appreciate you making moves on my wife."

He looked a little embarrassed at first, then recovering he said, "You folks are getting too big." Both Josie and I had the feeling that there would be more to come later.

Jane Carpenter was Josie's best friend. They had gone to high school together and were really close. Jane's aunt was moving to Arizona so Jane invited Josie to go along to help get the aunt settled. Everything was going pretty smoothly and Josie had never traveled much so I gave my blessing to the trip. It was really the first time Josie and I had been apart since we were married. I really missed her.

Even though the temperatures were the hottest in years, Josie had a fun time in Arizona and arrived home looking refreshed. Shortly after that Jane and her husband moved to Texas.

In 1985, just 3 days after he retired from Oldsmobile, Duane died. He had really been looking forward to retirement and was planning to take Josie and Mike on a fishing trip up north. Even though he wasn't really a blood relative, he was the cohesive factor in the family. With his passing our relationship with her family was on a fast downhill slide.

After the funeral the brothers told us that the next day everything would be divided and what was not wanted would be thrown away. Barry was the executor. I was rather surprised Josie was even invited to share in Duane's possessions. Josie asked if I would go along. I said I would, but inside I didn't trust any of them. The next morning we took Mike to Ma's and arrived at Duane's to find out that the brothers and their wives had gone through everything the night before and the place was empty except for the dumpsters, which were packed. I knew Josie was hurt. The only thing I could have used were some storm windows that Duane had offered me earlier. They were smashed in the dumpsters.

Later that year Josie's father's health deteriorated and he too died. Just before passing away he supposedly changed his will cutting Josie out. I'm not sure how that was arranged as he was on life support at the time. The signature on the will didn't even look like his handwriting. On that matter we later went to court and received an award that went into Mike's funds. Frank was noted for keeping cash stashed away and I always wondered who ended up with that.

Even though I never thought Frank treated Josie very well, I am sure he loved her. And, even though she had been hurt many times Josie looked after her father as she had her mother. I guess peace of mind was her reward.

On South Francis Street we had very little contact with Josie's brothers, but we had established some close friendships. Of course the Crumps on North Francis Street were just like part of our family even though they were just neighbors. Josie had grown up next door to them and had gone to school with their kids. Gary Crump was about Josie's age and Gary's sister Gwynn, had helped take care of Josie's mother when she was sick with cancer. The youngest boy, Levertis, was actually Mike's age; they were best friends.

Aaron Crump was 3 or 4 years younger than Josie. He remembers the first time he met her at a neighbor's swimming pool. The Stevens' both were teachers and because they had a pool all the neighbor kids congregated over there in the summer. Josie was about 10 or so at the time and for some reason the Stevens' son David and Josie were having a bit of an argument. Aaron remembers hearing this little girl tell David, "Kiss my ass!" It was the first time he ever heard a girl cuss and he would never forget it. Being brought up with 3 older brothers had turned Josie into somewhat of a tomboy; a tough one at that.

After Jane Carpenter moved to Texas, Tina Russell became Jo's best friend. Tina helped with the newspaper collections and during free time she and Josie would spend hours playing scrabble, watching TV and smoking cigarettes. At that time Tina was a single mother on welfare raising two sons, Steve and Josh. Steve was another of Mike's really good friends, with Josh usually being around in Steve's care.

Besides the Crumps there were some other good neighbors. Bob and his wife lived close by. They were in their 70's. Bob looked even older, though he was always willing to kick a soccer ball around with Mike. I remember once that Bob was away and his wife was upstairs in the house when a man broke in. When the guy tried to enter her bedroom she shoved a chest in front of the door to keep him out and called 911. The police said they didn't have anybody available to come. The thief finally took what he wanted and left. Later Bob found out that there had been three policemen at Dunkin Donuts less than a block away with their radios turned off. He was really mad about that one.

Right next door was Sarah and Richard. They were an interesting couple. To start out, Richard was just a pizza delivery man without much education. Somewhere along the way he applied for a higher paying job and "slightly" inflated his credentials on the application. He was hired for that job and from that one he moved up to an even better executive type position. Now with plenty of money, he drove expensive cars and eventually he left Sarah. When they were married they would come over for barbeques and Sarah would take part in the girl's scrabble games. We would learn more about Sarah later.

Finally there was Bart. He wasn't a neighbor but he was a good friend. Bart was the son of Chris, an Indian girl who went to school with Josie. Bart had a promising career going as a mechanic in the military. He was stationed in Europe somewhere, married to a girl that was a career soldier. They had a little baby and for some reason the wife went into a rage one day and slammed the baby against the wall killing it. The military hushed the whole thing up, with Bart getting a trumped up discharge.

Bart was always inventing things. If you knew the physics behind one of his projects, you would probably doubt its success. For instance, Bart mounted a motorcycle frame and motor on a fishing boat to turn the craft into a speedboat. He had rigged up a drive shaft from the cycle to a prop with an old oil soaked rag stuffed along the shaft to keep the water out.

The day when Bart was to try out his cycle boat on Grand River, a small crowd had gathered to watch.

I said to Bart, "Don't you think that rig is a little top heavy?"

"Hell I don't weigh that much," was his reply.

Bart's dad Dick, was there. Dick was a self inflated hick who seemed somewhat embarrassed by his son. On an occasion or two Dick had made a pass at Josie too. Well anyway, we all stood there watching as Bart revved up the engine. As he attempted to gain some speed the boat just seemed to settle in the river and went under with the engine still running, "blub, blub," until it finally died. "Dumb ass", said his Dad.

It took almost all of us to get the contraption back out of the river; Bart's dad grumbling all the way. Up on shore I managed to drop the boat on Dick's foot.

"Jesus Christ!" he said. I thought he deserved the painful dance.

As I said before, Tina was Josie's dearest friend and my pal was a guy named Pat. Pat worked as a mechanic on the night shift of a local Shell station. On a regular basis during the early morning I would stop over at the station for gas and coffee and talk with Pat about cars. He was a Ford fan and I liked Chevys. With that in common our friendship blossomed. Pat had originally trained to be an aircraft mechanic at LCC, but after graduation the only job's he could find would require him to move to Chicago or Marquette, which was in the Michigan Upper Peninsula. He decided to change to auto mechanics instead.

Eventually Pat would start stopping over at the house after his shift. He would have some breakfast and fall to sleep in one of our easy chairs. It became such a regular thing that Josie would chew him out when he didn't show up.

Pat soon was taking part in our card games. He, Tina, Josie and I were a regular foursome around that big table in the living room. He and I would do our best to gross out the girls, telling gory stories at dinner. Once, when no one was looking, I stuffed some noodles in my nose. Then I made a big deal of sneezing, and there were the noodles hanging from my nostrils. That was enough for Josie, she got up and left the table.

Pat and I also had developed a little "gay" routine which we acted out on shopping trips with the girls.

"Oh Pat, don't you just love these colors?" then I'd make some feminine gestures with my hands. Pat would reply with a high pitched voice, "No Bill, I just don't think those colors will match." We'd watch out of the corners of our eyes as the people around registered their disgust. Josie and Tina would just wander off to get away from the spectacle.

We really acted like a bunch of college kids. None of us did any drinking then, it was just self-generated fun from four people that liked being together. I think Josie really wanted to promote a little relationship between Tina and Pat. Pat seemed to be all for that, but Tina was wary of anything more than friendship.

Now that her father was gone, Josie had more time on her hands and was interested in establishing a good paying career for herself. She still kept the books on our newspaper distribution business, but I pretty much did the rest. She decided that what she would like to do was be a drug abuse counselor for young people. The State of Michigan had openings in that field in their prison system, however there was either a specific college or experience requirement or else one must be employed on the corrections staff for a year to transfer to that field.

I had received notice that they were looking for prison guards, but at 43 I had neither the desire for that type of work, nor the interest in the physical conditioning that would be required in training. Josie on the other hand, could see that if she was employed as a guard for a year that she could then put in a transfer for the drug abuse counselor's position. Both our friend Pat and I tried to discourage her on this prison guard idea, but she had made up her mind to pursue it. From earlier discrimination lawsuits that field was wide open to women and the wages were very respectable.

For the first time the Michigan Department of Corrections required that before any person was hired and trained to be a state prison guard, they must complete several credits in an approved Criminal Justice course. A Corrections Academy was then established within Lansing Community College to provide these necessary courses. Josie was late applying, but a lady by the name of Jennifer Braimer was instrumental in getting Josie's existing credits transferred and seeing that she was enrolled in the course. Although the credits required could be taken part-time, Josie planned to go at it full speed so that she could finish and be eligible for a job in the fall. Once she put her mind to something I knew she would succeed. She was not only very intelligent, she also had the drive to accomplish what she set out to do.

It was no surprise that out of over a hundred students, Josie graduated with honors. She was third in her class with almost straight A's. At the LCC graduation ceremony Josie received The Scholarship Achievement Award. I was really proud of her. Frank Elo was a deputy warden at Jackson and also an administrator for LCC's correction officer academy. He was in attendance at the graduation and after the ceremony he came over and personally congratulated Josie. "Some day this little girl will have her own prison," he said. For some reason the guy really made me feel uneasy.

On October 20th Josie was hired by the Corrections Department
and assigned to the State Prison of Southern Michigan (SPSM).
Now she had to begin training at Earl F. DeMarse Corrections
Training Academy. This training would take place in the building
that had previously been built for Michigan's School for the Blind.
It was a very large old brick and wood structure that at best could be
described as gloomy looking. If there were bars on the windows, it
could easily be visualized as a mental health facility of the early 1900's.

DeMarse was named after the first and only Michigan prison
guard that had been killed while on duty. That happened in the 70's.
At DeMarse Josie would attend classes relating to the duties she
would perform at the prison, plus she would receive physical
conditioning and training in martial arts. Part of her training would
actually take place in the prison. DeMarse was run similar to a military boot camp.

Again Josie proved herself to be one of the best. On February 6th
she graduated from DeMarse in the top ten of her class. Now she
would start her job as a probationary corrections officer in the
Central Complex of SPSM. This was the heart of this great walled
prison at Jackson; the place where they kept the worst of the human
race. I was not comfortable with this assignment.

. . . PAT . . .

Sometimes in the morning if I made a little extra noise coming
in the back door, I would hear Josephine holler from the upstairs,
"Who's makin' all the damn noise down there? Sounds like an
elephant." Of course it was all in fun. When she seemed to be sincerely angry was when I didn't show up. "Where were you yesterday morning? Couldn't you at least stop by and say hi?" Josephine
was a very pretty girl, but she didn't mind at all coming down in
her housecoat with curlers in. Guess she just didn't feel the need to
impress me.

In the living room Bill and Jo had an old lazy-boy rocker that
was really comfortable. At times I could slip in while everybody

was sleeping and get a nice snooze. After working all night it was a great place to recover.

Sometimes I would wake up in the chair to find the shoelaces of my shoes tied together or my shoes placed on the wrong feet. Once I even woke up to find my hair curled. Of course there was Tina and Jo howling with laughter as they hustled out the back door.

Whether we were playing cards or Trivial Pursuit at the big table, or just having dinner at some restaurant, we were a magical fun loving foursome. Jo was a very good cook, but since she started working at the prison the McCallum's had more money to spend and we all ate out on a regular basis. Occasionally, Bill and my antics at the dinner table would be bad enough for the girls to get up from their chairs and temporarily leave. Jo would say, "We can't take you two anyplace!"

Josephine was not one you could pry information out of, however during the table games she would give out tidbits of what was on her mind. She didn't seem to have much use for any of her brothers. Jim had stopped over once and apparently told her she wasn't running her life right. He seemed to be into Christianity then. Jo would tell how rough she had been treated by the brothers when she grew up and how she still didn't trust any of them. I think she had been smacked around a fair bit. Once she started to say something about her father, but stopped and didn't bring up the subject again. When she began complaining about her family, I'd say, "Fuck em—why deal with them?" That's all the further she would go with it.

My impression of Jim, was that he was a prima donna who never thought of himself as capable of being wrong. He treated me like so much dirt. What I remember of John was of him regularly being drunk or high.

I think Josie always wanted a sister and Tina seemed to fill that square, for they were always together. Jo was determined to get Tina and I together, but Tina didn't have that desire. Jo would say, "I don't know why she won't date a nice guy like you." "Because she's got better taste than that," I'd counter.

Once when she had just started her martial arts training at DeMarse she came home with her uniform on and I happened to be there. She was feeling pretty confident of herself. "I know how to defend myself now. I can even take your ass down." Well I was considerably bigger than Josie and I guess I kinda smirked at her boast. Tina said, "Let her do it."

"Ok" I said, and moved to the center of the room by the stairway. Bill stood over by the couch with a grin on his face.

Josie grabbed my right hand and put pressure on it with the intent of then twisting my arm around behind my back putting me off balance. Nothing happened. I explained that due to a severe cut I suffered once on that hand I had very little feeling there. "I knew something wasn't right because you should have gone down. Let's try it again with the other hand." She didn't have any better luck with that hand. In the process of her trying to twist my arm around I just grabbed her and threw her on the couch. Bill and Tina are laughing their asses off by this time.

"Give me one more shot," she said.

After her next failed attempt I picked her up and put her over my shoulder, heading up the stairs, "It's time I got a piece of this little girl," I said.

"Bill help me!" she screamed. All Josie heard from Tina and Bill was howling laughter.

In the beginning Bill and I tried to talk Josie out of being a prison guard, but she was determined to do it. Even though she had done very well at the Academy, we both questioned whether or not the training was adequate to protect her in there.

When she started working at Jackson she seemed to like her job and on weekends over a meal or a game session she would always be telling us about the funny things that had happened at work. I know that she was proud of the money she was bringing home and that she felt she was proving herself to her brothers. Bill and Jo were even talking about buying a different home. They wanted to be out in the country again.

. . . MICHAEL . . .

I loved living on the farm, but we ended up having to move back into Lansing. Even though I missed the hay silo and the big tree out front and the seclusion we had there as a family, I was excited about moving to the city. In Lansing I'd be closer to my friends and I was looking forward to that. Our new home on South Francis Street was just down the road from Levertis Crump's family and Uncle Duane.

The house was not big and spacious like the one we had on the farm. Instead of the wide-open spaces we were now situated behind Fish 'N' Chips and Quality Dairy in a neighborhood where the homes were very close together. My mother was right back in her old neighborhood. Maybe she found some comfort in that move; I'm not sure.

Uncle Duane was always a very generous man. When we had a family dinner over at his house he and Joyce, who was like his wife, would put on a huge affair. There was always plenty of food and laughs to go around. I remember those dinners at Duane's as the few good times we ever had with my uncles and their families.

I was told that back in 1929 Duane's family couldn't feed him so my mother's grandmother (Grandma Wilber) adopted him. Probably the fact that he had grown up without much food was the reason he liked to have plenty around for our dinners.

Only once did Duane get upset and angry with me and it was because Levertis and I decided it would be fun to tear some boards off Duane's neighbor's house. Duane must have heard the noise of our hammers pulling the nails out, or the sound of the boards hitting the ground. Anyway, he came around the corner yelling, "What the hell are you kids doing? Leave that alone!" We ran off leaving our tools behind. Later I went back and apologized to Duane. I'm not sure who ended up with the job of nailing the boards back on. Really, I'd say we were just average kids with vivid imaginations and a lot of pent-up energy.

I remember my Grandpa Frank as having a wide face and thin dark gray hair that he combed back over the top. He was a very

husky man who carried himself in an intimidating manner. There
was a faded military type tattoo on one arm. I can recall playing
with some big plastic cars in his garage while he sat and watched.
We never talked much. He seemed very closed up emotionally.
Because I was a kid, maybe he didn't know what to talk about,
or perhaps it was just his nature. Maybe when he grew up adults
didn't talk to kids much.

One funny thing I always will remember of him, was that any
time we went out to get breakfast he always had his eggs sunny-
side up and he would cover them with pepper. I would look down
at them and question how he could eat them. I wondered if all that
pepper on his eggs contributed to his stomach problems. At least he
did what he wanted to do.

Since we moved back into Lansing I saw a lot more of my grandmother, my father's mother. Her name is Margaret, but I've always
just called her Grandma. Considering all my relatives, she will
always be my favorite.

Grandma liked having me over and was willing to spend one-on-
one time with me. I'd take over my toys and stuffed animals and
play with them while she cooked us lunch or cleaned up.
Sometimes she would set her kitchen and dining room up like a
supermarket and I would pretend to shop and buy things. As she got
older, Grandma watched less and less TV, but around this time she
watched Three's Company, the news, and MASH. I would be there
most time when they were on and we'd watch them together. She
always cracked up at MASH, especially the character of "Frank
Burns", the uptight doctor.

When I was a little older I would ask her about the paintings on
the wall that she had painted when she was younger. She would tell
me about her life living out in Grand Ledge on this big farm of her
father's and how they would all go down to the Island and dance
and ride the roller coaster. I saw pictures of her when she was
younger. This one in particular was of her when she was twenty
years old. She was dressed as a flapper and her hair looked like
Myrna Loy or Jean Harlow's. She was very attractive and, from
what she said about her past, a very good dancer.

On occasion she would tell me about how she wished she could have pursued her career more as an artist. At a young age she was teaching art at a college in Kalamazoo and was a promising artist who was quite independent for her time. She had to give it up along with her independence once she was married. From her tone and how she put it, I think she harbored a lot of resentment for doing that.

Grandma and my mother didn't like each other too much. There was really no secret about that. I'm not sure who was the one to blame, but I do know that my grandma routinely criticized Mother's meals and dishes she would bring over for holiday get-togethers. My grandma was very stubborn and set in her ways. She was raised on a farm and was the eldest of four children. My mother was not one to tolerate Grandma's comments without saying something and the two of them were probably the two strongest willed people I would ever meet. More than once my father had to step in between them to settle things.

My father would tell me, when I was much older, that Grandma never had approved of any of his girl friends. She never even approved of his first wife, Carol, either. I experienced this firsthand when I reached the dating age and noticed how Grandma would critique everything about my girl friends. So I don't think any of it was really personal when it came to Mother, I just think it was the way my grandmother was. No woman was good enough for us or did anything as well as she did. I loved them both though and I accepted their relationship the way it was.

Levertis Crump was my best friend. I actually have pictures of us together as babies, so we pretty much grew up together, usually playing at his house or at ours. A favorite play spot of ours was this crawl-way under our porch that we used as a secret hiding place for our toys. We felt none of the adults knew about it.

Even at a very young age, Levertis had a lot of charisma. Not only did he have a good sense of humor, he more than once proved himself to be a very loyal friend. On one occasion in elementary school these two kids were picking on me, for what I can't recall. I remember them pushing me off of the monkey bars and falling head-first, hitting my head on this rock. I stood up and they began punching me. I felt something wet on the side of my face and my arm, so I put my hand to my head and it was covered in blood. The next thing I knew Levertis was there fighting the two kids off. A teacher took me to the office, called my parents, and at the hospital I had to have eight stitches.

Another close friend of mine, was Steve Russell, Tina's oldest son. Steve and I learned at a young age to take care of what we had because both of our families were pretty short on money. Steve was a year older than I was and I was a few months older than Levertis, but since I had no brothers or sisters I always thought of the two of them as my brothers.

There was this alley behind our house that Steve and I and Levertis would always play in. We'd ride our bikes and my big wheel up and down it to see what little adventures we could generate. Steve and I were pretty close and this one time we made a fort outside in my front yard with some railroad logs that were there when we moved in. We even stayed out there one night and only got discouraged enough to go inside when it started to rain.

Tina was over to our house a lot. She and my Mom were always together playing Scrabble or watching TV. The two of them were always laughing and smoking cigarettes.

I can remember all the nights with Dad, Pat, Tina and Mom playing Scrabble and Trivial Pursuit. A few times they would wake me up if I was on the couch and have me answer questions about super heroes or comic books.

Tina would go with Mom and help her empty the Detroit News coin boxes. They would be gone hours at a time. Later on, my father would tell me that when he did it, after she died, that it had only taken him half the time it usually took them. I think that was because they liked to ride around together and talk. The two of them were very close, like sisters. They were definitely best friends and thought of each other as I thought of Steve and Levertis–not blood relatives but still family.

Even though I spent a fair amount of time with my friends and Grandma, there were many times when I just played by myself. I'd go upstairs and play on Mom and Dad's bed. It was one of my favorite places to slip off into my own imaginary world. I had a very healthy imagination as a kid. I didn't get bored very easily and would always find something to do. With very little money and both of my parents struggling to make ends meet I had to make do with what we had and in my mind that was plenty.

The Christmas' on South Francis Street were pretty much like the ones out on the farm, just the three of us being warm and loving on Christmas day. With Tina around Christmas' were even a bigger deal, for now my mother had someone to go shopping with and to help decorate.

At Christmas time I was never the nosy type child looking for his presents before it was time to open them. But, there was one fateful Christmas when Steve and I were playing in my parent's room. We had some action figures and had them moving across this trash bag by their dresser. All of sudden the bag fell and revealed a big red sled. He and I looked at one another and the brilliant idea came into our brains to see what else was in the room. Needless to say we found pretty much every present they had bought for us. We put everything back carefully and I stopped Steve at the door, "Now don't say a word. They will be so upset if they find out about this." We agreed to keep it quiet and walked downstairs with our secret intact.

My mother said to Tina, "Well, we should go wrap some presents." Steve, not thinking at all, said, "Oh you mean the ones upstairs?" There was nothing I could do but put my hand to my head. Steve and I then had to sit through hours and hours of lectures about what we had done wrong. I think more than anything else that upset them, was that we had ruined the whole experience for them. I felt terrible about it. I think the thing that bothers me most is that I can't really recall if that Christmas was the last that I had spent with her. I really hope it wasn't.

Mom's brothers were another story. On Christmas and Thanksgiving holidays we would dress up and go to one of their houses for dinner, but no one would talk to us. I'm still not sure why they did that or why we continued to go. Sometimes we would show up and they would seem pretty normal, but even on those rare occasions they would be cold to us by the end of the night.

I even remember a couple of times when we came in the door and no one said a thing. Not one word. We would eat and then just leave. My mother tried her hardest to make things fun and happy. Not all of the get-togethers were bad, and we did have a couple good times over at Jim's, but overall they were not comfortable times for me. I was always happy once we got into the car. When you're young and trying to be nice and polite to people who really don't like you it's a tough thing. I don't know if it ever gets any easier.

I remember how it was after we left. Driving home with the snow blowing down on the car. I'd stick my head between my Mom and Dad in the front seats and look out the windshield. With the snow coming at us it reminded me of Star Wars when they would warp ahead into space, the stars just streaking by them. I would pretend that we were in space and that we were heading home.

My Uncle Jim had a very strong personality. He could be funny at times, but was always very dominant. With people around he would be friendly acting, but there was something very intense about him, even a little dark. Uncle Jim and Aunt Jane had this great dog, a German Shepherd named "Rex". Everyone called him "Rex the Wonder Dog". He was very smart and well-trained. Rex would carry a green tennis ball around and want to play any time I was over. Rex was really afraid of Jim and would cower when he spoke to him in a stern manner. If we were outside barbequing and Rex came close to Jim with the green tennis ball in his mouth, and Jim didn't like it, Rex would stay away from him for the rest of the day. On a later occasion Rex just wasn't there. I asked where he was, but never got a response from anyone in the family. This seemed strange to me, that the dog was "just gone" and no one knew why. I later heard that Jim had beaten Rex for being disobedient. After Duane and my Grandpa Frank died in 1985 we saw even less of Mom's brothers and that really wasn't such a bad thing.

When Mom was going to school for her new job our lifestyle changed. She took classes down at Lansing Community College in the Criminal Justice Department. Mom, Dad, Tina, and Pat were together on weekends, but the TV and Scrabble sessions during the week with Tina were pretty much over. Mom was busy studying all the time and Dad was taking care of the newspaper business. There were many nights when Tina was over helping Mom study and memorize different laws. Sometimes they'd be up to all hours of the night.

I think back on my parents and how they struggled to get by and it amazes me because they did so much with so little. We had to struggle to make ends meet and they worked hard and had crazy hours, but still found time for me and for all of us to have fun. When I think back to this time and place in my mind, I always think of them laughing. The biggest thing my parents had in common was their sense of humor. I thank God for what I gained from both of them.

Mom did really well in school. Tina and I sat together with Dad at Mom's graduation and I had some of my stuffed animals along too. I was proud of her when they called her up for some special award. She looked sharp in her new uniform. Pat and Dad called her the "Green Machine". Once, when she came home from class she was showing us some of the self-defense moves she had learned. She told Dad with a confident tone, "Take a swing at me." "Well, I don't know," he replied hesitantly. She urged him on, "Do it, give it your best shot." Dad brought up his arm and took a half-hearted swing at her and in short order she had wrapped her arm up under him and thrown him to the floor. He landed with a loud thud and sat there with this sheepish grin on his face.

I think mostly she was proud. I mean really proud of herself for accomplishing her goal; of wanting to do something for herself and her family, for going to school and studying her butt off and for not just finishing, but finishing third in her class. She wanted to become a drug-abuse counselor and she had made the first step in that goal. Mom's childhood was rough because she always had to prove herself to her father and her brothers and nothing she ever did was good enough for them. She had lost her mother at a young age and had to grow up too quickly. I too would soon learn how this felt and even thinking of that similarity gives me chills.

Birthday Party – Dustin, Michael, Levertis.

Another merry Christmas for Jo and Michael.

Graduation Day – Michael, Tina Russell and Jo.

Bill, Princess and Frank.

Brothers: Jim left, Barry front and John in back. Josephine on Duane's lap.

Michael and Grandma.

Michael and Grandpa Frank.

DARK CLOUDS

. . . PAT . . .

It was Monday night and the three of us were going out to eat. For some reason Tina couldn't join us. Bill was to drop Mike off at his mother's and we would meet him at the restaurant. I rode over with Josie in their Ford station wagon and it was almost fifteen minutes before Bill joined us at the restaurant. During the ride over and while we waited for him, Josie was unusually quiet. More than just being silent, she seemed troubled by something. I tried to fish around to see what was bothering her, but she was reluctant to say anything other than there was some problem at work. I hoped Bill could find out more.

This was the first time that I could remember, when Josie wasn't upbeat about her work. Missing this evening were the funny details of the days activities in the Central Complex and the cocky grin that was so characteristic of her good moods. Bill could sense her seriousness too, but she still was guarded about divulging any details. Finally she admitted that she was having some problems with a supervisor called Rakowski. She didn't elaborate. "What did this guy do?" asked Bill. I could see fire in his eyes. I expected her to clam up again because we all knew what a short fuse Bill had.

"This guy's been hitting on me for awhile. Today he said that I better be ready to put out tomorrow or I'd be dead meat". There was no question in our minds; she should not go back to work. In addition some black officer had been following her around too. He wanted to talk to her about carpooling together. She was smart enough to know what he was after.

It seemed ironic, that here she was working with all these bad prisoners yet her main concern was about her fellow corrections officers. There was no question in my mind, Josie really felt threatened.

All during the dinner we discussed the situation. Even though Bill and I were firm in our advice to stay home, Josie vacillated back and forth on what she planned to do. First she said she'd just ignore the guy. She assured us that she would go to the union if the harassment got any worse; that's what the union was there for. A minute later she would say she wasn't going back to work. It was around 9 p.m. when we got up to leave. I could sense that she still hadn't made up her mind. It certainly had not been a very pleasant meal.

Shortly after we arrived back at their home, I left to get ready for my night shift at the Shell station. I would probably see Bill sometime after midnight and slip back over to their place when my work ended at 7 a.m.

~ ~ ~ ~ ~

It was more than a night without sleep. Josephine must have felt that the turmoil in her life was becoming more than she might be capable of handling. What probably worried her the most was that her vulnerability was becoming evident to others. Partly, that was her fault. It was one thing to spill her guts to Tina, but it was unusual for her to let her problems at work be part of a dinner conversation with Pat and Bill. By the time she got home from the restaurant her tears had penetrated that hard outer shell. Bill could really sense her worry and fear.

"All the damn work I've put into school and trying to do good at this job and it boils down to just being a sex object!" she said.

"Hell don't go back to that damn place, quit," he said.

She assured him again that she would go to the union if things got worse. Bill didn't seem convinced. Josephine wasn't sure that going to the union would help either, but it was the obvious course to try. Dealing with Jackson's residents was bad enough, but she knew early on that would be a challenge. What she hadn't perceived was that dealing with some of the guards was becoming even more of a problem. Sgt. Rakowski wouldn't give up. His words would still linger in her mind, "Better be ready to put out tomorrow, or you'll be dead meat." It hadn't come across actually as a threat, but how could one interrupt the intent behind the remark. Josephine probably regretted mentioning Rakowski's comments to Bill. He was fully capable of coming unglued over such things.

Right now Josie was the major bread earner in the family and after so many struggling years, she obviously was reluctant to quit the job. She seemed determined to stick with it until she had the time in that job to allow a transfer to the field she really wanted to work in.

Over coffee that morning Bill again expressed his reservations over her going to work. The coffee and a cigarette gave her more support, even if it was temporary.

"Honey we need the money. This is a good paying job. I'll be OK and the union is there to solve these kind of problems." "Bill, remember Mike's only got half a day of school. He'll have the morning off. I'll hurry home and we'll go to the teacher's conference tonight."

Before leaving the driveway Jo lit another cigarette and inhaled deeply. She turned to see Bill standing on the porch, watching. They acknowledged each other with a half wave, and a try at a reassuring smile.

One has to wonder what thoughts went through Josephine's mind as she drove to work that morning. Certainly she must have again and again considered what the work day would be like. Perhaps her thoughts centered on the family and her marriage. Even though Bill and her had discussed having another child, life's immediate priorities had pushed intimacy out of their routine.

First the challenge of getting through school with good grades, and now the stress of becoming accustomed to working with hardened criminals and harassing co-workers. Sure they managed their schedules to have time with Mike, but Bill working nights with the newspaper and her on days at the prison were bound to take their toll sooner or later.

~ ~ ~ ~ ~

On Monday Warden Foltz would be attending a retirement seminar in Grand Rapids. After 29 years in Michigan's Correctional system, on May 1st he would be retiring. Of course it would seem a bit demeaning for a man of his stature to be learning the nuts and bolts of retirement alongside his employees, but this would only be the beginning of the lifestyle change he would soon encounter.

Dale E. Foltz would be considered by most, to be the dean of prison wardens not only in Michigan, but probably even the United States. Foltz was ending his tenure as warden of the world's largest walled prison. The prison was now separated into 4 separate complexes, each with a deputy warden, but still the overall responsibility was his. The deputy wardens provided insulation from many of the day to day administrative headaches, however Foltz was used to having his beeper go off day or night, seven days a week; whenever a deputy thought a fight or disturbance could get out of hand and blossom into something major. Nowadays prisons were overcrowded and understaffed—just the ingredients needed for something major to happen.

Shortly after the riots of the early 80's, they had asked him to take the warden's position at Jackson. He had been the deputy warden of the Central Complex in the middle 70's, so he had experience with the facility, plus he had proven himself as warden of Michigan's second largest walled prison in Ionia. Foltz had been warden of the Ionia Reformatory for over 10 years.

Michigan legislators were elated in 1928 when they had created at Jackson the world's largest walled prison. Foltz thought that despite the notoriety of heading such a large prison, the lawmakers had created a monster to manage. Even the deputy wardens had their hands full. For instance, just within the Central Complex there were five cellblocks, each having about 500 prisoners. Of course each cellblock contained a different level of inmate, depending on the supervision required, but still to keep track of all the potential problem areas was almost impossible. To say the least, it amounted to crisis management. To really manage prisoners effectively, just one of those 500 men cellblocks could use its own warden and should exist as a separate prison.

Getting funds to operate correctional facilities was a constant battle. There had only been one death of an on duty correctional officer in Michigan's history, so unless there was a riot or something else to arouse public sentiment it would be a continuous battle with the legislature to get more money for prison operations and expansion.

Foltz knew that the system was vulnerable. He met regularly with his deputies, and heard firsthand about their complaints and problems. He monitored misconduct and incident reports to identify potential trouble spots and worked with the deputies to correlate or change existing work procedures and rules to help alleviate these pressure points. Still, as hard as he tried it was nearly impossible to manage the system the way it should be managed.

Representatives of the Correctional Officers Union were regular visitors in Warden Foltz's office. Foltz felt that to get the big picture, along with all the reports coming up through the deputies, he needed to be aware of what the union had to complain about. He had never been a guard or even taught classes to the guards, so the union was his connection to the people that had direct control of the inmates on a daily basis. If the union representatives had reasonable demands, he would take matters up with his deputies or the head of the correctional system in Lansing. Rarely would he personally make adjustments based on union concerns. Foltz believed in the chain of command, just like the military, and to change something without the approval of a deputy would be violating that process. So, when the union brought up safety concerns regarding manning or security, he listened, but rarely took direct action. He knew that the union would always be asking for more than what was realistic to get funding for, but he listened.

A union steward named Halmich was in his office at least once a week with new ideas on how to improve security for the guards. Halmich was pretty sharp at analyzing problem areas, but putting his ideas into place required unrealistic funding requests that would get nowhere. Occasionally Foltz would even allow himself to hear individual grievances from the correctional officers. For instance, John Rakowski had recently broken up with a female that worked in the prison system. John had been deeply attached to the lady and was disturbed about their breakup. He wanted a transfer. Foltz didn't have the time to hear or handle many of those types of problems, but he did pride himself on keeping in touch as best he could with his people.

It wasn't just the Union looking for problems in the prison system, it was also the news media that kept digging into things. Some of the newspapers really disgusted him. Foltz told Deputy Warden Whelan once that every time he read the Jackson Citizen Patriot's articles on the prison it made him mad. That's why he refused to subscribe to the newspaper.

Soon it would all be over. In retirement he could be a full-time husband, father and grandfather. It would be a relief to be done with the stress, but it had occupied such a major part of his life, that he probably wondered how it would be when it was not there anymore. Maybe, in fact, he would miss it.

It would have been nice to end his career as the state director of corrections or even as the assistant, for he certainly was as qualified as the men there now. Director Brown and Assistant Director Bolden had both worked for Foltz at one time or another but they had been promoted over him and he now worked for them. Perhaps the fact that they were black had something to do with it, though no one talked about such a thing.

CENTRAL COMPLEX

MARCH 24 1987

Some of the prisoners called Merryman, Bubba, others just Mexico, which reflected his bloodline. From Red on the 4th gallery, Merryman had procured some wine (spud juice) and now he was sharing it with his buddy Hill, in Hill's cell. They were about the same size and weight, (5'7"—140 lbs.), but Hill was a couple years older and definitely had established a more impressive criminal record.

Edward Clay Hill, Jr. #C155098 was serving 18-40 years for assault to murder; 18-40 years for criminal sexual conduct in the first degree and 18-40 years for kidnapping two counts. All this was accomplished in his mid twenties. As a younger man of 18, he started his prison tenure from a larceny and concealed weapons charge.

Merryman on the other hand was in Jackson for a meager armed robbery and parole violation. He respected his friend Hill; not only for his impressive record, but also for the no nonsense way that Hill treated other prisoners. For a small man he was fierce and didn't take any shit off anybody.

It was a little before four in the morning and the prison hadn't come alive yet. They sat sipping the potent homemade alcohol and letting the affect mellow the start of another day. Soon they would head down for breakfast and their work assignment in the commissary. Hill was the foreman in charge of loading and unloading trucks and Merryman his designated assistant.

It was still very dark out as Josephine McCallum was driving to Jackson from her home in downtown Lansing. Probably the nicotine from the second cigarette was soothing her nerves and she was starting to reconcile herself to another day in the prison. It would give her peace of mind to picture Bill and Mike peacefully asleep at home.

Warden Foltz was also still sleeping. On this day Dale E. Foltz, warden of the huge Jackson prison complex would start his indoctrination for retirement. For 29 years he had been working for the Department of Corrections and most of that time had been spent as a warden.

Josephine McCallum punched in at 05:41. She always tried to be early. Her self-confidence was high when she felt that she was ahead of things, and in control. Sometimes her composure seemed to melt when she found herself in unfamiliar situations. In this environment, the importance of the appearance, as far as control and confidence, was paramount to success or survival in working with the residents.

Since actually starting on the job her assignments had been in housing. Her work had been about equally divided between 6 and 11 Block with a couple each in 4 and 12 Block. She worked in reasonably close proximity to the other officers and although she was in contact with the general population in those blocks, monitoring their activity, she didn't actively control resident movement. Today Josephine expected another day of the same duty.

The acting Captain of the day was Lt. Douglas McMurtrie. He held roll call at 05:50 and started giving out the assignments. Josephine would be relieved that at least Sgt. Rakowski had the day off. He wouldn't be hitting on her, nor would there be much meaning to his veiled threat of consequences she would suffer if she didn't submit herself for sex.

"McCallum, today you have the JCC gate," said McMurtrie. Jo acknowledge with a nod, but had no idea what the assignment entailed or for that matter where it was. McMurtrie added, "McCallum you also have dining room duty before the JCC."

Josephine didn't ask any questions of McMurtrie but after he was finished she immediately went to another officer, Brenda Wilson.

"Brenda, what's this JCC assignment, I have no idea what it is."

Brenda explained a little about it and told her that a real good resident porter worked in the area and would help her out. "You'll have a radio so this will come in handy." She handed Jo her walkie-talkie radio holder.

Sgt. Robert Cotton was passing out assignment keys. When Jo's turn came she said, "I need the keys for the JCC."

"Come back when you're through in the dining room," Cotton replied.

"Could you tell me where the JCC assignment is, I haven't been there."

"Go down the sub-hall to the south yard and the JCC building is to the left as you enter the yard. There is a JCC sign above the door where you enter," explained Cotton.

Shortly after that Officer Richard Rose saw Jo in the sub-hall. She approached him and asked where the JCC was located and what the duties were. He walked with her to the south ramp of the sub-hall and out the door where he could point to the doors of the JCC. He told her that her duties were to check ID's and not to let anyone in unless they had a detail form specifying that area or were listed on the call sheet. He reminded her to first report for the breakfast detail. Jo said, "Thanks a lot," and headed for the dining room.

Food Service Supervisor Follick arrived around 6 a.m. to start his shift. He would have 5 residents on his detail that were to start at 06:30. Michael James, Joe Cole, Carl Battle, Ray Merryman and Edward Hill would make up the detail. Hill was the crew foreman and Merryman was assistant foreman.

Hill was the last to arrive at 06:40. It was obvious to Follick that both Merryman and Hill had been drinking. He had trouble keeping them in the work area. Both kept running off and bickering and arguing with other inmates out on the serving line in the main annex of the kitchen area. Follick finally confronted Hill, "Have you been drinking?"

Hill responded, "If you don't stop squeezing me, I'm gonna kick your ass!"

Follick got a hold of K.C. Martin, his supervisor and told him that Hill was drunk and that he wanted to send him back to his housing unit.

Martin's response was "You don't run nothing around here but your mouth. If you send one nigger in, the other niggers won't work."

Frustrated by his supervisors response Follick got on the phone to Officer Butler in the Control Center, and told him about Hill's condition and that K.C. Martin wouldn't let him send the asshole in. Follick demanded, "I want a sergeant or lieutenant down here to shake the place down." Butler seemed unconcerned and said that he would send someone down when they were available. That was not what Follick wanted to hear.

Josephine worked the first and second window of the food service line. Her job was to make sure that the residents moved through the line in an orderly manner and didn't take extra food. Whether things went smoothly or not depended on the attitude of the residents on that particular morning. If they were of a mind to, they could make it hell for the monitoring officer. If the officer reached over to put the stops to an extra serving, it was easy to maneuver food or syrup on to the officer's uniform.

Josephine's co-worker at the windows that morning was Alfred Lee, a black corrections officer that had been pestering her since she went to work in Central Complex. Lee was continually trying to get her to car pool to work with him. She tried to be diplomatic with her refusal, but he wouldn't give up. She had complained to friends that she was sick of having him follow her around.

There was a problem with one inmate trying to take an extra tray of food and he was rather belligerent towards Jo when she tried to stop him. When she asked him to identify himself the man refused. Lee shook the man down and finally Josephine obtained the guys ID. She kept the ID for the purpose of writing a ticket on him. Lee offered to help her write the ticket.

By 07:20 the dining room was closed and the first truck had arrived at the commissary dock. The driver was Officer Charles Eddy. Eddy was in his early 50's and had worked for Corrections for 14 years. With him in the truck was Sabrina Johnson, a black girl who was doing on the job training (OJT).

After leaving the dinning room, Jo stopped to talk with Hearing Investigator Madley outside on the ramp by the south yard sub-hall. They exchanged a few words concerning a misconduct report that Jo had written and he had investigated. At about 07:30 Officer Baker also saw Jo at the corridor gate walking toward the Control Center to get her JCC assignment keys. In the Control Center the keys were issued to her by Officer Parker at 07:40 and he placed her key tag #524-c on the key hook in cabinet #3. He watched as she then headed to her assignment.

As the first truck backed up to the dock, Follick opened the commissary door and walked out onto the dock and then preceded into the JCC entrance, which was only ten feet away. Inmate Hill apparently had gone into the JCC. Follick told him to get back to his assignment and get the truck loaded. When he chased Hill out, Follick didn't notice anyone else inside the JCC entrance.

Sabrina Johnson left the truck cab and stepped inside the commissary next to some stacked boxes. She was watching the crew load the big aluminum boxes of bakery products when Hill stopped working and approached her.

"What's your name?"

"Officer Johnson."

"How long have you been working for corrections?"

"I'm on OJT," said Sabrina.

"Well how long have you actually been working here?" said Hill

"Six weeks."

"Will you be working here in central?"

"No I'll be in South Complex," answered Sabrina.

"If you come out here I'm going to be looking for you," he said.

With the loading complete Sabrina stepped into the back of the truck while Officer Eddy counted the racks of bread and rolls.

Hill followed Sabrina into the truck. He faced her and stood real close and she could sense the liquor smell on his breath. She backed away from him as far as she could, without getting off the truck.

"Why do you want to work in here? There's nothing but murders and rapers and thieves in here." Hill continued, "You know, they say I've killed six people and I'm in for triple life. I'm never going to get out of this place."

Sabrina wasn't sure what to say. "If you do the right things you might get out someday. You never know what might happen."

"Where do you live?" inquired Hill.

"I live close enough to get to work on time." Sabrina didn't like where the conversation was going.

"You sure got pretty teeth." Hill followed that with a warning, "You really don't know what the guys in here might do. They don't even respect themselves, so how can they respect you?"

"Yeah I know that."

"But you don't really mind?"

"Well I care but,---." Sabrina really didn't know how to answer him.

"My sister is thinking about working out here, but I wouldn't want her to. These guys don't respect themselves so they couldn't respect you or no other officer." It was the second time Hill said this and obviously wasn't getting the response he wanted.

"You know I'm liable to go out on you."

Sabrina countered, "I'm liable to go out on you too, you don't know what I might do." She wondered how Hill got the idea she would consider such a thing, however he'd been drinking.

The baked goods count was complete and Sabrina wanted the conversation with Hill to end so she left the truck bed and got into the passenger seat of the truck, closing the door. Eddy was still in the back. Hill walked up to her side and opened the truck door. Sabrina put her hand on the door to keep it from being opened very far. Hill placed his finger on the back of her hand and gave an affectionate rub. She snatched her hand off the door and he opened it a little further. He touched her butt with the other hand with the intent of sliding it under her. He couldn't do this, but instead ran his finger down her thigh. Eddy opened the other door to get in and Sabrina slid away from Hill. With her elbow she deflected Hill's arm and gave him a dirty look. Hill quickly closed the door and disappeared. Sabrina turned to Officer Eddy and told him what Hill did and that she didn't like what happened. She wanted to do something about it, but wasn't sure what.

Eddy response was, "All the female officers get treated that way by the prisoners."

Just then a female correction officer walked right by Eddy's side of the truck. Eddy remarked, "I've never seen her before." He was impressed with how attractive she was. The officer passed close enough for Eddy to read her tag, "McCallum." Jo didn't say anything, but seemed to nod at them. Sabrina said that she had seen her at the academy, and that McCallum was one or two classes ahead of her.

Eddy watched McCallum climb the steps and enter the already open door to the JCC entrance. Two black inmates Eddy didn't recognize were standing on the dock. They followed McCallum through the door and closed it behind them. It was about 07:45 when Eddy started the truck and left the dock.

Follick closed the commissary doors and they automatically locked. The inmates all seemed to be inside except Hill.

C/O Kidder's assignment was at the Bakery Gate. At about 07:45 a.m. he received a call from 4 Block asking why Hill had not shown up for Bond Court. Kidder said he'd look for him. In the commissary Kidder couldn't find Hill and asked Follick, where he was. Follick yelled out Hill's name, but there was no response. Follick told Kidder he would find him. After Kidder left Follick looked in the food service office hallway and cook gang area. Hill wasn't to be seen anyplace. Follick knew that Hill was supposed to have a bond court hearing that morning for some previous offense, however he didn't think that was where Hill was. Maybe he had gone to chow.

By the time the second truck, #530, had backed up to the commissary dock inmates were starting to arrive at the JCC entrance. One of the first was Archie Baker. Baker was a 37 year old black man who had an extensive record starting with armed robbery and ending up with several counts of criminal sexual contact (CSC), of which two counts of first degree CSC put him in for life. Today

Baker had a pass for work in the special activities office. The director, Mr. Campbell, had given it to him the previous day.

Baker stated that when he arrived the outside JCC door was unlocked, but the gate at the entry point was locked and there was no officer present. He waited in the lobby at the entrance as about seven other inmates arrived.

While the inmates waited for someone to let them into the JCC area, Officer Alfred Lee arrived at the gate. Lee asked if any of the waiting inmates had seen the officer that was supposed to be at the desk. No one had. Lee unlocked the gate with his passkey and went inside the gated area. There was an officer's coat hanging on the phone box. He removed the coat picked up the phone receiver then hung it back up and placed the coat back where it had been. Later, Lee would state that he only picked up the phone receiver to get the extension number. He said that when he removed the coat he noted the phone box had been unlocked. Lee also said he looked up the stairwell of the JCC and there were no inmates inside. He said he called out Officer McCallum's name and also peeked in the small auditorium door window, but didn't see her or hear any answer to his call.

Lee stated that after the main dining room was clear he had met with Jo briefly in the officer's dining room. She then left for the Control Center to pick up her keys. Shortly after that Lee went to the Control Center and was there until approximately 8:05. He said that he then walked to the JCC to see McCallum. That day Lee's assignment was in Cell Block 8. His duty started at 8:00 a.m. That cellblock was some distance away from the Control Center. It is unclear why Lee was intentionally late for his duty by going to the JCC. Perhaps it was just to strengthen his familiarity with Jo. She had thus far continually rejected his advances.

Before Lee left the area he relocked the gate. No inmates had been allowed to enter while he was there so they still had to loiter around until someone else let them in. Some waited inside the lobby, while others waited on the commissary dock.

Arthur Randall Blank was one of the inmates waiting to get into the JCC area. He remembers a short black officer unlocking the gate and using the phone. Blank, a 34 year old white inmate, was serving a lengthy sentence for armed robbery and a shorter sentence for assault less than murder. He stated that shortly after 08:00 Debbie Swihart, a teacher, unlocked the gate and let the waiting inmates in, then relocked the gate and left for her office.

Inmate Archie Baker now had access to the JCC area, however the door to the special activities office where he worked was still locked. Baker sat down at the desk by the gate to wait for someone to unlock that door. One of the last inmates in went over and reached into a pocket of the coat hanging on the phone box. Grinning he came up with what looked like an unopened pack of cigarettes. Baker told the guy to put them back or he'd probably get in trouble. Reluctantly the inmate returned the cigarettes to the coat pocket.

Archie Baker was now alone in the area and a little restless. He got up from the desk walked over to the auditorium entrance and stepped part way in through the unlocked door. He did not see anyone in the auditorium, but could hear voices. One was that of a female. At the same time he could hear someone unlocking the JCC gate and returned to the desk to see another instructor, Brian Innis, opening the gate.

Innis entered and left the gate open. Several inmates then followed Innis in and one passed by Archie and walked through the auditorium door. Archie walked back out the gate to the commissary dock and recognized the driver of the second truck. The driver was Roosevelt Henley, commonly referred to as Henley-Bey, a friend of Archie's.

Thirty eight year old Henley-Bey was serving life for armed robbery, with several other previous convictions spicing up his record. Accompanying Henley was Officer Jeanne Shappee. After saying hello to his friend Henley, Archie started talking to Officer Jeanne Shappee, kidding her about her last name and how appropriate it was.

The other inmate that had passed Archie and entered the auditorium was Kirk Douglas Leaphart, who was serving time for manslaughter. Leaphart was hot under the collar because Mitch

Badders, the auditorium supervisor had not put him on the call list to practice his music in the auditorium that evening. He was prepared to write a grievance against Badders if he couldn't get it changed.

Leaphart was the last inmate to enter after JCC instructor Innis opened the gate. He noticed an officer's coat hanging in the phone box area, but no officer was present. He entered into the auditorium and loudly yelled Badder's name but received no response. The only light in the auditorium was that from some dim lighting on the stage. Leaphart then walked down the stage steps and followed the west side aisle in the seating area to Mitch's office that was upstairs by the projection booth. Mitch was not there either. Again he called out, "Mitch!" Leaphart was determined to get this settled so he would just have to kill some time until Mitch arrived. He walked back down the aisle toward the stage.

Just to the right of the stage was an emergency stage exit with a set of double doors. As Leaphart passed these doors on the way to the stage stairs he heard a noise that he later described as a couple of thuds. He hesitated and was going to investigate inside, but passed it off as being nothing important. He proceeded up the stage stairs, then went over and sat down at the baby grand piano positioned in the center of the stage.

It was peaceful in the auditorium and for at least a few minutes Leaphart had the whole place to himself. Music was his pleasure in life; it helped to block out the rest of this life in Jackson. His sentence was not too long compared to the other inmates here and early next month he would be 29 years old. If he was lucky perhaps he could make a living playing the piano and singing once he was free. He still had time in his life to be successful, and Mitch had even allowed him to make recordings at the piano downstairs.

Leaphart started playing the piano lightly and was amazed at how the sound carried into the empty auditorium. Only partway into the tune Leaphart again heard the double thud noise from the stage emergency exit area. He stopped playing momentarily. Probably just normal sounds from an old building he thought. A pair of soft looking gloves on top of the piano caught his attention.

About 20 seconds later Leaphart's tune was again interrupted, this time by the sound of a walkie-talkie radio. That was a very familiar sound, in fact the most common in the prison environment.

The sound did not alarm him, so he continued playing.

Many of the guards carried the radios and usually had the volume turned up so that even though one couldn't understand the transmissions the voice noise was there.

A minute later he again heard the radio noise. The noise was coming from an area to his left. Leaphart got up from the piano and decided to see where the sound was coming from.

Leaphart found the radio on the floor of the curtain area. He hesitated beside it for a moment then proceeded towards the back wall and beside a short vertical curtain saw liquid smeared on the floor. It looked like blood. As alarmed as he was, he slowly walked to the stage and through the double doors from which he had originally entered the auditorium. Once he was outside the auditorium panic took over.

Inmate Harris had seen and heard Leaphart playing the piano. He was waiting outside when Leaphart exited the auditorium. Leaphart pulled Harris aside, "Man I seen a radio and blood on the floor in there!" Leaphart ran to the sub-hall where Sgt. Allen let him in to see the sub-hall gate officer. Leaphart didn't know the gate officer's name, but as he told him what he had found in the auditorium he could sense a lot of doubt in his listener. Then he spotted an officer he did know, Sgt. Hartsuff.

"Sgt. Hartsuff, you got to listen to me. You know I've never bull-shitted before!"

"What's up?"

"I'm not bullshitting, there's an officer bleeding in the auditorium!" Leaphart continued explaining as he and Hartsuff walked up the corridor to the Control Center.

THE SUSPECTS

While waiting for the second truck to be loaded with bread, Officer Jeanne Shappee noticed two commissary workers running back and forth between the dock and the JCC entrance. She knew both of them. The Mexican was called Bubba. His last name was Merryman and he had previously had a detail in the law library when she worked there. She had seen both Hill and Merryman several times before at commissary dock. Jeanne heard supervisor Follick tell Merryman not to go running off all the time. Apparently he had been doing it frequently. She said Hill acted agitated and a little antsy.

The second truck was about two thirds loaded when Follick noticed Hill come through the JCC entrance. He was bent over breathing very hard and soaked in sweat, some of which was dripping from his forehead. Hill was also holding his right hand.

"What happened to you?" Follick asked.

"A nigger just kicked my ass!" responded Hill.

"Get a pass. I'm sending you in."

For some reason Hill did not argue with Follick's order. Follick thought that was really out of character for him. Hill and Merryman then went inside the commissary and started arguing between themselves. He heard Merryman say, "You don't have to fight my battles for me." Hill left shortly after that for the kitchen area, supposedly to get a pass out.

Follick later reported that he felt uneasy about Hill's activities in the JCC area and that as the truck was about loaded he decided to go into the JCC and investigate. He started that way and quickly met Randy Vanepps and six other officers who were also headed to the auditorium to investigate inmate Leaphart's story of the blood, coat and radio on the stage. Follick joined the group. He recognized one of the officers as being the red haired female that had been stuck a while back.

The officers entered the auditorium and soon were on the stage. Vanepps picked up an officer's blazer in the center of the stage, examined it and said, "Does this look like blood?" The group spread out searching for an injured officer. Follick recalled his actions. "I stood there for a second and for some reason I cannot explain, something told me to go over and look down the emergency exit stairwell in the complete opposite corner of the stage area. When I walked over and peered down the stairway I could see a nude female laying at the bottom of the stairs. She was not moving or saying anything. I rushed down to the bottom of the stairs and saw that she had a man's belt wrapped around her neck. "I attempted to loosen the belt then check for a pulse on her wrist, and finally inside her armpit. At first I thought I felt a pulse, but then realized there wasn't any.

Although she lay on her back and right side, her head was contorted back and she was facing up. Follick noticed that her face was distorted, from what looked like a head blow with a heavy object. There was blood on her head and face with a large pool spread around her head. Follick backed away from the body and hollered up the stairway to the other officers that he had found her.

Hill was now at the Bakery Gate with a partially filled out pass for the Bond Court. Officer Daniel Kidder signed and dated the pass and watched as Hill hurriedly headed towards the back dock area.

At 08:15 Officer Randy McCormic logged Hill in at the corridor gate for his Bond Court call. Hill requested to use the restroom across the corridor and McCormic said he could. Hill was in the restroom for awhile, then he came out and left the area. In a few minutes McCormic saw Hill return past his station. Hearing Officer Snider would state that Hill never showed up for his hearing.

Next Hill attempted to get back into the commissary area. Officer Barr stopped Hill at the Infirmary Annex gate. Barr refused to allow Hill in because he did not have written authorization to be in the commissary. Barr thought that Hill acted excited and nervous and Hill touched him several times as he spoke. "My supervisor just came through ahead of me. I'm just trying to catch up with him." Barr didn't give in and Hill left.

In the Control Center, after hearing Leaphart's story of what he had found on the auditorium stage, Lt. Lawson dispatched a team of officers to investigate. Immediately after that he called Assistant Deputy Warden (ADW) Frank Elo. Elo grabbed a radio and informed the other two Assistant Deputies, Whelan and Grinage of the situation and then headed directly for the auditorium. When he arrived the officers were still searching for an injured officer, and he recalls seeing Follick enter the emergency stairway and hearing him yell.

When he arrived at the top of the stairway there was another officer standing beside Follick. Elo asked if there was a pulse. Follick thought there might be a faint pulse.

The other officer at the bottom of the stairway was Officer Norman Keesler. He had left 12 Block for chow and at the corridor gate Lt. Lawson had told him to accompany them to the auditorium. He had been searching through the rows of seats when Sgt. Hartsuff called from the stage saying they had found the injured officer. Two or three other officers were peering down the stairwell when Keesler rushed by them to aid the one officer by the female body at bottom. Keesler recalls the scene, "Near the bottom step an officer was squatted down leaning against the wall. He was on the second or third step. On the floor at the bottom of the stairs lay the body of a female, nude except for a bra and other small torn pieces of garments, which were around her waist. The body was lying on its back with the head and shoulders in a large pool of blood. The face was blood covered and to me not recognizable. Around the neck there was a leather belt approximately one inch in width. I heard someone call from the top of the stairs and ask if there was a pulse. I crouched beside the body and placed the index and middle fingers of my left hand under the belt around the neck lifting gently to loosen the belt, then turned my hand and pressed the same finger tips against the side of the throat next to the adams apple. I felt no pulse. I tried again, repositioning my fingers. No pulse."

"I looked to the top of the stairs and saw Deputy Grinage and Deputy Elo and I stated "No pulse.""

There was a large amount of blood around the head and on the floor and it had started to stiffen. I stood and leaned back against the wall. Within moments, probably two minutes, the medical team arrived. They immediately started CPR. Due to lack of adequate light several large flashlights were handed down the stairs at the medic's request. I held a flashlight in each hand shining a beam on the head and abdomen as the medics worked. After 10 to 15 minutes I heard a medic say, "Call the doctor on the radio and tell him we are discontinuing CPR." I turned off the flashlight and went back up to the stage area. I was told by inspector Moats to return to my block. The body was identified as that of Josephine McCallum."

Paramedic Brager was at the scene with RN Simpson and Connin. Brager describes the injured officer's condition.

"Her skin was cool and clammy and there was no sustained pulse. We attempted an IV and established an airway with an endotrachael tube. CPR was in progress. The IV failed so I inserted one mg. 1:0000 of Epinephrine down the endotrachael tube to stimulate cardiac activity. Cardiac monitor leads were attached and no electrical activity was evident in the heart."

Shortly after 09:00 a.m. the emergency medical crew notified Dr. Andy Steltmatter by phone and advised of the lack of cardiac activity and blood loss. At 09:15 a.m. the Doctor gave the official order to terminate life support procedures. Dr. Baumann, the Medical Examiner officially pronounced Jo dead at 09:30 a.m.

Deputy Warden Frank Elo recalls his actions. "At approximately 08:30 I made my radio transmission to Unit One (Control Center) that we needed an ambulance immediately. They asked the extent of injuries and I informed them that she had head injuries and that there was a large quantity of blood loss. I then made a second transmission requesting that State Police be sent to the scene. At 08:32 a.m. I radioed Unit One, after consultation with Deputy Warden Whelan and ADW Grinage and ordered the siren sounded to lock down the institution. At 08:33 a.m. I notified Unit One to notify Warden Foltz of the situation."

Elo started action to identify possible suspects. He requested a list of every prisoner that worked in the JCC, Special Activities, or anyone who would have been in the area that morning. He also requested call out sheets for any prisoners on call to that immediate area around the probable time of the assault. The radio log sheet would also reflect that at 08:40 a.m. Elo notified the Control Center to bring in about 20 off-duty officers. After the siren was sounded he had heard that they were having trouble clearing inmates from the south yard. The extra officers would also be needed to shake down possible suspects and examine them for scratch marks or other new wounds that might have resulted from a struggle with the injured officer.

Michigan State Police (MSP) Detective/Sgt. (D/Sgt.) Jerry Boyer was directed to assist D/Sgt. Chester Kozak in the investigation at Jackson Prison's Central Complex. He was there in the stairway when the medical team ended CPR.

"At this point the area was cleared and secured as best as possible. I requested the presence of the Crime Lab at this point to process the scene for evidence. I assigned MSP Sgt. David Hilliker to the door of the auditorium to obtain all names of parties present and refuse admittance hence of further personnel other than State Police."

Follick mentioned to several people of Hill's suspicious activity that morning and also that the belt around the victim's neck looked like one he had seen Hill wearing. It was a cheap looking belt with vinyl plastic material that was cracked. It had a red hue on one side and black on the other.

Eventually someone told ADW Elo that Food Service Supervisor Follick had mentioned a possible suspect. Elo immediately got in touch with State Police Detective Piziali and they met with Follick in the Deputy's office to hear what Follick had to say.

With Follick's information Elo asked Sgt. Cotton to choose some good officers for a pickup in 4 Block, where Hill resided.

At 09:15 a.m. Elo and the guard detail arrived at Hill's cell. Hill stood in front of his cell sink nude from the waist down. He appeared to be washing himself up. Elo ordered Hill to the front of the cell and informed him to get ready to move out. Hill then put on a pair of blue pants and shoes, grabbed a bag that appeared to be a potato chip bag and backed up to the bars to be hand cuffed by Sgt. Cotton. From there Hill was escorted to 5 Block, where at the dress in cage he was required to remove his clothes for a strip search. Those clothes were put in a plastic bag for analysis by the MSP crime lab. Elo noted that some of the clothes appeared to have bloodstains on them and that Hills right knuckles were freshly bruised.

Hill was quiet on the way to the 5 Block dress in cage, other than telling Sgt. Cotton, the black escorting officer, "It ain't that easy. You can't get me that easy." In the cage Hill said that he wanted his $1.35 in tokens and his cigarettes back. He also told Grinage, the black Deputy, to "fuck off", and that they would have to carry him to the slammer. Hill did however go to 5 Block without incident.

At 09:30 a.m. Tom Phillips was designated to notify Josephine McCallum's next of kin.

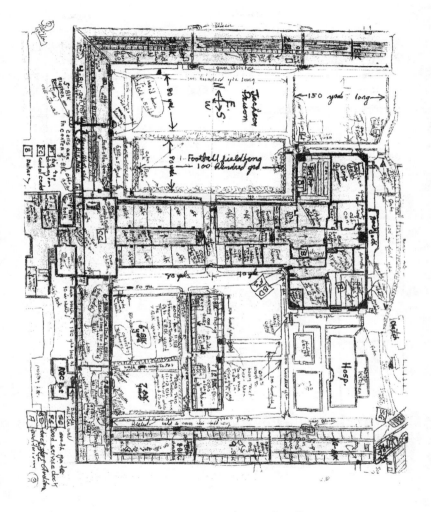

Prison layout given to Bill by a correction officer.

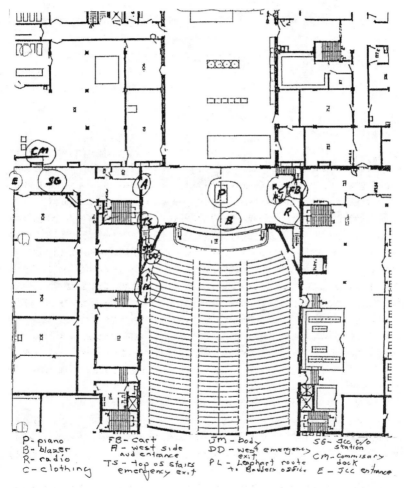

P - piano
B - blazer
R - radio
C - clothing

FB - cart
A - west side
   aud entrance
TS - top of stairs
   emergency exit

JM - body
DD - west emergency
   exit
PL - Leophart route
   to Bowers office

SG - Jcc c/o
   station
CM - Commisary
   dock
E - Jcc entrance

Crime area.

MARCH 24, 1987 – TRAGIC DAY

BILL – PAT – MICHAEL

Shortly after the alarm went off I got up and made coffee while Jo got dressed for work. Even though this was our normal routine I was unusually tired. Jo and I had talked late; then I went out to make sure the newspapers got dropped off.

To see Jo so upset about work was unusual. I didn't want her to go to work, but we didn't have the type of relationship where I told her what and what not to do. She had rationalized to us and herself that she needed the job; the union was there to protect her and she was a tough lady that would see this through as she had the other difficult times in her life. Besides, again, the pay was especially good. We sat down and had a cup of coffee and she was puffing on a cigarette. Recently I had an operation on my sinuses and wasn't supposed to smoke for three days. This was the third day and I again refrained from lighting up. But most certainly, the urge to was there.

"Why don't you stay home?"

"You know I can't do that. If I have a problem I'll file a griev-ance with the union," she replied. Then she added, "Don't forget Michael only has a half day of school and I'll try to get right home for the teacher conference."

I followed her out to the back door and waved as she drove out on South Francis Street. Michael would not be up for a while and I needed a little more sleep.

It was close to 9 when I woke up the next time. Michael was already up and playing with his action heroes. Pat was asleep in the chair. I whispered to Mike to be quiet and pointed to Pat, then went in and got dressed. I'd take Michael out for a nice breakfast, then he could play some more before I dropped him off for his half day at school.

We were regular customers at Sparty's. When we walked in the cook recognized us.

"You steal a car or something?"

"What do you mean?" I asked.

"The police called here a bit ago. Asked if you were here. I told them no."

"Know what they wanted?"

"Nope."

"Can't be a big deal."

The cook was always joking so I didn't give it much thought, but later when we were leaving he mentioned it again. Now I was curious as to why the police had called for me, and for that matter, how they knew I was there.

We had a nice breakfast, then left for home. Turning onto South Francis Street I could see something was going on close to our house. There were a lot of police cars around. Pulling in the driveway I could see that all the activity was at our house. The house looked normal; it wasn't on fire. I was instantly alarmed. Our friend Bart had stopped by to see me and exclaimed, "Bill you got a lot of company, what the hell did you do?"

"What in the hell–Bart, take Michael and stay here. OK?"

"OK, call me if you need me."

That's all Bart said before he grabbed Michael by the hand and led him out in the back yard to play ball.

A Lansing city police officer I knew, walked towards me. "Bill, you obviously know something's going on, could you please come inside." Another officer opened the door and followed me inside. My home seemed to be full of strangers and they all turned to stare at me as I came in. The only familiar face was that of Sarah, the neighbor. She had a distressed look on her face. There was a distinguished looking black man who stuck out his hand and said, "I'm Deputy Warden Dan Bolden." I swear, there seemed to be tears in the man's eyes.

The Lansing officer said, "I'm sorry to tell you Bill, your wife's been murdered at the prison."

Deputy Bolden spoke next, "There will be a thorough investigation and the department is here to take care of everything for you Bill."

It was as if someone had stuck a knife deep inside of me and was twisting it around. I don't remember how I responded, that's a blur now. I do remember that there was this great mix of panic, fear and loss all rolled into one that invaded my innards. I had to get Mike out of here. That was the immediate priority. I left them all standing there, and once outside I called for Mike. A news reporter could sense an action intercept; me coming out of the house and Michael from the side yard where he was playing ball with Bart. Out of the corner of my eye I could see Mike's back. Apparently he hadn't heard me call and was still playing ball. The reporter was in front of me now, leading with his microphone. "How does the boy feel knowing his mother was...." He didn't get a chance to finish his question as my fist found his mouth first, and then there was a long throw of his microphone.

"Come on Michael, let's take a ride." I grabbed his hand; confusion was his expression.

At first we drove along in silence. He was waiting for me to say something. I was trying to think of the right words to use. The tears starting to leave my eyes were not giving me much time to speak. As we were still on the highway I pulled over into a small city park and shut off the motor.

"Mom is gone from us Michael. She has gone to heaven and won't be home again."

I could see my words sinking in. He could see me crying. It was his turn to cry and he repeated my words as a question, "She won't be coming home again?"

We drove to my mothers. I knew that she could provide now, what I couldn't, insulation from reality with love. She took him into her arms and he held on tight. We all awkwardly looked at each other. She put him down and Mike went looking for his toys.

"Ma I must get back to find out what's happened." "Michael, grandma will take care of you for a while. I'll be back to see you soon."

Damn, I hated to leave him. I was afraid that my grief would only compound his. I had to have time to think; find out what had happened, what I should do next. It was about 10:30 a.m.

I went back to the house and talked with the people there. Later I started calling family and friends to let them know what happened. I called Tina and told her. At first there was only silence, followed by a choked, "I'll be right over." Next I got a hold of Jo's close friend, Jane Carpenter in Texas. She screamed and dropped the phone.

The police had the house blocked off, but by now there were many news reporters in the street. They shouted questions as I got out of the car, but I ignored them and entered the house. There still were a lot of people inside. The living room was small anyway and it really seemed crowded.

Tina soon arrived. Somehow they let her in without me identifying her. Probably Sarah, the neighbor, told them who she was. Tina had a questioning expression on her face as we met. There were tears in her eyes; we hugged. She was led off somewhere and Deputy Warden Dan Bolden was again with me.

I don't remember the questions I asked him, or the information he provided at that time, but I did feel that he was genuinely concerned and caring. I was assured that there would be a full investigation. There also was the promise that we would be well taken care of and wouldn't have to worry. The department was there to help us through this and take care of everything.

Pat arrived outside and it appeared the State Police were not about to let him in. I opened the door, "Let him in, he's family." Pat gave the police a mean look and pushed through. We had only a brief conversation before he was led off too the other side of the room.

. . . PAT . . .

I told the State Police to get the fuck out of the way, that I was a close friend and going in. They thought otherwise until Bill told them I was a relative. All I knew was that Tina had said something had happened to Josephine at the prison and for me to get right over there. That's all she said before hanging up.

When I got inside I only talked with Bill for a few minutes, before someone led me away for questioning. There was something about the people in there that made my skin crawl; the hair stand up on the back of my neck. People I didn't trust had invaded the sanctity of Bill and Josephine's home.

There was a big table in the living room that had always been the center of our fun, for cards, Scrabble or just talk. The four of us had sat there so many times laughing and enjoying each other's company. Now Tina sat there by herself answering someone's questions; her grief was evident.

It seemed like the phone rang a lot. Bill would answer, but there seemed to be no long conversations. Later, when it rang, some of the police would crowd around him and after the call he'd tell them what the call was about. They kept a log.

Of course they questioned me about how I was related to the family and so forth. I tried to find out what had happened to Jo, but the most I could learn was that she had been murdered and there was an ongoing investigation. Eventually the questions about the family led around to the status of the marriage and how well Bill and Josephine got along. At first this didn't bother me. "They got along just fine." My answer obviously didn't satisfy the guy for he kept fishing around with other questions of the same nature, even getting specific.

Now I was pissed off, for I didn't like at all what this guy was insinuating. "I told you their marriage was fine, all right!" The guy immediately retreated from that line of questioning and we talked about my work and automobiles. In the background I could hear the Deputy Warden assuring Bill that the department was there to help him and take care of everything. It also seemed that there was a lot of rooting around by some of these people. They were even looking into drawers all over the house. I really felt uneasy. Bill looked agitated and nervous.

Eventually Bill grabbed my arm. "Let's get some fresh air." I felt uneasy about leaving the house to these people, but Tina was there to watch.

"I'm not supposed to smoke today because of that operation, but I got to have one."

"Sure." I said, and reached out with my pack. He lit the cigarette, inhaled deeply and let the smoke ease out. I didn't really know what to say. We stood there in silence as a car came up the back alley toward us. The police hadn't blocked that way off. It looked like there were two men inside, a black and a white. When they got close the black guy leaned out the window and said to Bill, "One down and one to go." Bill lurched towards the car and the driver shifted to reverse and spun his tires retreating down the alley. Bill picked up a small rock and with a lucky shot hit the driver's window. Some of the police came over to check out the disturbance and left in pursuit of the vehicle.

I heard later the cops caught up with those guys, but neither of us ever heard who they were and what they were up to. Bill then told me that a lot of crank phone calls were coming in. Some were muffled voices issuing threats. He didn't go into detail.

Back in the house there was a State Treasury representative talking with Bill about Jo's insurance coverage or something. He asked if there was a bathroom he could use and then excused himself. Tina must have been watching the guy because later she caught him in their bedroom looking through Josephine's underwear drawer. That confirmed my feeling of unrest concerning these folks. Also there was a mirror like piece of glass on the piano where Jo used to position figurines. She would always let us know that we should keep our hands off that. The glass was now clear, and the figures were in a pile on the back as if someone had opened the top of the piano to look in.

I made up my mind that as long as these people were in the

house I would be there to watch. The State Police were only in the house for a few hours the first day. After that they just supplied security on the outside, controlling access to the house. Even though the news media was kept out of the yard, whenever anyone left the house and backed into the street you were surrounded by people with microphones and cameras asking questions.

From what I could tell the people left in the house were correction officials or those having something else to do with the State. When Bill left the room for any reason there was an effort by them to rat through things and I did my best to stop that activity. They didn't like me because I wouldn't leave. At one point they threatened to haul me off in handcuffs. I said, "I'd love to have you try and do that."

For the rest of the week I stayed at Bill's house during the day and then left for work each night. I vowed to stay there as long as these assholes were hanging around the house. There was always someone yakking to each one of us as if that person was assigned to keep us busy and separated; Tina at the table, Bill by the window and me near the opposite wall.

After a day or so they were pestering Bill about all the funeral arrangements. They wanted to really make it a big thing. It seemed to me that it was more for their image rather than respect for Jo or Bill.

Sarah was around quite a bit. Several times I saw her and Tina talking. That surprised me because before Tina never really liked Sarah and would bad mouth her regularly. Sarah and her husband used to come over and play that stupid word game Scrabble with all of us; right there at the table where Tina sat.

Various prison employee groups were contributing money for the family to defray costs and also for a memorial scholarship fund. One young lady who had been a classmate of Jo's came to the house no less than three times. Each time she would be at the door crying so much she couldn't talk. After the last time that happened I thought she might not have it all together mentally. She was a guard at the prison in Ionia and had collected $500 from those employees.

By midweek Jo's brother Jim arrived at the house in his Eaton County Police uniform. I guess he got in by flashing his badge. Bill wasn't there at the time, but I was. Jim wanted to pick up a few things in the house. I brought those plans to a halt and he left. A state trooper asked, "Is that Mrs. McCallum's brother?"

I lied, "Don't know who he is." Jim did come back later, but left after a short conversation with Bill.

. . . MICHAEL . . .

That morning Dad took me to breakfast at Sparty's Coney Island, which is just off Pennsylvania Avenue. We went there quite often, usually for breakfast. I remember having a couple cartons of chocolate milk and a big stack of blueberry pancakes. It was nice having the morning off from school.

When we arrived home there were a bunch of police cars around the house and a helicopter overhead. A family friend named Bart led me away from Dad to play catch with him. While we played Bart didn't say anything. That seemed strange. Dad went inside with the police.

Shortly after Dad went in the house he came back out and asked me to take a ride with him. I knew something was up, but I wasn't sure what was going on. We got into our '66 Bel Air, that Mom used to drive all the time and headed down the highway.

We rode for a while before Dad said anything. I knew something was really bothering him though, because he looked sad and there were tears in his eyes. When he told me my mother had gone to heaven he started to cry and I did too. I really couldn't comprehend my mother not coming home again, but the thought of that possibility disturbed me deeply.

My father then took me to my Grandma's house. Grandma gave me a big long hug and after a while my Dad drove off to do things. I'm sure Grandma was surprised to hear about my mother, though we didn't talk about that at all. Grandma was a kind and loving person who always seemed to like having me around. That day we just slipped back into our normal routine as if nothing had happened. She seemed extra attentive to me. She fixed lunch and we ate under the apple tree in the back yard.

I only spent one or two nights at Grandmas. I didn't particularly like sleeping there, because where I had to sleep was her sewing room. Ever since I was a very young child it always scared me at night. It seemed like weird shadows were always present there and that frightened me. Usually I'd wander into her room and crawl up in bed with her.

There were a lot of people at our house during the day now. At night they went away except for the police cars. In the morning Dad would take me to Grandmas, returning late to bring me home. One of the first nights back home, Tina's boys, Josh and Steve slept in my room. Josh still had diapers on, but he was a big kid. Steve and I played together in those times. I remember saying to Steve, "I have to tell you something about my Mom." Before I even told him he was holding back tears. When I told him he cried. I cried too. Perhaps he already knew she was gone and just hadn't said anything. That was one of the hardest things I've ever done.

One day a corrections officer returned with the old green Ford station wagon Mom had driven to work. Josh saw it out the window and said, "Josie's home".

. . . BILL . . .

The next day I went over to the Crumps. Rubin saw me drive up and met me at the car. "Rubin, Josephine has been killed at the prison. I should never have let her go in." He said he had already heard the news. Rubin was well aware of what I was talking about for Jo had also mentioned to him the previous evening that she had been threatened at work and might not make it home today. Maybe then the statement didn't carry much weight, but it did now.

The Crumps, and the Welbes had been friends and neighbors for so many years. Jo had grown up and gone to school with his oldest child, and his youngest, Levertis, was Michael's best friend and close to the same age. Rubin didn't know how to console me, but offered to do what he could, anything I needed. That wasn't necessary to say, as I already knew that they would always be there for us.

It was on the first or second day when Jack Welborn came to the house. He came with one of his aids, Don Prang. Jack was a State Senator who headed the Senate Committee on the State prisons. He was a distinguished looking gentleman with a western flair in his attire. He introduced himself and asked how I was doing. Of all the people around there he was the one that acted genuinely concerned about our welfare. Everyone else was eager to help, but they seemed to have a hidden agenda. Several were very interested in looking around the house, for what, I don't know, and Deputy Warden Bolden seemed engrossed in the funeral arrangements. He was determined to make it a "very special happening."

"Bill you can have as many limos as you want."

"But I can't afford this, I don't have much money," was my reply.

"Don't worry the state will take care of everything. The world will be watching. We have to show them we have pride."

I didn't particularly understand his comments. I thought to myself, who was to benefit from this big happening anyway?

Josephine was only the second State prison guard to be killed in the line of duty, the first being way back in '73. She was what they wanted to exemplify; a serious, young, attractive, smart family person who had chosen to be a state prison guard as a career. This funeral ceremony, at least in their minds, would show how much they cared for her and how important she was to them. Although I had to be involved in the uncomfortable details of picking out a casket and agreeing to visitation times, there were other things cropping up that invaded my time of grief. The first being when they brought the station wagon home.

At first I didn't think much about it, other than remembering the last time I had seen her in it leaving for work. Eventually, when I got around to take a close look at the car, I could see that someone had literally torn it apart on the inside and then attempted to put it back together. The putting together part of it was shoddy, to say the least. The door panels were loose as well as the dash, with wires out of place and the radio didn't work. Pat even discovered that the inside of the tailgate housing had been removed. Screws were obviously rusty and broke when the person tried to remove the panel. It was still loose and didn't fit properly. The car had been rifled. Wherever there was a cavity, it had been exposed. Someone was definitely trying to find something and there was no explanation offered. I was angry.

According to Pat these people were snooping around my house; someone searching for something had ripped my car apart and there was the issue of the phone calls. The message someone or some people were trying to send was that there might be more to happen, to me or to Mike. We should watch our step. There was also an indication in these calls that there was more to Josephine's death than was evident on the surface. Even Senator Welborn had alluded to that possibility.

I started to ask more questions and see what the newspapers were saying about Jo's death. The Jackson Citizen Patriot led the way with front-page headlines, "Prison locked down after guard slain." The staff writer, Bradley Flory, gave those details that had been released to the media by the Corrections spokeswoman in Lansing, Gail R. Light. At that time the family was still being notified, so the dead guards name was withheld. They did say that the female guard's body was found at the foot of a stairway.

The Patriot writer detailed the other recent attacks at the prison. In early March another female guard had been treated for three stab wounds received in Block 4. On February 8th Officer Mary Szarej was beaten inside a cell in the North Complex. In January Officer Bruce Goll was treated for stab wounds incurred in cellblock 12 in the Central Complex along with Officer Sharon Drayton who a week earlier had received minor injuries with neck stab wounds. All of these attacks except one were in the Central Complex where Josephine worked.

In the Patriot article Fred Parks, president of the statewide union for prison guards was quoted as saying that he understood the correction officer was working alone. "That is one of our protests, no officer should work alone. It is a dangerous situation," he said. No one had mentioned anything about all this to me. Were they trying to spare me grief by withholding details or were they trying to keep me in the dark.

The day after Josephine's death more specifics came out in the papers. State officials had already told me that they had some suspects. A Detroit News article said there were four. Union officials were again beating the drum about her being on the assignment alone and that because she was a new guard on probation this assignment was counter to the union contract. Anonymous prison employees said there was a belt wrapped around her neck and that she had been beaten badly; might have even been sexually assaulted. Some correction officers were quoted as saying that prison overcrowding, lenient discipline and officers working without partners made correction officers vulnerable to violence. Robert Hughes, the former president of the MCO Union chapter at Jackson stated, "The kind of clientele we're getting in prisons just don't give a damn. I've been here six years and I've never seen anything like this. They're going to kill guards."

It seemed that within the department these were conflicting opinions on how a probationary employee should be supervised. Spokeswoman Light said, "They should have been checking on her, if they were not with her." Warden Foltz said that McCallum's supervisor was a sergeant, but it's not clear how frequently he got around to check on her because he had other duties." Warden Foltz also said McCallum had a radio and, "That was the best device you can have."

It was obvious to me that the warden was trying to say that supervision was supplied through the radio. Correction Officer Hughes sure took exception to that when he said, "That radio doesn't mean much. They can grab you so quick you don't even have a chance to use it." Even the warden's boss, Director Brown, interpreted intensive supervision to mean "visual contact."

The politicians were starting to come forth with statements to show they were doing something. Governor Blanchard asked

Attorney General Frank Kelley to review policy and procedures involving prison guard's safety. Blanchard said, "We will not rest until the facts of her death are known and the guilty party or parties are brought to justice."

State Rep. Phillip Hoffman urged the department to reassign female guards in maximum and medium security prisons until an investigation into the death was complete. Senator Welborn, whom I had met at the house, said that he was concerned that the rookie guard was working alone. Unnamed prison officials said that was not unusual to have someone like that working alone.

Of course there were anonymous guards making statements to the affect that women didn't belong there. The Director of the Michigan Department of Corrections took issue with that opinion. "We've been through that. Females are part of the resources of our society and I need all the good help I can get."

One newspaper quoted a 37-year-old Central Complex female guard, who had worked there for 3-1/2 years, saying that she had been threatened by inmates' dozens of times. In one incident a prisoner remarked, "I sure hope I'm around when you're knocked out so I can get a little piece of you." This woman said that guards are reluctant to talk to the media because of a corrections policy that says they will be accountable for statements made to the media.

By Thursday the search for the killer had narrowed down to an inmate named Hill, who worked in the commissary. A friend of his named Merryman was also a suspect. County prosecutor Joseph S. Filip said Hill was one of the suspects, but Brown, the Corrections Director, and several guards who asked not to be identified stated he was the prime suspect. The prison continued their lock down of the Central Complex and it's 2,368 prisoners. The regular force of 125 officers was increased by 15.

On Thursday, the date and time of the funeral was published; 10 a.m. Saturday the 28th, at the Resurrection Church on Michigan Avenue in Lansing, with burial at St. Joseph Cemetery.

Apart from what now was becoming a controversial death, many nice things were being said about Josephine. The dean of Lansing Community College, James Person, said she was an excellent student who finished 3rd in a class of 100 with nearly straight A's. "She did a beautiful, beautiful job." He said they were establishing a scholarship in her name.

Deputy Warden Frank Elo was affiliated with the Correction Officers Academy. He said, "She was an excellent student and a dedicated guard. She was the kind of student every instructor dreams of."

I remember what Elo had said at Jo's graduation, "Someday this little girl will have a prison all her own. I'll make sure of that." I think now that he was instrumental in having her sent to that hell-hole at Jackson.

One employee who didn't want to be named was quoted in the Thursday Detroit Free Press as saying, "Jackson tends to be like a city dump. It's the place where all other prisons like to dump their garbage inmates. If an inmate threatens to beat up a staff member at another prison they send him to Jackson. So, we have a big concentration of troublemakers here. It's one of the reasons other prisons run so well."

From the news articles I had a pretty good idea of what had happened to Josephine and what the governor, warden and politicians were going to do to fix things. It was unfortunate that after three serious assaults on female guards since the first of the year and warnings coming from the union for several years, that it took Jo's death to start any corrective action. I sure wasn't willing to make that sacrifice. I'd give anything to have her back and to hell with that prison and the politicians.

We held a visitation at the funeral home. Mike and I were positioned over by the coffin while all the Welbes brothers and their families were clustered together nearby. As people passed by to pay their respects the Welbes could be heard whispering and occasionally giggling among themselves. I didn't say anything to them about it but I thought their behavior was rude. When the visitation was over they left as a group and didn't have anything to say to us. That's the way we had been treated at the holiday get-together's in the past when Jo was alive—I guess I just expected something different from them now. That didn't happen.

Something else happened at the funeral home that brought me out of grief to a point of rage. I went out to get a drink of water and caught part of a conversation that was taking place on a nearby phone. It was Sarah our neighbor talking; "Dan, I've done everything you said; given you stuff and talked to everyone and made a list of who came and went from the home. When do I get my permanent position?"

Shit, I couldn't even trust Sarah. I literally ripped the phone cord out of the wall. Sarah made a fast exit and didn't show up at the funeral. I found out later she was a part-time secretary with Corrections. The only Dan I knew was Deputy Warden Dan Bolden, who had been at the house. I had to wonder, what the hell's going on here and whom can I trust.

"Alone ... afraid"

by Bill McCallum

Life changed today.
My life died today.
Our life took a turn today,
her life died today.
She left us alone today:
She left us afraid today.
She was the center ...
    she was the hope.

But now we are alone–
    now we are afraid.
The shining fun of life is gone ...
    the Dark Red Resolve is mine.

She was alone,
she was afraid
She died there–alone ... afraid ...
         Why?

This poem was written by Bill McCallum and published in The Keeper's Voice in March 1988.

INVESTIGATION

After the siren blew and the prison went into lock down, established procedures were followed to get the prisoners back into their cells and to account for all of them. Deputy Whelan tape-recorded a message to be broadcast on the prison radio hookup.

"This is Deputy Whelan. We have had an unfortunate incident occur this morning here at SPSM. One of our officers was brutally attacked and killed in the auditorium. The Michigan State Police Crime Lab is currently on the scene. Of necessity, we have had to lock the institution down until we can sort out what happened. I assure you we will attempt to return to normal operations as soon as possible. We ask your full cooperation. Thank you."

According to Deputy Elo he met with a State Police representative and people from his Internal Investigation Office (IIO) to examine a list of possible suspects and determine the direction of the investigation.

Although the Michigan State Police would handle the crime investigation, prison investigators would have to formulate a Critical Incident Report for the institution. Security Investigator (SI) Dan Verlin was put in charge of the report. Another investigator Cindy Lindemyer would aid Verlin in interviewing witnesses.

To start the investigation Verlin had a list of all inmates and correction officers that had been in the auditorium, plus all inmates that were in the Special Activities building that morning. During lock down inmates had been shaken down and examined for new cuts or bruises and possible blood on their clothing. Three prisoners were taken to 5 Block for administrative segregation. They were; Thompson, who had multiple scratches on his neck, McGee, with one new scratch on the back of his upper arm, and Carter who had blood on his clothes. The other commissary workers, Edwards, Hill, James, and Merryman appeared to have no broken skin injuries according to LPN Jim Chamberlin, but were placed on administrative segregation in 5 Block because other witnesses had put them in the area or because they had easy access to the crime scene. The clothing they were wearing and that in their cells was confiscated for the MSP crime lab.

Shortly after the lock down a search was initiated for a weapon that could have been used in the murder. Nothing was found, however Officer Priscilla Mann did find a set of keys in a food service hat inside a trash barrel outside the south yard sub-hall area. This was approximately 40 yards from the Special Activities Building.

The Michigan State Police Crime Lab personnel arrived at 10:45 a.m. Although the auditorium had been cleared when the siren was sounded, prior to that, numerous prison personnel had walked around the stage and crime scene area: those officers searching for the injured officer, medical team personnel and the two deputy wardens. Blood had been walked in and tracked by different people and some of McCallum's clothing had been handled.

Officer McCallum's shirt, shoes and socks were found at the east end of the stage next to a pillar. Buttons from her shirt were strewn across the stage in different directions, and the strings on her shoes were still tied. Her tie was found some distance from the rest of the clothing. It was obvious that there had been a violent struggle as the assailant or assailants tried to remove her clothing. The radio Leaphart had heard while he was playing the piano was in the southeast corner of the stage. Her blazer, laying on center stage was soaked in blood. Personal work notes and papers of Officer McCallum were strewn about near her clothing. Blood was smeared on the floor near a heavy flatbed cart in the northeast corner of the stage and several spots were later found toward the front of the stage. McCallum's pants were found beside her body in the stair-way. They were turned inside out as if they had been removed from her there.

Initially corrections officers associated with the search, or those that had contact with McCallum that morning provided handwrit-ten memorandums to Security Investigator Verlin. Later he or Cindy Lindemyer would interview them in addition to the inmates that had been workers in the commissary that morning. The Michigan State Police would eventually again interview some of the same people that the prison investigators had talked with, but in several instances they would simply rely on the information pro-vided from the prison internal investigator.

At 09:30 a.m. Tom Phillips was charged with notifying the next of kin, however a little over a half hour later the records would indicate that he came to the Control Center desk and asked that a locksmith unlock Josephine's car so it could be shook down, sup-posedly for anything that had a phone number of her parents or next of kin. That was strange, considering her home address and phone number and husbands name was on her employee file records and readily available.

It was around 11:37 a.m. when Warden Foltz met with Deputy Whelan and department heads to review the situation. Forty-five minutes later Josephine's body was transported to W.A. Foote Memorial Hospital in the city of Jackson.

Henry A. Kallet conducted the autopsy at Foote Hospital. Dr. Baumann, who had pronounced the death, was there as well as Detective Sergeant Brown and Chief Technologist Fluker of the MSP. Also present representing the prison were Jeff Pritt and Bill McFarlan. Dr. Loren Kelborne, Foote Hospital Pathologist wit-nessed the examination as well.

By anyone's description, even those practiced in viewing autop-sies, this was a grim scene. The injuries visually evident depicted a violent death with much suffering. Dr. Kallet dictated his observa-tion of the victim using body part terminology that the layman might not be familiar with, but to those in attendance there was lit-tle doubt as to what he was referring to. Occasionally he would interject an opinion as to how the damage had been done. The fist of a right-handed person would have caused the laceration to the left corner of her mouth. The same for the right lower jaw. Both eyes were black from blows and the lower nose was injured. Kallet noted that the head had been in motion when it struck something, like the corner of a table; thus causing a skull depression by the left ear. The left ear was almost split in two. Bruises were evident on the left side of the face, which was swollen and distorted. Her lips were extensively bruised, as was her right lower jaw.

Dr. Kallet concluded that more force than necessary had caused this death. Repeated blows to the head and the skull fracture had incapacitated the victim, compression from the belt around the neck and manual strangulation finally ended the life. Blood in the lungs and brain lacerations with extensive cerebral hemorrhaging were the end result.

It was a violent animal like rape. The bruises inside the uterus were extensive. Dr. Kallet said, "A woman would not tolerate this type of abuse." He pointed out that the laceration of the left nipple and abrasion below that breast appeared to be bite marks. He noted the cloudy fluid in the vagina. It would be analyzed, along with other swab samples from different parts of the body. These specimens along with fingernail scrapings were surrendered to Chief Technologist Fluke of the MSP.

Two days later, MSP Detective Sgt. Norman Brown served a search warrant on inmate Hill for the purpose of collecting evidence. The prison doctor, Dr. Sandra Stritmatter and her assistants, Alfred Simpson RN and Chris Connin RN conducted the physical examination on Hill in the 5 Block nursing station. The medical team collected samples for the sexual evidence packets, head and pubic hair, saliva, a blood sample. The whole procedure was witnessed by prison investigators Dan Verlin, Lt. Gary Barker, Deputy Warden Herbert Grinage and prison employee Dennis Parks, who video taped Hill the entire time. A few minutes later, except for the medical personnel, the same people observed Hill being finger printed in the State Police office. Videotape was made of that procedure also. Later that afternoon Hill was moved from Jackson

Prison to the Huron Valley Prison. Although there was much to do before Hill would be brought to trial, there was little doubt in anyone's mind, that Hill was guilty.

It was early in the afternoon on the 26th. Harold Boyer, the porter of 5 Block, was sweeping the ground floor when a kite (paper airplane) came down from the second floor. The prisoner in a ground floor slammer said to Boyer, "Give me the kite."

Boyer responded, "I'm not giving you anything." Boyer leaned down, picked up the kite and threw it back up to the second floor.

Boyer knew the ground floor inmate was Hill, and he despised him. About three months before Hill had completely embarrassed him in the commissary and Boyer harbored considerable anger about that incident. Boyer had been sweeping a band of trash out towards the back dock after 5 Block finished their meal. Hill stood in the kitchen by the commissary door. Hill said, "I'm gonna grab your ass." And, that is exactly what Hill did as Boyer moved by. He reached out and squeezed Boyer's butt.

"If we were in a different area I'd get rid of you," snarled Boyer.

Boyer had been doing his best for a long time to keep out of trouble. He had landed a porters job and wanted to eventually get out of this place. A fight with Hill, no matter who was to blame, could ruin his good record and possibly land him in solitary. So, instead of retaliating he swept his pile out to the back dock and helped dump the rest of the trash accumulated from the 5 Block meals. Since that time Hill and Boyer had passed each other several times in the commissary and only traded mean looks.

Boyer continued his sweeping up to the desk area and when he returned the kite was back down on the ground floor.

"Just sweep that kite in here," said Hill.

"I'm not giving you anything you're not suppose to have in the slammer."

The slammer is a type of solitary cell used when segregating certain prisoners from the rest of the population. It was referred to as a quiet cell. The cell had an outside door that could be shut cutting out any noise the prisoner might make. At this time the outside solid door was open.

Again Hill asked, "Why don't you give me the kite? There's something important on there I want to read."

Boyer again told Hill he wasn't giving the note to him, but instead swept it up against the wall with other trash, then scooped it all up with a shovel and deposited it in the trash bag.

Hill issued an angry threat, "I'm gonna kill your white ass just like I did that bitch the other day."

"That's all you can mess with is a female guard. You can't mess with a real man."

"I remember you. I grabbed your ass out in the kitchen a while back and you didn't touch me. You ain't gonna do nothing now either," said Hill.

"If I had 5 minutes to get into that cell with you I'd make up for what happened then and what you did to that officer guard."

After just looking at Hill, Boyer got mad and slammed the solid door shut so he wouldn't hear from him again. Officer Borkowski stepped around the corner right after that and told Boyer that he wasn't supposed to be talking to prisoners in the quiet cells. Borkowski said that he could get fired for that. Borkowski also said that he'd heard part of the conversation and asked what it was all about. Boyer told him about the kite incident. Borkowski said, "That guy's in trouble. We're not supposed to communicate with him. Where is the kite?"

Boyer went to the trash bag, fished it out and gave it to the guard.

Borkowski unfolded the kite and read the short paragraph that had been printed on prisoner stationary.

'Dig Homeboy. If that's you them --- accusing of that murder watch your food boy for real. They said on the news they have a prime suspect: 27 yrs old and in here for rape, robbery & murder. I don't know if that's you but do like I said.' "Shorty Mack"

SAYING GOODBYE

On Saturday, March 29, 1987 a mile and a half long convoy of cars and buses made its way north on US 127 from Jackson to Lansing for Jo's funeral. Police reported that the procession heading down Michigan Avenue to Lansing's Church of Resurrection was one of the biggest the Capitol City had ever experienced. Not only was it a collection of State prison workers, but also those representing correction officers from Canada, and other states. Most of the corrections officers wore their green blazers.

The 700 seats inside the church were quickly filled and soon lack of even standing room forced hundreds outside. Loud speakers were set up outdoors for those to hear the service and a priest even served Holy Communion on the sidewalk.

I'm sure that the tribute to Josephine made Deputy Warden Dan Bolden very happy, for it was so important to him to show the world that they really cared. I will admit that for all of us it was impressive to see how many folks had shown up to honor Josephine. What I remember most was the tears in the eyes of those that really knew her; the Crumps seemed to react as if it had been one of their own children.

Corrections Officer Eldon Roushey gave a stirring eulogy and Rev. William Koenigsknecht conducted the service. The Reverend's message was how Josephine was a victim of a breakdown in society—how the prisons were crowded with those who care little for life. I know he was talking about the inmates, but I also felt he was leaving out another group of derelicts, some of her supervisors and co-workers.

After the service Brenda Wilson came up to me. Brenda had brassy red hair, and reminded me of Lucille Ball. She had been the last corrections officer to talk with Jo. Brenda kept saying that maybe she was to blame for Jo's death, for telling her about the porter at the JCC that would help her. Maybe that had made Jo vulnerable. I assured her that in no way was it her fault. Later Brenda would become a close friend and for a while, a source of information for me.

Although I had been promised as many limousines as we needed for the service, I ordered just one. That was a smart move on my part, for the State didn't cough up money for any part of the service. I paid the bill from her insurance money.

Governor Blanchard came over to our limo and stuck his head in one of the rear side windows to pay his respects. I got out of the front seat and told one of the men with the Governor that I'd like to talk with the Governor. He said, "The Governor doesn't want to talk with you." The guy was big and obviously one of the Governor's bodyguards.

Corrections officers, most of whom I didn't know, served as pallbearers. At St. Joseph's Catholic Cemetery they played Amazing Grace with bagpipes. An honor guard saluted her and a squad fired a volley of shots followed by the playing of "Taps." They folded the flag that had covered the coffin and presented it to me. All the time the tears kept coming from my eyes and I kept wondering what was going through my boys mind. I wished that somehow I could shield him from all of this.

Although I had requested that no pictures be taken during the service, on the second front page of the Sunday Detroit Free Press, there I was with my eyes closed holding the folded flag with my arm around Mike who had his face pushed against my side. There was also a picture of Mike, Tina, and myself together on the front page of the State Journal. The press was stationed some distance away, but I guess they used telephoto lenses.

The Free Press writer, Chris Christoff, interviewed several

correction officers at the funeral. Randy Hoenes told about working with Jo. He said she was a "good officer that asked pertinent questions and paid attention."

Barbara Stahl met and chummed around with Jo in training. She said that Josephine was looking at the job more as a career opportunity than just a job. "She was a real logical person and an extremely private person. She talked a great deal about her son and even stayed home on the night of our academy graduation party because he had the flu."

Others told about how intelligent Jo was and that she had received a trophy for graduating third in her class.

Of course all the state officials from Governor Blanchard on down through the many wardens were listed as attending the funeral, but I don't remember any of them coming over and saying anything to us. I guess it was just important for their reputation to be there.

We had a dinner after the funeral that Fred Guetschow provided. He had also furnished the food for our wedding, and this time he again put out a remarkable spread for us. Although I insisted on paying him he steadfastly refused. "No way Willy, you don't owe me anything. What are friends for?"

Before Jo was killed Michael had made several gifts for her in school. There was a little bottle, a wind chime and a coupon book. Each coupon offered a service, a back rub or something. He really was confused as to what he should do with them. We ended up taking the bottle to the cemetery where he put it and a note on her gravesite. The wind chime he gave to me.

Later I went back to the cemetery and read his note to her. He simply said, 'We're doing OK. I miss you a lot. Dad's cooking is getting better.' I stood there and cried for some time.

. . . MICHAEL . . .

Sometimes people close the door on part of their lives; just tuck it away in some spare room where its unpleasantness can't confront them. I didn't do that intentionally, but once it had happened I was determined that the door stayed closed. I missed my mother terribly. But it was something that was private and I couldn't share. How could anyone understand the empty feeling that her absence had left with me?

I have a sharp memory, but the funeral to this day is only a blur. Like a silent movie I remember a lot of people in uniform, them folding a flag and giving it to my Dad: people hugging or patting me, but saying very little. Also, I can remember sitting in the back seat of this limousine when the governor stuck his head in the window and Jane Carpenter almost caught him in the face with her cigarette. That's about the extent of my recollections, other than how sad people seemed to be.

I didn't go back to school that year. Time was spent with my Grandma, my friends and Dad. He still was running the newspaper delivery business, but that happened while I slept. Even after the funeral, reporters would keep stopping around and there were strange phone calls from people we didn't know. Dad was loving and became quite protective. He seemed restless and more on guard than I ever remembered before. When we were at a shopping mall or car show and I wanted to wander off with my friends, it became standard procedure for him to brief me on what to do if a stranger approached my friends or me. It was ingrained in my nature at an early age to be watchful of other people. Eventually I would understand my Dad's concern.

My teacher's at Fairview, Ms. Macatee and my classmates sent me a small glassed in replica of a garden with a small ceramic bunny in it and some nice cards telling me they were thinking of me and hoping that I was doing OK. I remember the first time my mother met my teacher. That day they recognized each other as former classmates. They planned on a get-together to catch up on old times and would have been able to see each other again at the parent teacher conference, but that didn't happen, for that was the day she died.

Dad and I started going to see this lady, Carmen Salinas, a psychologist, about once a week. Sometimes we'd visit with her together—many times it was just me in her office. I wasn't used to anyone asking me questions about my feelings and I would take my action figures along for support. She didn't seem to mind, when at times I paid more attention to them than I did to her. I felt very uncomfortable there. I still didn't understand what was really going on. I just knew I didn't like to be there. Several visits into the therapy I just began telling her what I thought she wanted to hear. Sometimes I think kids can be smarter than adults give them credit for being and I was no dummy even at that age.

That summer we moved from South Francis Street to another house outside of Grand Ledge. Dad said that it was a home that he and Mom had considered before she passed away. They both were looking forward to a place in the country and with her job they could afford one. There had been insurance money associated with her job, so that was providing for this new place and Dad thought that she would have wanted us to have it.

After Mom was gone we gained one new and real good friend, Senator Jack Welborn. All of a sudden we were scooped up and made a part of his family. Jack was warm and most importantly straightforward. He started off by taking me on a personal tour of the Michigan State Capitol Building. Dad had a little suit for me to wear and I felt very special that day. Jack even took me up to see the inside of the dome. The public tours didn't even take in that attraction.

The capitol visit was just the beginning of my association with Welborn. Soon he was having Dad and I at his home for dinner. Jack owned a big farm over by Kalamazoo. The farm was out in the middle of nowhere, but he had built a large beautiful home there. Jack's wife, Dorothy, was just as nice as he was; a very caring lady. His son, who was a lot older than I was, lived right next door and came over several times while we were there. It seemed that we had been friends with all of them for a long time. It was a stark contrast to my uncles, who didn't give a damn about us, or ever speak to us again.

Our visits to Welborn's farm became a regular thing. I was even welcome to bring friends along, so Levertis would occasionally come too and we would wander all over Jack's farm. Once we were out quite a while and got a little disoriented in our direction. Soon we heard this motor sound coming towards us. I think our imaginations ran a little wild as we both panicked from the sound. It was especially frightening for me because of all the threats we were receiving. The sound came closer and over the hill came Jack on his quad-runner. He didn't seem at all disturbed that we had wandered off, just stopped to see if we were all right and would like a lift back to the house.

Mom's friend Tina, never came into our house much again. I think she could not accept my mother being gone. Her son's Josh and Steve were at our place often though. When school was out those two would even stay a few weeks at a time with us. Of course Levertis, always seemed to be around too. Dad made my friends seem very welcome. He was always treating us to pop and pizza and taking us to the movies. In this time frame I developed a keen interest in the movies. It was a sense of escapism. Ever since I was a young kid anytime someone asked me what I wanted to do I said, "I want to be an actor!"

We had neighbors close around us at the new place so we weren't that isolated, but still we had more privacy than we had on South Francis Street with an alley on 2 sides and a road in front. We also had an unlisted phone number, but Dad did work out a deal with Jack Welborn to have a phone in his office with call forwarding to our place. That way we could still get calls without having someone find out where we lived. There were people out there that didn't like us for some reason, and they called. One person tried to muffle his voice, "We're gonna get the kid." Others were just hang-ups.

Dad didn't try to alarm me about what was going on, but he was always cautioning me to be careful. I don't think he knew why we were being threatened, however people were telling him things about my mother's death and he would tell Jack Welborn everything he found out. Jack was chairman of a State Senate Committee overseeing the prison system. Maybe the connection between Jack and my dad scared some folks. I think eventually Dad let it be known that he would be receptive to anyone who wanted to provide information on what was going on.

The day we moved into the house in Grand Ledge one of the neighbor kid's mother mentioned that she went to high school with my Mom. Reality set back in and at that moment I knew her death and that loss was something I would live with the rest of my life. I also knew the knowledge of that and her memory were things I would fight to keep sacred and to myself.

Funeral – Bill, Michael and Tina Russell (behind Bill).

AP/Worldwide Photo

HOW IT USED TO BE

FROM A FORMER
CORRECTIONS OFFICER

In the apartment complex where I live there are some Jackson corrections officers living above me, and also a couple on the floor below. Last summer I was out catching some sun by the pool and I heard a couple of them discussing work.

"Man, I'd like to see some action around 'The Big Mama'—like they had in the old days".

The other one chimed in, "Yeah. It's boring as hell."

I thought to myself if only they knew how it had been back then they wouldn't be saying that. If I told them they probably wouldn't believe me anyway. They think they're invincible. Maybe if only there was some way I could lend them some of my reoccurring nightmares. It has been 13 years since I set foot in that prison, but it seems like only yesterday that I was part of that hellhole. I still can't shake free of those memories. I doubt that I ever will.

It's funny, because I had grown up in Jackson, right down the road from the prison. When we heard the sirens from inside, we knew something was wrong and they were probably locking the place down. But, having the prison there seemed so normal, we never gave it much thought. A lot of the local folks worked there, but I don't remember them saying much about what went on inside.

The year was 1976 and my wife and I had our first baby: I was working for the railroad. The job required a lot of nights away from home and I wanted to be around more. I decided to quit and find work that was closer. In that time frame the prison was hiring guards on a regular basis. There wasn't much of any interview; you just walked in the front door and picked up an application.

Training consisted of one or two weeks of basic classroom indoctrination. There was no OJT in the prison for us. They did show us this film on the riots in Attica, New York, where a lot of folks were killed. That was kind of scary, but they told us that only one guy had been killed on the job in Michigan's prison history, so it seemed like a reasonably safe job.

As I think back on it, I don't think any amount of classroom training would have prepared me for the rude awakening of actually being in the place. More accurately, I would describe it as a severe culture shock.

I went to high school on the outskirts of the city of Jackson and I don't recall there being any blacks enrolled in the school. It seemed to me when I walked in for work that first day, that 80 or 90% of the Jackson inmate population was black. So now, I had to not only deal with the criminal culture, but also a race of people from the inner city I had no familiarity with. The corrections officer force at that time was just about all white males.

The first day I was assigned to 5 Block. That was the segregation detention block, in Central Complex which was the heart of the prison. These prisoners had all done something wrong within the prison system to get there. The noise in this block was almost unbearable. I'm sure that outside the prison, the yelling inmates could easily be heard on Cooper Street. I couldn't believe what I had gotten myself into; and for a little over four dollars an hour pay. I definitely had misgivings about having left the railroad.

As I was given assignments in other cellblocks I could see that the public perception of what went on in the prison here was probably pretty misguided. I think most people would picture stone faced guards with a baton pacing back and forth in front of cells full of bad guys. Not true here. Other than 5 Block most all the cell doors in the Central Complex were open and inmates roamed freely within the prison. Various cellblocks even mixed together out in the yard and for meals.

Inmates had work assignments in the prison factory making automobile license plates and office furniture. Also there were school classes and other work areas, but there seemed to be no control of inmate movement. They were free within the prison 16 hours a day. It all was part of the current rehabilitation philosophy within the system. The thought was if they're to be rehabilitated, they shouldn't be locked in their cells all the time.

If there was a reason to put an inmate in his cell, the locks were so bad they could be easily jammed open anyway. The locking system was terrible. Only at night, when the dead bolts were closed was the prison population actually locked in. Of course, if a guard was stabbed or something else of that nature and there was a general lock down, the dead bolts held them all in.

There didn't seem to be very many guards at all and we were right in the middle of the inmate population with only a radio to defend ourselves. We were at the mercy of the inmates. In due time I learned the basics to survive here and it didn't involve cultivating the tough guy image, but rather working out some friendships and agreements with the inmate leaders. It was a seat of the pants survival technique.

Most all of the factory work gave the inmates easy access to metal pieces that could be fashioned into weapons. There were several inmate gangs and their method of settling disputes was to simply stick the opposition. Of course correction officers got stuck regularly too, but the bulk of it was inmate against inmate. In 1980, 22 inmates were killed in the Central Complex alone. Going to work and witnessing blood shed was routine. I remember one day when one inmate hit another in the head with a half cement block. The guy's head just caved in.

There was a lot of overcrowding in the prisons. Double bunking within the cells was common. Staff was really short so it was a definite recipe for trouble. Each cellblock normally held 400 to 500 inmates and for each side of a block there would be one guard. Imagine, 50 cells in a row five floors up, for one guard.

In the late 70's and early 1980 I was working in 2 Block located in the North Complex. Now that area is referred to as the Egler facility. Those cellblocks face out toward the prison wall with their own entrance outside, while the other blocks all were part of the inside. At that time the North Complex was supposed to house a less dangerous individual. That was a laugh. The classification system was as bad as the cell locks. Hell, an inmate with a record equal to the worst in Central Complex might be classified for trustee status. A few bucks would buy about any classification they wanted.

In 1980 the North Complex also had 10 modular units to ease the overcrowding. Each modular held about 30 inmates and they were not locked in. Their classification was supposed to be less dangerous. What a joke that was. These were the worst that enjoyed the most freedom allowed within the prison system. I had been assaulted several times, but I did what was necessary to survive each day. The inmates knew that there was little advantage for them to kill a guard, so the thought was to keep the guards in line and use them as necessary.

There were two black gangs, both based on supposed religious beliefs. One group claimed to be Muslim, and I can't remember what the other group was called, but the meetings of each gave ample opportunity for drug business arrangements and actions against rival gangs. Because these meetings were supposed to allow opportunity to practice religion, there were no guards present. I don't recall there being any white gangs. That race was in the minority anyway.

Finally in May of 1981, after inmate and guard stabbings had reached an unheard of level, the swing shift guards took action on their own to force some authority on this free wheeling operation. It happened after the night meal before the evening exercise period. All the administrators had gone home for the day so there was no one to object when the guards performed a lock down of the Central Complex and dead-bolted the cells. The cons were in for the night and they were pissed.

The next morning I arrived for my shift and sensed that something was definitely wrong. The prison administrators had found out what happened on the previous evening and decided the safest course of action was to allow the situation to return to normal. In other words allow the cons to take back control of the prison.

Although I had worked there for over four years, I was not in the mainstream of guard activity. Most of the people on my shift had no idea what the other guards had planned. Eventually we were the ones that bore the brunt of their actions.

The inmates were openly defiant towards us the next morning. The spud juice was flowing freely in the open and the attitude towards us was, "What are you going to do about it?" "Fuck you!" Of course the cons had access to the phones, so in short order the other major prisons in the State found out about the unauthorized lock down that had been conducted by the guards. The whole situation was festering into something big. I'm sure the administrators were wringing their hands, but we were the ones in the middle of the mess.

Although I didn't know what the renegade guards were up to, I agreed with what they did. Stabbings were occurring daily and something had to be done to bring some authority to the prison. Drug flow within the prison was rampant, and just like outside the prison, crime follows drugs, except in here the punishment deterrent was non-existent. I believe the warden at that time had previously been a psychologist. His dream world of rehabilitation was really just a time bomb ticking.

By the time the spud juice and drugs started to take affect the inmates moved from passive defiance to riot like activity-breaking and burning stuff. The administrators took a wait and see type of approach to begin with, but eventually it was obvious to everyone that there was going to be a major activity here. I don't even remember what the inmate issues or complaints were, other than the previous lock down by the guards. All I know was that they were angry and going to raise hell to vent their anger.

Over the course of three days a full-blown riot took place and it was scary. Really, we were just unarmed spectators with a front row seat, because we were right down there in the middle of everything.

There was lots of gunfire from the guard towers, but it was aimed at the ground as a deterrent. I'm sure the inmates knew this too, because it didn't stop them from tearing things apart and burning anything burnable. The guards were pretty much left alone.

If they had attacked us, probably the shooters would have aimed to kill or injure the attackers.

The prisoners in 1 and 2 blocks broke through the window in the back to gain access to the inside of the prison to join forces there. None of the inmates could get over the main wall, but there was a worry that they could climb up and over the administration building to escape. Stationed on the rooftops were scores of heavily armed State Police.

Some guards in the North Complex locked themselves in the corridor and were more or less hostages, but no guard was killed.

There was a group of inmates that congregated in one end of the yard that wanted nothing to do with the rioting activity, but the others did enough to make up for their absence. All the modular housing was burned to the ground.

I remember that our Captain that day had been a Marine in Vietnam and he was yelling over the radio for us to hold our stations. With over a thousand convicts raising hell in our area there was little we could do but watch and wait—and worry.

They finally had fire trucks in to douse the fires and the inmates. Supposedly negotiations took place, with the riot finally fizzling out. The inmates were doubled up in the North Complex cells and all of them were dead-bolted in for the rest of the summer. They were fed in their cells and didn't get any yard time.

As I recall the administrators initially tried to blame the guards for what happened, however over the summer more thought was put into the cause, since the media, politicians and general public were putting pressure on the governor to do something.

Prior to the riots the emphasis was on rehabilitation and the fashionable thought was catering to the inmates demands and allowing lots of freedom. Teachers were raped and stabbings were so common—it finally became apparent that establishing some authority would be a good thing. Also it was decided that Jackson was too big and would be divided up into separate entities and operated as such.

Some of the ringleaders from the riots were separated out and sent to Huron Valley, others to Ionia or Marquette. A lot of fence went up around the North Complex.

After the riots many of the prison guards called it quits. That gave me the opportunity to move up to the rank of Sergeant. Of course the promotion required me to work inside the Central Complex, but hell, I couldn't perceive it being any worse than where I'd been—plus I'd be making a few extra bucks.

We were already understaffed so there was a major push to hire more guards. Among the new-hires were an increasing number of females. That certainly added a new dimension to the work environment. Many of the male correction officers and probably several of the wardens felt that women had no business working in a men's prison, however, lawsuits aimed at providing equal employment for women gave the administration little choice in the matter.

Some inmates didn't appreciate having female corrections officers around; invading the privacy of their cells. These inmates could serve forth with a wide variety of profane verbal harassment that could be quite intimidating. Most of the other inmates I think enjoyed having them there. In fact many would offer to look out for them and offer a thin shell of safety in this threatening environment. "Baby, it's dangerous in here. I'll look out for you. I'll see that you're protected."

Then there were the sweet-talkers, the inmates that eventually could lure a female officer into some kind of relationship. For a girl that was not particularly attractive, to be complimented and made to feel special by some handsome dude brought her under his control. There were always little favors that could be done to make life on the inside easier and normally there would be a succession to bigger favors that could result in an officer being blackmailed or threatened if they didn't cooperate—and maybe bring some drugs in. Inmates would routinely call these women at home.

You'd have thought that after the riots there would have been a multitude of new operating guidelines and retraining for the guards. That was not the case. For those of us that had learned to operate by the seat of our pants, there was no change; that's the way we continued to work.

It was tough enough doing the job, but now with all the new hires we were loaded up with large groups of OJT trainees to follow us around. If they had sent someone from the academy to guide them around it would have worked OK. Instead they just dumped them on the Sergeants to provide some kind of training and exposure to the prison environment. We had our hands full as it was, and now we had to look out for these folks.

In this time frame, rumors had it that on numerous occasions about half of the guards would show up for roll call hung over or still with a buzz on from booze or drugs. Although it doesn't do anything for the reputation of those officers, think a minute about the environment these folks were faced with day after day. For some, it took that insulation to just muster the fortitude to show up for work—all for a minimum wage. The rumors were true.

While I'm addressing rumors, let me touch on another, that of intimate relations between male and female correction officers. Let me assure you that did happen, and quite frequently. Some of the Captains, Lieutenants and for sure the Sergeants were involved in this behavior. When the OJT female correction trainees were brought in for exposure to their future work place, the supervisory personnel would have their pick of those that had the promise of promiscuity. Once these gals finished their schooling and were at work those that pleased a supervisor were provided a cushy assignment for favors granted. It wasn't unusual for a Captain in the Control Center to be absent from his post for an hour or so while he checked on one of these ladies at her work station—returning with a smile on his face.

With one broken marriage behind me I too was one of those Sergeants trolling for something new, and quite successful I might say. If the walls in the auditorium projection booth could talk they would have some real tales to tell. It was in this time frame that one of the new hires doing OJT really caught my eye. She was black, quite attractive and seemed responsive to my interest. Over a short period of time we saw a lot of each other and eventually a romance blossomed. We approached Warden Gingrage with our intent to get married. He didn't give us any grief and offered to make life easier for us by moving her to a separate facility. We all realized it would be an almost impossible situation for us to work in the same prison.

What a change my life had taken. I had never been associated with blacks growing up and now I was not only working in an environment that was predominately populated with blacks, I was married to one too.

Not all of the new female guards were approachable. Josephine McCallum was one of those. She was pretty enough to turn heads and a lot of people were hitting on her. In fact there was one black Sergeant that was quite infatuated with her. He was a handsome, smooth talking charmer, but he didn't have any more luck than anyone else. I didn't even try. Although she had new and green written all over her, she was not outgoing and really quite reserved. If I'd have thought it would have held promise I might have been right there like the others. To many, McCallum's reservedness just made the challenge more worthwhile.

I had just transferred to day shift and I was the Sergeant on 5 Block that morning. About 8:30 I was walking up the corridor to the Control Center (CC) when all of a sudden an inmate stops me. This guy was a pain in the ass. His name was Leaphart and he always had some kind of a grievance or something just to bitch about.

"Sgt., Sgt., you've got to listen to me!"

"What's up?"

"I'm not bullshitting, there's an officer bleeding in the auditorium!"

Well I was headed to the CC anyway so I told him to come along and he could tell someone there about it. Leaphart really seemed to be disturbed. He said that he'd gone to see Mitch about a grievance and had seen a coat lying on the floor with blood on it. We had to pass through the corridor gate and the officer there was Ray McCormic. Ray was an asshole and tried to stop me from taking Leaphart through because he didn't have a pass. I told him as a Sergeant that was my decision, which was pass enough. We stood arguing for a few minutes, but finally he opened the gate and let us through.

In the CC Leaphart told his story to Lt. Lawson. Lawson immediately dispatched Sgt. Hilliker and myself with a crew of officers to the auditorium.

When we arrived at the JCC gate there was no officer at the desk. That certainly wasn't right. The auditorium door was also unlocked.

I walked around up on the stage: it was really dark. I didn't expect to find anything, but then my foot hit something. I reached down and picked up a coat. From the coat my hand was wet with a warm liquid. It was blood. Next we found the radio and then spread out to search more extensively. Soon she was found at the bottom of some stairs leading from the stage to the seating area.

She lay on her back and right side, completely nude except for undergarments around her waist. There was a lot of blood on her face and where her head laid. A belt had been tightened around her neck.

In this prison I had seen a lot, but now I couldn't bring myself to take more than a fleeting glance at her. Medical help arrived and they immediately started all the pertinent steps to keep her alive, however there were no signs of life.

Soon the emergency siren was blown for a lock down. The staff on the scene took the names of the prisoners in the area. Eventually these prisoners were strip-searched and their cells checked. Inmates were also examined for cuts that might have resulted from a struggle with the downed officer. Two inmates had new cuts and were placed in 5 Block for investigation and two others; Merryman and Hill were also put into 5 Block segregation as someone had seen them in the area. The State Police were now on the scene and in charge of the investigation.

It wasn't long after McCallum's death that I had the opportunity to take over as the dining room Sergeant. The previous Sergeant, Phil Lee, had been beaten so severely that he never again returned to work. I'm not sure exactly what race Lee was, maybe some black, but a lot of Indian. He was a short man with an in your face style when it came to dealing with the inmates. With that attitude it wasn't difficult to make enemies. I guess the inmates finally got their revenge on him.

They called the inmate's dining room "Big Top". As I recall, it could seat 500 or so. As dining room Sergeant I was responsible for setting a schedule that would get all the inmates fed and out of the dining room so there was ample time to get ready for the next meal. My strategy was to call enough cellblocks to really saturate the facility. As soon as one inmate finished eating there was another waiting for his spot at the table. Even though only 500 could be seated, with those in the serving line and the inmates coming and going I would have as many as 1,500 involved at one time. Some inmates would skip meals rather than be exposed to such large groups. With little guard supervision, it was too easy for one con to stick another then melt into the crowd. Yes, there were gun turrets in the dining rooms, but there was really little they could do if a fight broke out—and the cons knew this.

Movie night in the auditorium was another situation that was conducive to inmates getting stuck. While the movie was going on only a few were actually watching it because other activities were occupying them.

Once the movie ended and all the lights came on, when the cons stood to leave that's when it was easy to carry out a contract on someone. It really was an insane situation.

McCallum's killing was in the headlines for some time. Before that happened, a guard getting stuck was not big news for the media.

There was plenty of speculation as to what happened to her—both from the media and the Jackson employees. I remember the day very well, and there are some things I'm very sure of. One 140 lb. drunk inmate did not do all that damage to her. I couldn't have done that sober. It would have taken at least three or four of them.

I also know that there was no way that McCallum should have been assigned that position in the first place. The area was isolated and known to be dangerous. Was the schedule changed purposely to make her vulnerable or maybe because she hadn't been sensitive to someone's advances?—maybe. I personally don't think it happened because someone planned to have her harmed. McCallum hadn't been there long enough to create the type of enemy that would want her killed. I would have no idea who would gain anything by killing her.

I guess I'm convinced that McCallum was a victim of circumstances that were way beyond her capability to deal with. Possibly she unexpectedly walked in on a drug deal or someone's sexual liaison. Whatever happened she suddenly became a severe threat to some individuals.

Even though McCallum's assignment was changed at the last minute, it wouldn't be unusual at all for that to become common knowledge in short order. Word travels fast in the prison system—from officer to inmate and from inmate to inmate. In fact, most inmates that would have just passed her in the corridor would have tried to strike up a conversation and find out what her duty was for the day.

Another question of course is how her assailants got to her. Did they hoodwink her into allowing them through her gate? Did she leave the gate open while she cased her assignment or were they surprised when she entered the auditorium? If so how did they get in to begin with? Only the last question could I supply a knowledgeable and plausible answer. There was a passkey that opened numerous doors through the prison—several in the auditorium. Along with the correction officers many inmates had that key. I know for a fact that officers have sold or traded the keys to the inmates for favors.

Leaphart, the inmate who had found her coat and stopped me in the corridor, was fearful over reprisals from whomever killed McCallum. He received a transfer to another facility.

Josephine McCallum's funeral was the biggest I have ever seen in Lansing. There was a huge procession down Michigan Avenue.

That fall another officer was killed. It was the first time I had ever seen both main gates open at the same time, as the ambulance was rushed through in an attempt to save Jack Budd's life. I stood there asking myself, how many more times is this gonna happen? Jack was on 5 Block when he was killed. He was said to have been abrasive to the inmates there, but he was probably still angry from having lost a friend that spring. If people could realize how the inmates on 5 Block were yelling and carrying on all the time—who wouldn't tend to hate them?

For the next two years I became more involved in the Corrections Officer's Organization (MCO), ending up as a Vice

President. We tried our best to increase staffing levels and improve security for the guards. It was a constant battle with some, but very little improvement. Deputy Warden Elo and I went head to head over those issues. He was the warden that was involved the most and was not hesitant to insert himself into the middle of an inmate conflict. He was a Vietnam Veteran and I respected him, but he was also a staunch supporter of the system. Maybe that's why he's still there—definitely a survivor.

Warden Foltz retired shortly after McCallum's death. As the main warden he had a huge job, but I don't think he knew what was going on. He never was one to be down in the trenches like Elo.

I hear Warden Bolden is still around. He's another one that must have been politically correct, because he's survived in the system. I've seen him at Correction's parties and he's a real cool cat!

Probably the individual that did the most through the MCO to improve security was Robert Halmich. He was a former con himself and was relentless in his efforts to change things. He didn't care who he pissed off doing it either.

Senator Jack Welborn did a lot to bring to the public's attention the severe problem in Michigan's prison system, while Governor Blanchard either didn't know, or tried to make believe the problem didn't exist. The fixes that trickled down from his office were aimed mainly to repair image not the problem, and there was significant effort from his Attorney General, Frank Kelley to avoid a Grand Jury and keep a lid on things. Despite federal investigations, no one knew how high up the prison corruption might lead. For years the white buses (Snow Birds) shuttled massive amounts of prisoners between Michigan prisons for questionable reasons. Unwittingly I had even played a part in it all. Deputy Warden Jackson had on several occasions directed me to escort a certain inmate to his office for meetings. Later that warden was indicted for corruption.

In 1989 I took stock of my situation at Jackson prison. Things really hadn't changed much. Inmates were regularly sticking each other and myself, like many other guards were in the middle tackling the knife wielders, trying to keep them from killing each other, for who knows what reason. Officers were still getting stuck and eventually I'd probably get it too. Drugs were widespread. Probably the reason I'm still alive is because I just didn't write up or turn inmates in when I found drugs on them. Yes, I flushed some of the stuff down the toilet, but to write them up would have done no good. The administration's position seemed to be to pacify them and let them have their drugs. What scared me the most was the widespread availability of alcohol. Alcohol in certain inmates made them very violent and dangerous. Spud juice was readily available and it wasn't unusual for a guard to occasionally slip in a pint of liquor as a favor.

I was divorced again now, and spending more time at the Roadhouse drinking to insulate myself from the job. It was time to leave. I quit and within three days I moved to Florida. A year later I was asked to return as a witness for Hill's trial. I told them I didn't want to come. They said they'd subpoena me if I didn't volunteer.

They paid for my flight back to Michigan and I testified, but I doubt it was worth the State's money. I just didn't have much to offer. I was surprised by a couple of things at the trial. The State Police never took any fingerprints, and the South Yard Sergeant, who was supposed to be McCallum's supervisor that day was never questioned much. I don't think he had any part in the murder, but I do think he knew a lot about what happened, probably more so than anyone else. He was the granddaddy of the black corrections officers and very aware of what went on around there.

Well I'm back in Michigan now and have been for several years. I am in really poor health with no insurance and no job and the doctor says maybe only a couple years left for me. I've been trying to get Social Security and Medicaid without much luck. Seems ironic, but I've thought of getting a water pistol and attempting to hold up a bank. At least in a Federal prison I'd get some good health care.

I have one bright spot in my life. My son and I have forged a good relationship and he lives nearby.

If for any reason, my travels happen to be near that prison, I take some alternate route so I don't even have to see the place.

I question the value of reliving all this crap now, but at least my son and others may have an idea of what we went through in those years at Jackson. God, how I'd like to forget!

VOICES—FRIEND AND FOE

J found out that early on, the State Police investigator asked for the family to come in so he might give them an update on the investigation. I wasn't informed of the meeting, but the brothers all showed up. Although I don't know the exact details, I would guess that the bothers told Piziali that Josephine's husband was a real old SOB who didn't give a rat's ass. Piziali never made any attempt to meet with me. Later on I would read in one of his letters to Welborn, "How kind and caring Josephine's brothers were." They sure bamboozled him.

There was plenty of information coming in from all directions, even if it wasn't from the State Police investigator. The Jackson Patriot reporters were routinely quoting unnamed employee sources that described how bad the situation was in the prison and how the administration had screwed up by putting Jo, as a probationary corrections officer, in a remote one person assignment. I was hearing similar things from phone calls I received from the people who worked there. Many wouldn't divulge their name and most of those that did identify themselves, requested anonymity. I know that Senator Welborn was also privy to a lot of information too, and although he didn't share many specifics with me, I could detect from what he did say, that there might be a lot more to the story than what the newspapers were saying. He wanted me to brief him on any tips I might receive.

There were still those calls of a threatening nature. They had started coming in almost immediately after Jo's death. The most surprising threat was the one from two dudes that drove up the alley in the truck. I was standing on the back porch breaking my smoking absence to settle my nerves, when from the vehicle window the one guy said, "The bitch had to die and you're next." With tires squealing they had retreated back down the alley, but not before I planted a lucky rock shot on the drivers window. I then went inside the house and came out with one of Mike's ball bats. I stood there on the porch thinking to myself, "Now what the hell are you going to do with this bat?"

I can only describe my state of mind as to one of confusion and a feeling of weakness and vulnerability for not knowing what was going on.

I enlisted the help of an attorney, who according to the Lansing State Journal, was one of the 'movers and shakers' in the Michigan legal community. Just judging from what the MCO union officials were saying about negligence on the part of the prison administrators, and what I was hearing over the phone, I determined that we needed legal representation.

It was obvious that Senator Jack Welborn was a very caring individual who was sincerely interested in Mike and my welfare, but other than him, I really wasn't convinced that the official investigators were wholeheartedly trying to find out why Jo had been killed. Too many things didn't add up. Why was I a threat to anyone? Did they think that maybe Jo had told me about improprieties at work or was it because there was this obvious bond between Welborn and myself and perhaps that alliance would create problems for those that had things to hide? Were we a threat to the administration, the inmates or both?

One thing was certain, the location of our house on South Francis Street, with a road in front and an alley on two sides, certainly left us open to harassment. The police presence would only last so long, and it seemed that about everyone, especially the news hounds knew where we lived. If there was going to be any kind of stable life for Mike there would need to be another move. Jo and I had wanted to relocate to the country anyway, so I settled on a small home west of Grand Ledge—it had been one we both had looked at and considered.

For the first time in a long time I did not have money problems. Jo's work benefits came through along with a life insurance settlement. I'm sure Jo would have shuddered to think about me trying to manage a large sum of money, but I believe she would have approved of the house that I bought.

We had close neighbors at the new place, but it wasn't at all like being in the city, and it held the promise of some security from those who might want to harm us.

Although I had moved Mike away from his friends, I went out of my way to make sure that they had transportation to our house, and believe me some of them were there most of the time. When I needed to be absent he was either at their house or my mother's.

Our new phone number was unlisted, however at Jack Welborn's suggestion, there was a phone in his spare office that after a ring or two would forward the call to our place. He knew that I wanted to keep the information calls coming in, without divulging our new residence. I still remember that number: 517-372-5751. Jack said that he could tell that I was getting a lot of calls because he could hear the phone ring from his office. I think that for his own reasons, Jack wanted to know everything going on in the prison system, and I was providing just another conduit of information.

The first night after we moved to our new place, someone broke into our garage. Mike and I had gone out for supper and when we returned I noticed that the little door going into the garage was ajar. I had left it locked. My '66 Chevy II was parked inside and as I looked around I noticed the passenger door open with the glove box light illuminated. The envelope containing the registration and insurance had been removed from the glove box and opened. Some of the papers were on the car floor. There were footprints other than my own near the car and a closer look revealed screwdriver marks where the garage door had been jimmied open. I called the Eaton County Sheriff Department.

About 45 minutes after my call a sheriff's deputy arrived. I told him we had been broken into. He wanted to know what had been stolen and how we knew a break-in had occurred. I said I couldn't see that anything had been taken, but I did show him the screwdriver marks, footprints and the open glove box. He didn't seem impressed, but made out a report and left. Shortly thereafter, a couple of neighbors came over. They had seen the patrol car in my yard, and wondered what was going on. From what they said, there never had been a break-in in the neighborhood before.

I called Welborn and told him the details about our garage intrusion. He said it sounded like someone was just checking to see if we lived there. That made sense, but wasn't very comforting. "Keep me advised," he said.

It wasn't long after Jo's funeral that I received a call from Judge George Economy. At one time Jo had worked part-time in his office. After he offered his condolences to us he told me that I needed to get my butt down to probate court and file conservatorship for Mike, before anyone else did. I had questions, but he didn't offer anything additional.

When I arrived at probate court I tried to see the Judge, but he wasn't in. I told the clerk that I needed to sign up as conservator for Mike; whatever that was for. I thought that being his father I would automatically be in charge of his affairs until a certain age. Apparently that wasn't the case. The paper work was quite involved and it took some time to complete the process. I was required to report his income each year and how it was disposed of.

That all was fine with me, but I was still curious as to why the Judge went out of his way to call.

As I left the office area, there getting off the elevator were the uncles and aunts, Jim and Jane, Barry and Carol, John and Corey.

I more or less acknowledged their presence as I skirted around them for the elevator.

Jim said, "What's going on with you?"

I didn't answer.

"Hey! I'm talking to you."

"Just taking care of business guys."

Jim stepped toward the elevator, but the door was closing. I found out later that he had called to inquire how they could get conservatorship and that's why I had been alerted. For Mike's best interest they wanted to control his money. Right! When Jim found out they couldn't file he raised a disturbance and was asked to leave. That was only second hand information of course.

That August of '87 I lost our newspaper delivery business. Even after Jo's death there was no interruption in the service we provided because I had good drivers. Jo and I had turned a marginal enterprise into something quite profitable but there was the complaint from our manager that we were getting too big. That complaint however came after Jo rejected the guy's romantic advances. Then after her death, I was approached by a representative of the higher-ups in the newspaper, to provide exclusive rights to Jo's story. I told him that my attorney didn't want me to do that. Shortly after my refusal to do the story, one morning our papers were never dropped off to us, so we had nothing to deliver. Any missed delivery was grounds for canceling our contract and that's exactly what happened. I heard that they ended up in some dumpster, but more likely they probably got turned back in for the recycling money. I tried to fight it, but by August they had taken all our routes and I was out of a job.

Sometimes I guess things happen for a reason. Without the newspaper business I could be a full-time father to Mike and at the same time maybe find out more about why or how Jo was killed. I wasn't sure that the State Police were doing that thorough of a job. Maybe if I had heard the investigators side of it I might have felt differently. But I doubt it. Trying to put all the pieces together from the phone calls and tips I was receiving, certainly just gave me the impression that things were being swept under the carpet for who knows what reason. I knew that it would be very difficult to sort it all out because I had little knowledge of the prison system at that time. Later I learned a lot about it.

In the next few months I made a sustained effort to get the word out to prison employees and even the inmate population that I was willing to listen to anyone who could shed more light on Jo's murder. My association with Welborn helped fuel my effort because he already had the reputation as a crusader to improve the prison system. Because Jo's murder was still news, the media was more than willing to interview me and that helped as much as anything to keep the calls coming.

My attorney then—"the mover and shaker of the community", didn't like my yakking to the press, but soon he took over the headlines with word we were suing the state for 30 million dollars. I think from that time on many people looked on my efforts as a way for me to get rich from my wife's death. For a while it sure slowed down my information flow. I'll admit that if the state somehow screwed up in my wife's work assignment, that made her vulnerable to be murdered, there should be some compensation for Mike and I, but $30 million was a little much. Looking back on it though, such an enormous amount brought the newspaper headlines that offered priceless advertising for my attorney, whether we got anything out of it or not.

We were still receiving some threatening calls, probably because more and more we were being enlightened on the prison secrets. I'm not sure whether or not the threats even had anything to do with Jo's death, but I considered it necessary now to arm myself for both my sake and Mike's. I applied for a concealed weapons permit with Eaton County and Sheriff Art Kelsey went to bat for me to get one. I started packing a Glock pistol with an 18 shot clip.

The fact that I now carried a concealed weapon was not a secret and I didn't want it to be. In some of my newspaper interviews I was quite open about it and that bit was carried in print. Maybe the news would make someone think twice before planning to try something against us.

Because of my notoriety now, I was being solicited to become involved in a crime victims support organization and other groups that were being formed to support employees that were being harassed and discriminated against in the prison system. I was quickly learning that there were many women in the prison work place that had been assaulted and sexually harassed. Like Jo however, women were extremely reluctant to do anything about the harassment.

Ann Flesher started one program through Employee Services, specifically for women workers in corrections that were assaulted on the job. In a letter she analyzed the lack of success achieved by the program.

"The women in the group were highly suspicious of me and each other and never really developed the necessary trust level to become cohesive and supportive. Group members were frightened that information discussed in the group would get back to their work site."

"The stress and pain among these women was extremely profound. Many were immobilized by their fear and anger, but had a continued sense of loyalty to their fellow officers. The fear and sense of loyalty made it difficult for them to talk about their experience or the job in the group. Their stress levels negatively affected all the women's spousal relationships. Many had developed physical problems, the least of which were difficulties with sleep and eating. All the women talked about feeling like they could not trust anyone, and all expressed fear and anxiety about the idea of returning to work."

Ann Flesher was later employed by Michigan State University in the Counseling Center as a therapist for the sexual assault program.

Jack Budd was Jo's classmate all through correction officers training. In fact, they use to study together. Dave Walton, a writer for the 'Keepers Voice', (correction officials newsletter) recalled that Jo had been harassed by her Sergeant as long as 10 days before her death and had asked for Budd's help in deflecting the Sergeant's advances. Jo was completely nauseated by the Sergeants actions and demeanor. Of course this had been going on long before I found out. Jack was really upset by Jo's death and he was one of the officers calling me with information. He also had his problems.

On November 27th Jack Budd called, "Bill, there are so many weapons around here. We don't have any and they have them all. It's nice to know that somebody is trying to help us, because we're sure not getting it from middle management."

Budd's last call came on December 3rd. "I can handle myself, but I'm afraid for my other people here. I've got a real knack for finding weapons. I'm scared because I'm too good at finding weapons."

Two days after Christmas James L. Miller, an inmate nicknamed "Money Mike" or sometimes "Ninja Miller," stabbed Jack Budd to death. Three months prior Budd had removed 4 knives from Miller's cell and Miller had forwarded a written complaint about Budd harassing him. Inmate Curtis Lewis said that he had heard that Miller had planned for a week to kill Budd.

Budd supervised the porters in 5 Block and there had been a lot of them hanging near Miller's cell, probably doing some kind of illegal business. Jack told them to stay away from Miller, that there was too much traffic around there. That probably added to Miller's anger.

Officer Daniel Dyer escorted Miller from his cell three levels down to one of the ground floor shower cells. Another officer, Michael H. Rife locked Miller in the shower cell and removed his cuffs. Almost immediately Miller broke the cell door open and slugged Rife, breaking his nose.

Miller started on a slow trot to where Budd normally would be posted. Budd instead was 180 feet down the cellblock signing door cards, a procedure that shows each cell has been checked. Spotting Budd, Miller broke into a run. "Stop that son of a bitch," yelled Rife.

An inmate porter, Monte Lee, was mopping the floor when he heard the commotion. He turned and saw Miller running at him with a "horse," (knife). Lee placed the mop in front of him for protection as he thought Miller was going to stab him. Miller instead went past and started attacking Budd. Budd pushed Miller away, but he came back at him. Before other officers arrived and helped Budd wrestle Miller to the ground, Budd had been stabbed 5 times in the neck and shoulder area. Finally Budd said, "I've got to get out, I'm hit." Budd then collapsed on the floor. Soon after he arrived at Foote Hospital, he died.

In a hearing after Budd's death, Judy Cotlon, who reviews inmate misconduct tickets, said she learned that Budd was to be murdered, but administrators ignored her; brushed her off like so much dandruff. Another officer, Tim Ryan, an employee for 15 years, said, "Guards are afraid to take action because prisoners will file lawsuits against them or take out contracts to have them killed or assaulted."

I talked with Jack's widow, Betsy, and expressed my sympathy. I felt sorry for her. They had a young son and she had diabetes that was progressively getting worse. There had been a lot of strain in their marriage and now she had to deal with Budd's death, her own illness and to raise her young son. Over time we became close friends.

Fortunately for Mrs. Budd, there was Senator Jack Welborn. He was the type of caring individual who entered the eye of the storm to comfort and make things better. He was not the standard politician doing good things to enhance his public image; he genuinely cared. Senator Welborn was still there for us too. Mike and I were treated like part of his family. And, when he introduced me to some of his neighbors in the rural community around his farm, it wasn't, "This is Bill McCallum, whose wife was murdered in Jackson." I wasn't his trophy to haul around, but just a friend.

In January C/O Rich Loomis was passing out mail when from behind he was stabbed four times in the neck. There had been two murders in less than a year and now another stabbing. The newspapers were having a field day with all of it and good old Senator Welborn was keeping the pot stirred. Of course all this had been going on for years, but nobody seemed to care, except Welborn. Now people were starting to listen.

In one January '88 newspaper article Senator Welborn was commenting on the present state of affairs at Jackson: ' –gangs with hit lists, illegal drugs, prostitution, sexual harassment, homemade weapons, inexperienced correction officers left alone with the most violent inmates, even cellblocks with broken locks; all these elements have been known to exist in Jackson, and yet the environment there is nearly as ripe as it was when Josephine McCallum was bludgeoned to death.'

Welborn was constantly criticizing the Correction Commission that Governor Blanchard had created. He labeled it as an ineffective committee that the Governor could hide behind when things went wrong. The Governor would receive credit for taking action by recognizing, and sending problems to the commission. When things appeared better he could bask in the glory of improvement, and when the situation worsened it was because the commission hadn't recommended action and was studying the matter.

Early in January a Lansing State Journal editorial stated, 'Governor Blanchard's position on disarray in the state's prison system has been less than precise. Attorney General Frank Kelley doesn't like the idea of a grand jury inquiry as requested by some legislators and civil rights groups. Mischief he calls it.'

The news media was now digging into their files and bringing out past events that might shed more light on the present status of the prison system. Not too long ago a Jackson inmate had success- fully sued the state after he had been raped in the Honor Block. Former Corrections Officer Griffin testified at that trial. He had been a 14-year employee who spent the last 4 years working in the Honor Block. That block supposedly housed medium and close security inmates on good behavior. Griffin said that he never felt safe there, "It was full of drug dealing, drug using and booze". Assistant Attorney General Michael E. Stafford described Griffin as a "disgruntled former employee and an idiot." Roy T. Reynolds of the Jackson Patriot put that article together.

After Jo's and Jack Budd's deaths one newspaper reported that Senator Welborn now had an obsession with visiting the State Prisons. He might show up at the front gate at 2 a.m. and ask to inspect the prison. Not only was he concerned about security with- in the prison he was also interested in unfair inmate treatment. He took time to talk to inmates, corrections officers and anyone else that had a beef with the system. The prisons have an effective com- munication system so word got around fast and there were always bits and pieces of information coming to the Senator's attention. He bragged once that he had snitches in every prison. The media thought these visits were something new, but I knew Jack had been doing this for a long time.

My physical appearance was quickly changing. My hair was thinning and I had put on about 40 pounds. While Mike was in school, my full-time endeavor was conducting my own investigation into what had really happened to my wife. I was continually taking calls from my hot line, meeting prison employees in various places to hear what they had to say and keeping abreast of all the new stuff the media was digging up. I had parted ways with my attorney. He disliked the media attention I was receiving, and he had proved ineffective with the civil lawsuit. Later I would learn that a younger partner of his firm had received an appointment by Governor Blanchard to be the Eaton County Probate Judge. More things would surface later.

The Jackson prosecutor was having problems selling the use of the new DNA testing of the blood on Hill's shoes and clothes as evidence for trial. An earlier State Supreme Court ruling had rejected its use in a different trial. The prosecutor was delaying the trial until he could gain its submission. Otherwise, they might fail to get a conviction, as the other evidence was quite circumstantial.

A husband and wife team, Randy and Francine, ran Ranraar Research. They had established contact with many inmates, and seemed to be the inmate's link to the media, attorneys and other investigators. Randy seemed concerned about my wife's death and offered to help me investigate her death.

In addition to calls, someone sent me a package containing inmate letters intercepted within the prison. I was astonished to read some of the letters. Together with all the contacts I had made on my own, some of the stuff seemed quite plausible. At least, I had new theories to evaluate, which was more than the official investigators were willing to consider, even though we offered this information to them. Their case seemed open and shut on inmate Hill. Here is some of the information that filtered down to me from the inmates.

From the Buchanan Branch of the NAACP in the Central Complex there was correspondence from their Executive Board directed to editorial writers in the state's newspapers.

In this letter they first criticized prison administrators for having the "mind-set" that they were running prisons solely for punishment and rejecting rehabilitation programs. They continued by pointing out that scores of inmates have been killed, however no one seemed to care until a female guard was murdered. Also they stated that the 1981 prison riot supposedly was caused and participated in by disgruntled prison guards.

In direct reference to Josephine's death, one letter stated that an inmate clerk from JCC saw two male correction officers come out of the auditorium and quickly slip back in upon seeing the inmate. They contended that the radio found close to Jo's body was not hers, but that of another officer's, and was used to bludgeon her to death. Also they stated that her blouse had been carefully unbuttoned, which proved the rape theory invalid.

According to this letter Jo's keys were found in a trash bin inside the Control Center, dropped there by one of the officers involved in her murder. The keys were wrapped in a hat similar to what Hill wore.

The auditorium was referred to as a well-known brothel scene for sexual orgies between male and female correction officers. And, that the auditorium was always thoroughly locked for that reason. The letter alleged that other guards had at numerous times raped female guards.

Other letters by specific inmates seemed to support a theory of guard involvement. Sgt. Lee was said to have left the Control Center that morning with scratches on his face and hands, with something under his coat. He talked to a lieutenant there and later that's where Jo's keys were found in a trash can. The radio next to Jo's body had belonged to Officer Lee, and it insinuated that both the Sgt. and Correction Officer Lee both were involved, yet on the other hand it also was stated that the skin found under her fingernails was that of a 'European'. Because both Lee's were black this pointed to white officer involvement too. Supposedly blood drops of the same type as Jo's were found on Sgt. Lee's clothes and the carpeting of his car.

One inmate who claimed to be Merryman's (Mexico) father told how his son had been falsely accused and was being portrayed unfairly as gay. He said that inmate Hill was being beaten down at Huron Valley in an effort to make him confess. Also, a blond pubic hair had been found on Jo's body, and, "These foul bastards are doing all they can to keep the truth from the public in general, and her family, in particular. You can credit the power of the screw's union (MCO) has over the media for making every effort to cover up the truth and focus attention on the hated prisoners. Much of the blame for this can be attributed to the likes of Welborn and State Rep. Hoffman who is a tool of the MCO."

That particular letter told about dozens of pictures that were discovered showing sex acts between guards. It went on to detail numerous sexual assaults on female guards by other male guards. When one female corrections officer went to her supervisor to complain of an attempted sexual assault by another guard, the female supervisor supposedly made this statement.

"McCallum was stupid and that was why she was killed. She was a dumb bitch who let the prisoner in. She got hers because she wouldn't keep quiet—see if you can!" The corrections officer said she would file a report. "Do it and I'll have your job and you'll never work in this state again."

The inmate's letter went on to state that the female supervisor was free with her beliefs and morals, concluding that 'we as female officers should put out and remain alive.'

Another piece from inside read like this.

'Listen, I don't know if you can use this information or not, but I know you were closely involved with the Josephine McCallum case. Well, I won't admit this in open court or anything, but Hill didn't kill her. It was done by 3 officers; one black, Sgt. Lee, who transferred a couple weeks later to the Southside. A white one named (last name) Lee and another one that still works in central. I'm not sure of the last ones name yet. They went into the auditorium thru the quartermaster door. They were going to scare her into dropping her complaints. One of the officers hit her in the head with her radio and she started to scream and even beat on the quartermaster door. She was grabbed and accidentally suffocated. She was hit a couple more times.'

'She then was raped. The C/O's masturbated and each ejaculated inside her so that it would appear sexually motivated and it would complicate identification of semen. They then pinned it on

Hill because he was in the area. This may be hard to believe, but it's true. And, if you made them look further and question the quartermaster officer, he'd verify they went through that door (maybe he would). But that's what happened.'

Much of this sounded preposterous but some of it jived with other things I'd heard. Separating fact from fiction became a daily chore, but I felt there was truth in some of it.

1989–A NEW YEAR OF CHAOS

On the anniversary of Jo's death, I received a very touching handwritten letter from John Hawley, a Deputy Warden of the Marquette State Prison.

"Although I never personally knew Josephine, her death has had more impact on me and my job than any other single thing that has touched my 21 year career with the Department of Corrections. Her death marked the darkest day of that 21 years.

I think about her and her fate every day as I try to make a safer place for us to work at Marquette Branch Prison. I have praise for the courage that you have also shown in trying to make a safer environment for our employees.

I know that Josephine must have been a good wife and mother and her loss was a senseless waste of life. I just want you to know that she didn't die for nothing.

I will continue to pray that God will touch you and your son and bring you peace and comfort."

I was interviewed by several of the state newspapers. One interview was featured on the front page of the Lansing State Journal, and another received a lot of coverage in the Detroit Free Press. I expressed my frustration with the fact that my wife's killer or killers still hadn't been brought to trial. Hill was in custody serving prison time for another offense, with the prosecutor biding time until he could obtain a ruling to allow the new DNA testing as evidence in court to convict him. Everything focused on Hill, but based on a lot of other things I was hearing, there was much more to the story that wasn't being addressed.

One newspaper said that I was on a crusade against the leaders of the Department of Corrections by backing those state lawmakers who felt a federal grand jury was necessary to clean up the State's prison system. Phil Jurik, a reporter for the Lansing State Journal, said that, 'Prison problems and his 28 year-old wife's death have consumed McCallum; reshaped his personality. He's angry. He no longer works. Most of his time is spent on this mission. He has become a fanatic. "I can't let her memory go," he says.'

I pressed the point that Jo had been sexually harassed, and that probably there was a link between that and her assignment to an isolated position. I told the reporter about the death threats and the fact that about 30 people call my hot line regularly with information. I was quoted as saying that I held the system as responsible in her death as the guy that killed her. Also I mentioned that I now carry an 18 shot 9mm pistol with me for protection.

On the other hand Robert Piziali, the state police detective in charge of the investigation said he had heard all the rumors about McCallum's death and there was no evidence to support them. In a Jackson Citizen Patriot article he was quoted, "There is no indication that anyone had anything to do with it, other than the individual charged."

Welborn and I weren't the only people complaining about Michigan's shoddy prison system. At a public hearing in January over a hundred correction officers, prison employees, retirees and family members told their stories about how bad working conditions were inside Jackson's big prison. Most of those complaining placed the blame on the Corrections Department Director, Robert Brown.

Following Josephine's death there was a considerable amount of pressure on Corrections Director Brown to take some kind of action. According to Brown, an internal investigation into the conditions surrounding the homicide was the obvious thing to do. Brown selected Joseph Abramajtys and Evert Elkins to take a look at the operation of SPSM. Abramajtys was a deputy warden at a medium security Michigan prison who had turned down the opportunity to work as a deputy warden at Jackson several years prior. He was a former school administrator who had conducted what ADW John Whelan described as an excellent inspection of SPSM back in 1981. Elkins was a lieutenant when he first worked for Warden Foltz at Jackson. Now he was a deputy warden at Huron Valley Men's Facility in Ypsilanti. Foltz remembered him as a good loyal employee.

Both Abramajtys and Elkins lost their creditability with Warden Foltz and Deputy Warden Whelan when their report was published at the end of June. Neither of the investigators came to the now retired warden or the deputy warden with any news as to what their findings might be. The report was submitted directly to Director Brown who almost immediately released it to the press. The report turned out to be a scathing review of SPSM policy and supervision. From key control to putting probationary officers in isolated assignments, the report was an unexpected blow to both Foltz and Whelan and what really sent Whelan into orbit was a statement within the report quoting him as saying that he wasn't going to process a critical incident report every time "a female officer got her tits or ass grabbed."

Whelan told both Brown and Foltz that he never made that statement and that it was just Abramajtys trying to add some spice to his report at Whelan's expense. Foltz said that kind of language might be typical of Whelan in an informal conversation, but he always knew Whelan as an honest man, and if Whelan said he didn't make the statement, he didn't.

In their efforts at damage control both Whelan and Foltz were now very critical of the investigators. Foltz hinted that both investigators might be trying to settle accounts with Whelan, who in the past had investigated and found things wrong with the facilities they worked at. He also indicated that Abramajtys was the type of guy that thought he knew about everything, and if there wasn't something he knew it probably wasn't worth knowing. Whelan said that Abramajtys didn't know diddly about Jackson Prison; that he had no real background in investigation and no experience in a maximum-security prison. Foltz even suggested that Abramajtys had forced Elkins into signing the report.

Foltz stated that 10% of the inmates and corrections officers make the whole prison system look bad. Probably those were the folks the investigators had talked with. The inspectors had made general statements and drew conclusions without detailed documentation; that was wrong.

Despite the criticism of the report Director Brown was able to temporarily allow blame for things to fall at a level below him. Conveniently Foltz was already retired and now Whelan, who had a bad back and other health problems, was also talking retirement. Whether things changed or not, at least Brown now would have different people in charge.

A year after the Abramajtys/Elkins report came out, Dave Walton, writing an anniversary tribute to Josephine in the Keeper's Voice (newsletter for corrections officers), stated that only lip service had been paid to the exhaustive in depth 40 page report. He quotes Director Brown as saying, "...it is not a comfortable report for any of us to read. It describes conditions, some of which have resisted long standing attempts to remedy, which nevertheless must and will be remedied." Walton then points out that seven months later another corrections officer at the same institution is murdered.

In reference to Brown's remarks about his discomfort in reading the Abramajtys/Elkins report, Walton writes, 'His discomfort is nothing compared to actually living the report.'

In this article Walton describes that it was common knowledge by Jo's co-workers that she was being harassed by one of her sergeants and that it had been going on for 10 days before her death.

I had numerous discussions with Dave Walton over the years, however this outspokenness over various prison issues eventually caused him to lose favor with both the union and correction system.

A good share of the inmates felt unsafe at Jackson too. Gordon Kamka, a consultant on prison management said that the danger of violence was especially prevalent at state prisons, in Jackson and Ionia. He said that there have been times in recent years when 18 percent of the nearly 5,000 inmates at Southern Michigan Prison have asked for protective custody from other inmates. He said that was an extremely high figure.

Reading from an earlier state police study's summary section, Kamka related the persistent problem of sexual pressure on inmates —blacks on whites, blacks on blacks who are young and effeminate appearing. Most of the problem results from 'skating'— inmates being allowed to roam at will. Kamka went on to quote the state police report, 'drugs are prevalent and there are many unreported rapes.'

That spring of 1988, Jack Welborn received the Golden Eagle award from the American Federation of Police. This was certainly a well deserved and a very prestigious honor for his efforts to clean up Michigan's prisons. Among the previous 19 recipients, were President Ronald Reagan, Vice President George Bush, Speaker of the House Jim Wright and former Supreme Court Chair Justice Warren Berger.

In accepting the award Senator Welborn acknowledged all the help he had received from his senate committee and various other lawmakers plus his staff, but he also specifically acknowledged information that came from within the prison system. "I could never have taken on the problems we have had in our prisons without the hundreds of correction officers who have written me, phoned me, or whom I've met personally on one of my unannounced tours through practically all of Michigan's thirty-four prisons."

Jack also praised his wife for her support. "I thank my wife Dorothy who has put up with the midnight phone calls from prisoners or staff, who when we go on vacation ends up sitting in the car reading a book while I'm making a 45 minute tour of a prison that ends up taking three hours."

I tried to make life for Mike just as normal as I could even though I thought there was an unknown threat out there. Occasionally that threat would rear its ugly head.

As I recall I had some of Mike's friends spending the night. They were asleep downstairs, but I was awake. I listened to an occasional car pass on the road. The front window was partly open. I loved the smell of the country air. Our road did have a little tendency to be noisy from time to time. It wasn't unusual to hear tires squeal as some young stud was out feeling his oats through his car's horsepower. I could relate to that. For some reason, I felt a bit jumpy and uncomfortable this evening. I got up from bed and headed for the bathroom. Suddenly I heard the crunch from the gravel in our driveway. 'Could the kids be out there?' I wondered. The front window curtain was closed, so I parted it and looked out. There was a pickup truck parked in our driveway. From the neighbors yard light, I could see it was orange—like a state highway truck. It had hub caps on the front wheels—none on the back.

My shotgun was clipped on the back of the piano where the kids couldn't see or reach it, but instead of getting that I picked up my Glock and still in my bathrobe, headed out through the back garage door. I don't know whether the guy in my yard was black or white, but I am sure that his intent was to hurl the half cement block in his hand through our front window. After the block hit the house he started running back to the truck. I yelled at him to stop—that didn't slow him at all. The truck wheels were spinning as it backed out of the driveway.

My neighbor's house was directly on the other side so I couldn't do anything. In that instant my judgment was probably pretty clouded. I didn't want to stop these people by aiming at the tires, but I did want to scare them away and hurt them. Now out of the driveway, they had it in a forward gear exiting to the north. I opened up at the passenger door. It was at such close range I couldn't miss and there were thuds, probably from bullets impacting the door. The side window shattered. The shots were at an angle, so I doubted if I'd killed anyone.

The truck raced away to the north. I moved back towards the house and waited in the bushes to see if it returned. Surely the shots woke up the kids and they would be terrified. I went back in to check on them. The noise hadn't fazed them, but to my surprise Michael had been sleeping on the living room couch. He was now standing there wide-eyed wondering what had happened.

I called Welborn and woke him up. After telling him about the incident I said, "Jack I think I really wanted to kill those guys."

"OK—keep an eye out and we'll talk about it tomorrow."

I went back outside and looked down the road. Panic set in again as I could just make out a truck sitting down by M-43 with the lights out. Suddenly the lights came on and the truck made the turn heading west on the main highway.

Again I called Welborn. "Why would they be sitting down at the corner Jack?"

"Why don't you look around outside in the morning and we'll check the hospitals and see if anyone has been treated for gun wounds."

I checked the clip on my pistol. Only four shells were left. Needless to say I didn't sleep that night. I just sat on the couch until morning.

In the morning I found glass from the truck window out by the driveway. So not to wake the kids I just rode the bike down to the corner to look where they had stopped. On the road was a puddle of what looked like blood. There was a tire track going through it, probably from another car.

We checked the local hospitals for any gunshot admissions. Up at Carson City there had been treatment for a puncture wound suffered by a correction officer at that facility, but that was all. Later the neighbor came over and mentioned that he had heard what sounded like fire crackers that night. I said, "Yeah, I heard them too."

Nothing more ever came of that incident, other than the fact that I was more watchful and fearful that this was not the end of it. Maybe "paranoid" would be a better description of my mood. I also felt very alone and I missed Josephine terribly. I really didn't know what was going on.

On another occasion Mike and I were headed home on the old Saginaw Highway. It was a dirt road, but sometimes we used it as an alternate route into town because the kids thought it was fun bumping along on it. We were headed home not to far from Benton Road, which was our road, and all of a sudden we had this black and white truck following right on our butt. I thought I heard gunshot noises so I pushed Mike down and stepped on it. I roared around the corner on to our road and sped right past our house. The truck behind gave up the chase and turned off. As much as I liked racing, this shit was getting scary.

It was in that first year after Jo's death that Mama McNamara and her husband were killed in a one car crash coming home from the U.P. of Michigan. I had met with Mama Mac several times at Napoleon's Coffee Shop. She was another link to the inside information I was receiving.

Mama Mac was in her 50's and a training supervisor at Jackson. From everything I heard she was extremely well respected by both the inmates and other correction officers. She told me she figured Josephine was going to get in trouble. For one thing she thought Jo was afraid at work and she thought others could read into that. She also said Jo was quite opinionated and would rarely listen to advice. Coupled with all that, she said Rakowski and others were hitting on her like vultures.

Mama Mac's husband Charles, I believe, was a counselor for the prison system. I had talked to her just before her death. She told me that her husband was soon retiring and that he had collected enough stuff to really knock Bob Brown and the system on their asses. Mama Mac talked rough, but that was the first time I had ever heard her use profanity. She said her husband kept good records and that once he retired they couldn't hurt him. I didn't know what information her husband had collected, but I often wondered afterwards if their death was more sinister than just a car accident.

Back in the Central Complex of SMP at Jackson, life went on as it had for so long. AP writer, Jim Mitzelfeld, was part of a prison tour conducted by the new warden, John Jabe. Mitzelfeld's observations vividly portrayed what it was really like inside. Walking near 5 Block, the new Warden Jabe cautioned the visitors to walk under the bulk head to avoid getting hit with stuff thrown out of the cells. That stuff could be uneaten food, milk cartons, urine or feces. Along with the mess on the floor came the stench of it all, body excrement and a sour milk combination accompanied by the drone of yells, screams and whistles that echoed through the building.

Warden Jabe explained to the tour group that these inmates in 5 Block were there because they disobeyed prison rules, assaulted other inmates or attacked a guard. They would spend all of their day, except for one hour, locked in their 6-1/2' x 10' cell. Each was allowed a short exercise period and shower outside of their cell.

There was a lot that Warden Jabe didn't tell the tour group about 5 Block. He didn't remind them that on the base floor where they were walking was the route that Jack Budd's killer took as he ran down to stab Budd to death. Jabe didn't tell them that as bad as this block was, inexperienced new guards were routinely assigned there. Such was the case involving Stephanie Baraboll, a probationary corrections officer.

Baraboll, who had worked only two months in the Central Complex, was assigned the gallery in 5 Block as a door signer. Just after she had served the evening meal she proceeded to leave the gallery. In the stair corridor she excused herself as she walked around a porter named Holloway, who was bent down with a dustpan. He immediately straightened up and started attacking her. As she fell she screamed, but realized the noise in the block was too loud to be heard. She blew her whistle and that's the last she remembers until being revived. Baraboll suffered a broken nose, cut lips, head injuries, torn neck muscles and severed nerves to her right arm. It took three months for her to recover. Her injuries might have been much worse had not an officer and inmate from base heard her whistle and rushed up finding her in a pool of blood.

At Holloway's trial he threatened Baradoll. "I'm not through with you yet Baradoll." Stephanie asked Warden Foltz not to be assigned to 5 Block again while Holloway was there. Foltz agreed but Deputy Warden Whelan did not. He told her if she was going to be that easily intimidated, she should find another line of work. Whelan sent a bristling memo to Foltz. 'Need answer from you. I think it's a mistake to let her tell us where she is or isn't going to work.'

Some inmates were in 5 Block because they wanted to be. For self-protection it was probably a safer place to stay than the blocks designated for those that requested protection from other inmates. An assault against a guard would pretty much guarantee a trip to 5 Block and that would lend for a better image with your fellow inmates than pleading for protection in another block. People might think that you were spilling your guts on some illegal activity. That certainly would be grounds for a hit contract.

Nor was it evident here in 5 Block, the despondency that was associated with inmate segregation. Attempted suicides were relatively common. A young inmate in his early 20's had first tried a broken piece of a light bulb to cut his throat. When that didn't work he tried to saw through the vitals with a piece of mirror glass. A sweatshirt wrapped around his neck hid the wound, but as the blood slowly ran from his body it trickled out to the bars. When the guards discovered the situation their comment was, "Well, that's one we don't have to count tonight." That didn't turn out to be the case though, as the fellow survived for another opportunity at it.

An older inmate wrapped himself up like a mummy with toilet paper and begged the guards to ignite him. No one at home would answer his collect calls anymore. He wanted to end it all. One guard thought it was funny as hell and laughingly asked a fellow corrections officer to get a lighter. Another guard thought it was a sad situation until she learned that the guy was a convicted child molester. Then she thought it might have been a good idea.

After reporter Mitzelfeld's tour group left 5 Block, they entered other cellblocks. The prisoners in the rest of the prison roamed freely about in street clothes; many in leather jackets, sweat suits and designer sunglasses. Along with Warden Jabe was ADW Frank Elo. Elo told the group, "Basically, if a guy wants to be out of his cell, he can be out of it most of the day."

The reporter remembered that a few months before two hooded inmates had attacked a guard with a knife, critically wounding him, then using the crowd of inmates for cover, had slipped back into their cells.

Inmates far outnumbered the unarmed guards, which lent to the reporters feeling that this being thought of as a safe, secure facility, was only a mirage.

'At one point, an inmate joined the tour group. The inmate leaned against the gallery railing smiling. He wore a green BMW cap, a windbreaker with a "Universal Studios" logo on it and large rubber boots. He drank coffee from a Michigan State beer mug.'

"Let me tell you the main problem in here," he said. "The security is outrageous. There's no security at all. Guys are constantly getting stabbed in here."

Senator Welborn felt that an obvious way to curtail violent behavior within Jackson's walls was to start limiting personal possessions of the hard-core inmates. Not only would that reduce the resources to fashion homemade weapons, but also it would be an incentive to foster good behavior to get those 'luxury' items back. He also felt that those prisoners under 'close' custody should wear prison uniforms rather than street clothes. Welborn introduced legislation to incorporate his views into law, however Deputy Corrections Director Dan Bolden offered to institute these changes through prison policy instead.

Almost immediately prisoners got wind of the policy changes before they were even written, and filed a lawsuit. After reviewing the inmates lawsuit Ingham County Circuit Court Judge Giddings issued a restraining order prohibiting the corrections department from implementing the new policy. Welborn reacted venomously to the judge's decision.

"Score another one for the Michigan's most dangerous prisoners, the ones who continue their crime sprees behind bars. Without pulling a gun they stole the heart of a circuit judge in Ingham County. Judge Giddings upheld their claim that bad behavior should not result in a bad prisoner suffering the loss of his TV or be forced to wear prison clothing. His restraining order was no doubt a heart warming victory for those who think there is no such thing as a bad criminal."

Senator Welborn continued by saying, "Giddings came to the rescue of the poor misunderstood murders, robbers and rapists who stood to lose a few comforts the next time they threw urine and feces into the face of a guard or stabbed or raped an inmate. Not yet understanding the type of heart that bleeds for the heartless, I am going to reintroduce my proposal in the Legislature."

Frustrated with the lack of interest from the Governor and Attorney General to clean up the prisons, Senator Welborn and his counterpart on the Senate prison committee, Democrat Christopher Dingell, headed to Washington to make a plea with the Justice Department for some help. They detailed evidence of the numerous rapes, murders, drug use, civil rights violations and corruption.

Welborn wanted a grand jury. Attorney General Frank Kelley indicated that the State could handle it's own problems.

Although it didn't become public knowledge until the spring of
1989, the previous fall, a task force had been put together to investigate Michigan prison problems. State Attorney General Frank
Kelley was put in charge of the task force, which included the FBI,
U.S. Attorney's office and the Michigan State Police.

Michigan State Police Director Col. Rich Davis was quoted as
saying that the investigation inside the prison system was "a mam-
moth undertaking." A federal investigator said, "The system has
been rotten for years. It goes all the way up and down the line."

The federal investigator was certainly right when he indicated
that the problems at Jackson were not a new phenomenon. A previous five-volume confidential 1973 State Police report and a similar
1982 Justice Department report pointed to severe longstanding
management problems.

I knew that this new task force would never have come into being
had it not been for the continuing pressure Senator Welborn and his
committee had exerted to get something done. Probably letting
Kelley be in charge was a face saving effort to allow the Michigan
public to think that Blanchard and Kelley were leading the charge to
improve things. It didn't fool everybody. One news reporter head-
lined his column by stating that Kelley and Blanchard were doing
everything possible to stay ahead of the 'Federal steamroller.'

Now, the new news at this time was that back in 1987, just
before Josephine was killed, an extensive federal investigation led
to the indictment of 19 people, including three prison officials
involved in a huge marijuana ring. This investigation received little
attention and the report was not available to the public. Reportedly,
none of the 'big time' drug dealers were prosecuted, but the current
investigation would start where the earlier probe left off.

In the Detroit News, reporter Rachel Reynolds did an excellent
job of bringing all the prison's dirt to the surface. She interviewed
an unnamed attorney who had reviewed the '87 federal report.

The '87 report read like a novel. Convicted triple murderer
Ronald Wiltse, who was one of the drug kingpins, offered to help

investigators in exchange for a transfer to a federal prison. Wiltse owed his teammate, Rodolfo Rios, $80,000 and it probably looked like a healthy time to cooperate with the feds.

Wiltse detailed how he paid prison employees, visitors and other inmates to smuggle drugs inside of Jackson State Prison, Kinross Corrections Facility and Marquette Branch Prison. He said he made about $5,000 a month dealing marijuana.

A husband and wife escaped prosecution by becoming federal informants too, detailing how they smuggled drugs from Texas in a customized van, which had a secret floor and panel compartments to hide the material. This lady, though married, had fallen in love with Wiltse in 1982, while visiting a friend in prison. From 1984 on she and her husband hauled drugs for him back to Flint. There, they cleaned, packaged and distributed the drugs for Wiltse, who called in his instructions from the pay phones in the prison yards. The drugs were then mailed to couriers outside the prison who mailed back payments. The lady kept detailed records recording names and dates on all of the transactions. Her records were given to federal investigators.

One courier named in the ladies notebook, was John Haddix who operated a paper supply business. The lady said that Haddix hollowed out reams of paper where he packed drugs and mailed the boxes to the prison paralegal office. Haddix's son James was the inmate working in that office that then turned the drugs over to Wiltse.

According to James Haddix, Wiltse, whose nickname was 'Runner' controlled everything from drugs to arranging 'hits' within the prison. According to Haddix, "This guy (Wiltse) had it all, did it all."

Acting on information supplied by Wiltse, federal agents seized the last drug shipment hauled up from Texas by the husband and wife team. Along with marijuana the investigators found cocaine, heroin and two Uzi submachine guns.

Wiltse, who declared himself Jewish, even enlisted the help of a rabbi's assistant to smuggle drugs in by hiding them in the cloth band he wore around his waist. Wiltse would meet the assistant in the Jewish section of the chapel. Other drugs were brought in by inmate's wives hiding them on their bodies in condoms.

When prison officials searched Wiltse's cell they found two automatic pistols hidden in the wall with ammunition clips wedged inside the TV.

In early January of 1989 prison officials were boasting that prison violence had declined in the last year; how that more than 1,500 newly hired state prison guards had allowed the state to start to tame Michigan's prisons. Although assaults with weapons at most of the prisons had declined significantly, there was a 'huge' increase in the use of knives at Jackson. Director Brown said that the materials to make knives were smuggled out of the prison industries program.

The present task force was continuing their investigation and although prison violence statistics might be reported down, drug trafficking and corruption seemed healthy as ever. One task force member told the Detroit News that one large drug ring was currently masterminded by a convicted murderer and as many as 20 guards were involved at different levels. Prison officials had even helped this inmate expand his drug operation by transferring him between Michigan prisons. Official prison records indicate that he had been transferred 29 times between 1980 and 1989.

Stephen A. McCreary was the inmate who had traveled around Michigan prisons organizing his drug business. His last transfer came at the direction of Central Complex Deputy Warden Wayne Jackson, who facilitated his move to the medium-security Western Wayne Correctional Facility, from where he escaped.

In early 1989 McCreary was recaptured. He was driving a BMW that he purchased after a trip to Hawaii and Florida. McCreary spilled the beans on his drug operation and how he had bribed the deputy warden. According to McCreary, after he had been transferred to SMP in 1987, he was called into Deputy Warden Jackson's office. According to McCreary Jackson said, "I run this place. What can I do for you?" McCreary asked Jackson to be transferred to SMP's medium security North Complex. Jackson allegedly responded, "Forget that. I'll try to get you out of here." After several months of negotiations McCreary's stepfather made a $7,500 payment to Jackson in a donut shop parking lot.

Jackson was being charged now, for accepting a bribe, but state police detectives were grumbling because they felt State Attorney General Frank Kelley had prematurely released news about the deputy warden's involvement and blackballed their investigation, which might have led to people much higher in the chain of corruption.

Meanwhile the Corrections Department received more bad publicity. The Warden at Huron Valley, which housed some of the state's most dangerous criminals, had lost the prison master key and much more. According to Olivia Pitts, a Sergeant at the Cotton facility, her and Warden Travis Jones had been having an affair. In October police responded to a call from Pitts claiming Jones had assaulted her. In December police again received a 911 call from Pitts claiming she was being raped. When the police arrived Jones was naked standing behind Pitts, holding her arm that was wielding a large kitchen knife. Jones claimed that Pitts had drugged his wine knocking him unconscious. He said that Pitts then stole his clothes and the Huron Valley master key.

Director Brown fired Jones, saying, "Jones was a disgrace to the department." In early 1989 Pitts was awaiting trial for stabbing Jones.

In the spring of 1989 while the media was embroiled in the story of the two errant wardens and the task force investigation, life within Jackson's Central Complex continued as it had in the past. On the first of February, inmate Kimbrel lured C/O David Bowers away from his workstation. Kimbrel grabbed Bowers and put a screwdriver to his back threatening to kill him if he didn't do as told. The inmate couldn't find any cuffs on Bowers so he left Bowers in the cell and closed the door. Kimbrel then grabbed a female correction officer and put the screwdriver to her neck and threatened to kill her. Bowers got the cell door opened and followed the inmate to the lower level where Kimbrel held the female guard. A scuffle resulted with Bowers being stabbed twice in the chest and four times in his left arm.

The Jackson Citizen Patriot reported on March 15th that in a one-week period an inmate had been stuck by another inmate every day.

On February 6th, an inmate sat eating his breakfast cream-of-wheat and another inmate approached with a shank and stabbed him straight in the heart. Reportedly it was a payback for an earlier altercation.

One former female corrections officer kept a daily record of events she was aware of and her various problems.

3-03-89	2 stickings today
6-03-89	Male corrections officer fell out on bulkhead with heroin and marijuana found in his system; also received harassing phone calls
6-24-89	Stabbing in 4 Block D.O.A.
6-25-89	Stabbing, 6 Block—stabbings increase to 5 or 6 a week all summer
7-29-89	Plot to kill corrections officer discovered. Four inmates, 3 shanks (weapons) 1 snitch.
8-17-89	Male C/O exposed his penis in front of me. I have medical tests (treadmill) now carry nitroglycerin.
9-11-89	Stress test positive
9-25-89	Angina attack at work
10-29-89	Riot demonstration (I was not notified and working alone at the time)
12-19-89	Increased angina attacks
1-17-90	Scheduled for heart catheterization
3-02-90	Dr. report, heart chest pains from stress

That was not the end of this correction officer's ordeal. She was asked by a female deputy warden to snitch on fellow officers who were corrupt. She performed this service, but in the end it backfired on her and her health deteriorated into a nervous breakdown. A year later she was fired.

One good thing happened in 1989. Mike and I acquired a new friend named Commador. Commador was an English Bulldog puppy. We still had our other dog, LW (Little Woman), but figured she needed some company. My buddy Jan Barnes sold the pup to us. Jan's girl friend wouldn't let him keep the dog, so he let me make payments to buy him.

Once when we visited Senator Welborn, Commador walked right over and pissed on Jack's briefcase. "Must be a Democrat," laughed Jack. He knelt down with some paper towels and wiped his case off. When I sent in his registration papers I listed him as Commador "Jack" in commemoration of this event.

Michael
and LW.

Commador Jack Smasher
of Thunder Bay.

Saginaw Exchange Club – "Officer of the Year Awards".
Michael, Bill and Dennis Martin (Saginaw County Deputy Sheriff.)

Bill addressing a Corrections graduation class.

THE TRIAL

Three years after Josephine was murdered Judge Perlos ruled that blood and DNA tests could be used as evidence in Hill's trial. The prosecution had been waiting all this time for that decision; trial date was set for Monday, April 24, 1990.

When the trial began Hill was being held in maximum security at an Ionia prison and transported each day for the trial. That lasted a couple of days, until they figured it would be less costly to keep him in his old home, SMP, at Jackson until the trial was over.

I attended every day of the trial, but was also late each day because I had to get Michael off to school before I left.

On the first day of the trial I tried to introduce myself to Piziali, but he seemed quite rude. He just walked off, muttering, "He couldn't please everyone." The next day I really got his attention. I had been running late that morning; first dropping Mike off then getting delayed in traffic. Because I was running so late it slipped my mind to lock the Glock in the trunk. When I sat down on the opposite end of Piziali's bench the Glock and holster loudly thumped against the wood back. Piziali heard the noise. He motioned me toward the hallway.

"What you got there?" he asked.

"I have a permit to carry it, but I was running late and forgot to put it in the trunk."

"Go do it," he snapped.

"Jesus Christ!" I replied.

I never brought the pistol in for the rest of the trial, however in times to come that little incident would lead to the loss of my weapons permit.

Early on in the trial, a surprise visitor showed up. It was Merryman, (Mexico) Hills old inmate buddy he had been drinking and working with the morning Jo was killed. In fact, Merryman had met Hill coming out of the auditorium, Hill saying to him, "Some nigger just kicked my ass!"

Well I'm not sure of the whole story, but because Food Service Supervisor Follick had stated that Merryman had not been out of his sight that morning, the State Police had eliminated him as a suspect. For some reason they just let Merryman sit in administrative segregation for a long time. I heard he had thrown some urine in Elo or somebody's face. That's not solid information, but what did happen was that Merryman got an attorney to protest his unlawfully long incarceration in segregation. I heard that not only did he get a release from prison, but also a nice cash settlement.

When Merryman showed up in the court hallway, he was either under the influence of alcohol or drugs, and was dressed in a white, silky looking outfit. I remember the letter from the inmate referring to Merryman as his son, and its rebuttal to the accusation that the boy was gay. Judging from his attire, he sure fit the image.

Piziali spotted Merryman and before he could make a grand entrance to the courtroom Piziali was escorting him to the stairwell saying something like, "Get your dumb ass out of here. I told you to stay out of here."

Leaphart was one of the prosecution's first witnesses. He had been the inmate who had been playing the piano in the auditorium, who had heard the radio, found the bloody blazer and alerted C/O Hartsuff. At least he was scheduled to be a witness. They tried to drag him to the witness chair without success. While visibly shaking, Leaphart told the judge that other inmates warned him that if he testified he would be dead. That word came down from Hill, and Leaphart was convinced it was a credible threat. He did look at Hill and said, "You can die in the box!" Hill just smirked.

Another inmate, Willie Lyles Bey also refused to testify. He had been in the commissary that morning of the murder, involved in a dispute with one of Hill's buddies. Other than those two, the prosecution had some 87 people scheduled to lend circumstantial support to the key evidence in the trial, blood and semen.

Of course I was not privy to the official investigative reports, so other than the newspaper coverage and my informants a lot of the information that came up in trial was really quite different from what we discovered.

The defense attorney, Engle, brought out that a blond pubic hair was found in the zipper of Jo's slacks. Sergeant Eddy, one of the truck drivers had noticed two large black men following Jo into the JCC entrance. Engle's intention from the start was to convince the jury that more than one person was involved. That was a theory I had heard from many people.

Correction officers testified as to the time when Jo picked up the keys to the JCC and who had talked with her or seen her at various locations.

Food Service Supervisor Follick testified that Hill had acted both antagonistic and playful that morning before he disappeared from his job. Follick also described Hill when he reappeared later, gasping for breath and sweating, with his burgundy T-shirt all rumpled.

Supposedly two officers checked on Jo between 07:50 and 08:10, calling her name with no response.

Hartsuff said he was shocked to find blood on his hand from picking up the blazer. Nursing supervisor Chris L. Connin stated that the belt around her neck was so tight he had to have help loosening it.

Throughout the trial Hill looked almost bored by the proceedings. Occasionally he would converse with his attorney, but for the most part he sat quietly, almost unconcerned, even when the medical examiner described Jo's injuries.

Dr. Kallet testified that vigorous intercourse had taken place on her; more than any woman would willingly tolerate. He also said that semen and blood on McCallum's blazer matched Hills blood type as did the swab from her vagina. McCallum's blood type was also identified on Hill's shirt; some from what looked like the brush of a hand and more that appeared to be from her hair on his chest as he was dragging her to the stairwell.

When the scientific comparison from the blood and semen off of the clothes were analyzed in terms of DNA testing, Hill finally lost his relaxed demeanor and could be heard making loud comments to his attorney and nervously moving his feet. Perhaps he realized at that time that he was nailed for sure.

In his closing statement Hill's attorney admitted that the blood on Hill's clothes probably belonged to McCallum, but he continued to press the theory of more than one assailant. Could it really be possible—that in such a short period of time one person Hill's size, could convince McCallum to unlock the door, rip off her clothes, beat and rape her, drag her across the stage; finally strangling her with his belt? And why was Leaphart even around there? He knew that Badders was not going to be in until noon. Inmate Archie Baker said he heard a female voice in the auditorium at 08:25. Hill would have been gone by then. Why wasn't there tests conducted to see if the semen from other inmates was in her. There were several sets of prints found, some matched Hill's and McCallum's, others a couple of other inmates. Why didn't they run the other prints through the FBI computer system to find additional matches?

The prosecutor held up Hill's shirt where holes existed from the swatches removed to identify Jo's blood. He did the same with Jo's pants where Hill's fluid was identified. The circumstantial evidence now seemed to fit.

It took a week for the chief prosecutor, Ed Grant to parade through the 63 of the 80 some witnesses he had lined up, but only three hours for the jury to reach the guilty verdict. When the foreman announced the decision I yelled, "All Right!" I had a whole row of supporters. Several were from a victim rights group that had been providing me with moral support for most of the trial. We all hugged and celebrated. I didn't see it but one reporter said that at the time he saw Hill just yawn.

After the trial Hill's attorney said that some of Hill's off the cuff statements really damaged his defense. One happened two days after the slaying. They told Hill he was being transferred out of Jackson for his safety. Hill said to Piziali, "The inmates here don't care what I did and won't do anything to me."

I was allowed to make some remarks prior to Hill's sentencing. Basically I said that justice had been served even if it took three years. I could finally explain to my son who was now 11, that his Mom's killer had been convicted. Hill seemed to scoff at my remarks.

An assistant prosecutor reviewed a psychological exam conducted on Hill in 1985 after he was convicted of the attempted rape of three women in Detroit. The report read, 'Hill is predisposed to anti-social behavior and has no respect, regard or value for human life.'

On May 31st Hill was sentenced to spend the rest of his life in prison with no chance of parole. In a statement to the court Hill proclaimed his innocence. "Others at SMP know the identity of the true killer. I didn't kill her, and I'm quite sure there are plenty of people who know it. Police found an inmate available and they didn't look any further." On the TV nightly news they carried the rest of his statement. "That I was the only black person in this court room"—as if race had some way clouded the jurors decision.

With his hands and ankles shackled Hill was led past his silent mother and brother. Later his mother would tell reporters that she didn't believe her son killed McCallum or even believe he tried to rape those women before in '85. She didn't even feel he was a violent person. "He is very brilliant. He plays the piano and he sings. He has a beautiful voice."

One would have thought that with Hill's conviction we would have had closure and gone on with our lives in a normal manner. That didn't happen. I still believed that there was much more to what happened to my wife with additional people involved. I continued to pursue my personal investigation based on what I was hearing from those inside. I knew that my nosing around in this prison stuff was still keeping Mike and me in a risky environment, but I was too committed to the whole process to stop. Hill's conviction did little to change things. Too many people had too many things to hide and as that one unnamed federal agent said, "The whole system, top to bottom has been rotten for years."

For Michael my protective shield would soon be unavailable and in the next few years he would enter his own personal hell. I'll let him tell you about that.

SCHOOL TIMES

MICHAEL

Because I hadn't officially finished the 4th grade in the spring, the school administrators felt I needed to start the next fall with the 4th grade even though I was taking 5th grade classes. Dad tried to talk them out of it, but didn't have any luck.

I found out much later that before I arrived to start classes, the teacher had informed the class about my mother's death and advised them not to bring up the subject. Not having to talk about that was just fine with me, as it had all been front-page news only a few months before.

Going to school in Grand Ledge seemed to work out OK, at least for the first few years. There were still some things that happened around home that were troubling. Shortly after we moved in Dad discovered that someone had broken into the garage and had opened the car glove box.

I had never seen a gun around our house before, but now I knew Dad kept a pistol handy. The next time I saw him with it was about a year later. I was sleeping on the couch in our living room when something banged against the huge front window. I was immediately awakened and I sat up to see Dad holding his gun. He moved around to the back door and I heard him exit. I remember sitting there in silence wondering what was going to happen. A few minutes of silence passed, and then that was shattered by "popping" sounds. I heard a car squeal out and then Dad came in. He told me everything was okay. I didn't know until the next day that Dad had shot at the guy. Outside along the road we examined what looked like some pools of blood on the ground. He said he'd told Jack about it.

There was also the time when we were chased down old M-43. We were coming back on the old road rather than the paved highway. It was around 9 p.m. and I kept dozing off; then I heard a series of pops and felt Dad's black truck accelerating. He reached over and pushed me off of the seat to the floor. "Stay down Mike." Now Dad was weaving the truck back and forth. In the side mirror I could see flashes and headlights close behind us. Once we turned on Benton Road, Dad accelerated again, driving right by the house. By the time we got down to the main highway, whoever was following us was not there anymore.

I started the 6th grade at the Beagle Middle School. The 6th thru 8th grades were taught there and the school was located right in Grand Ledge. My second year at the Beagle School drastically altered all the rest of my school years and it started harmlessly enough at a school social event.

You'll have to understand that when I went to Fairview School in Lansing, I hadn't ever experienced racial prejudice. My best friend, Levertis, was black and going to school with people of color was normal for me. At Grand Ledge a good friend of mine was Justo Hernandez and so I thought it would be nice to invite Levertis along to the school dance with us so he could see my new school. It never dawned on me that Levertis would be the only black kid there or that it would make any difference if he was.

At the dance there was a D.J. and a few parents to chaperone. Only a few kids actually danced. Little groups of friends formed around the gym floor and finally somebody got out a basketball to shoot some baskets. Eventually someone suggested a little three on three competition. It was Levertis, Justo and I against three of the popular top jocks of the class. At first there were only a few bystanders, but as the tempo of the half court game increased most everyone started to circle around and watch. Levertis was really a good athlete—Justo was not bad either. I wasn't very tall, but I was scrappy and the three of us played well together. Levertis was looking like a pro dribbling that ball between his legs going around the opposition with ease. We were really kicking their asses, the score being pretty lopsided: 11-3.

These boys didn't particularly like getting had with all their friends watching. It was obvious their self-esteem was melting like snow in a furnace. I heard the word nigger mentioned by the kid guarding Levertis. I looked at Levertis as if to say, "Should we do something?" But he just waved me off and ignored the remark.

Whoever made the last point had possession again after an opponent checked the ball. Levertis tossed the ball out to this kid who wasn't ready for it. The ball caught him on the chin. The kid threw it back hard right into Levertis' face. Now they both started charging at each other and the fight was on. I was trying to restrain Levertis and some parent had the other kid, but from his buddies and some voices in the crowd I heard, "Kick that nigger's ass!" "Show that nigger!"—"Fuck that nigger up!" I was infuriated at all of this and I started yelling at them, that I would kick all of their asses.

Finally things settled down and the social event came to a halt without further incident. Shortly thereafter I was called into the principal's office. Really the assistant principal ran the school and Mr. Jones, the principal, just filled the principal's position. When his door was closed, Mr. Jones nonchalantly mentioned that I shouldn't bring "those kinds of people" around here.

"What!" I was shocked.

"You know what I mean," he said.

At another dance, I got after a kid that also called Levertis a nigger. This kid was a real "redneck". When we went out to the parking lot his father's truck was parked next to my Dad's. Immediately his old man started spouting off the same crap that I'd been hearing from his kid, that I was a damned "nigger lover". It wasn't hard to see where the kid had picked up his views.

My circle of friends really got small. Of course Levertis was back on his home turf in Lansing, but Justo and I had to deal with the folks in Grand Ledge. Several of the boys in Beagle School had older brothers in high school that also got the word that a 'nigger lover' was causing problems in town.

It was a couple months after the basketball game when the next incident occurred. Justo had choir practice that ended after the day's classes. I waited for him to finish and then we planned to go to the library to study followed by a walk to his place for a little TV. We had common interests and were very good friends at the time and both of us worked hard at school. The high school was a half-mile down the road and school classes had ended for the day there too. We were ready to leave for the library when another student warned us that there were some cars full of high-school kids outside that were waiting to kick our asses.

We peered through the door windows and sure enough there were 3 or 4 carloads of boys. It looked like some had baseball bats. I recognized the two Higbee brothers, who had reputations for getting into fights with anyone, anytime. They had failed their grades numerous times and looked old enough to be in their twenties. For sure the others were at least 17 years old and on up—more than we were ready to deal with. They didn't move and we stayed in the school. Finally the choir director came out. She walked out to the cars and warned them that if they didn't leave she would call the police. They finally pulled away. When they were out of sight we made our exit. Unfortunately they were waiting not far away. The chase was on. Justo and I ran where the cars couldn't go. Eventually we traversed enough back yards to find hidden refuge behind the city police building. That was just one of many such incidents.

At first there was a part of me that liked these confrontations. I was the outlaw, the Billy The Kid type, with the attitude, if you fuck with the bull, you'll get the horns. That mindset would change in time.

I'm sure my school problems lay heavy on Dad, plus things happened that continually made us both aware of our vulnerability. One evening we decided to go out and eat and took our English Bulldog, Commador, with us. Commador loved to ride in the car and we would take him regularly. LW was our other dog from when we lived on the farm. Riding in cars didn't suit her at all so she stayed home.

Before we left I had been busy organizing a bunch of comic books that were stacked on the living room end table. When we came back home everything seemed normal. Dad was in the kitchen checking the messages on the answering machine when I noticed that my pile of comic books was off the table and spread around on the floor. "Dad." I pointed to the comic books on the floor. He instantly knew something was wrong and without saying anything he motioned for me to stay put. With pistol in hand he moved through all the rooms upstairs and then to the basement. When we left, the basement sliding door was open; now it was closed. He opened it slowly and there sat LW at the bottom of the stairs looking very frightened. No one was in the house now, but they had been there.

We scoured the house carefully and found nothing amiss except the scattered comics and a scared dog. Finally when inspecting the office area across from the bathroom we found an 8x10 picture of myself missing.

Although there were conflicts, I made it through the Beagle Middle School intact. I had very few friends, but for the most part the others realized that I would swing at the drop of a hat, which gained me a certain amount of respect. I hoped that respect would transfer with me to high school and it might be a more peaceful experience. I was wrong. It is human nature to want to fit in and be part of the mainstream. Sometimes this can be accomplished by establishing a common enemy to the mainstream. I was that enemy.

My freshman year was just under way when an event took place that would set the course for my high school years. A popular kid, named Paxton, (he had thrown the basketball into Levertis' face, two years prior at the 7th grade dance) was standing by his locker as I went by. Rumor had it that this guy had been making his 'nigger lover' remarks about me already and saying that he kicked my 'nigger friend's' ass. It was time to address this problem right now.

Usually, in this sort of situation I would never be the aggressor, but I couldn't let his comments go without saying something. I walked right up to his locker and tapped him on the shoulder. I questioned him about what he said. Paxton backed off with a grin on his face and threw a fake punch. I uncoiled one right into his face. With no hesitation I was on him with the intent of doing some significant damage. Unfortunately one of his huge football friends grabbed me from behind holding my arms down with a bear hug. Paxton came at me with a punch to the nose. The big kid let me go and I stumbled back feeling my nose running. I looked down to see the blood dripping down on my tennis shoes.

The blood was now in the water and the sharks were circling. From now on, I was the token town "Nigger Lover" and they would be messing with me on a regular basis. As my freshmen year ended it was becoming harder and harder for me to live a normal school existence. Once my sophomore year started the harassment grew. It wasn't just once a week either, at one point maybe 8 or 10 times during the day things happened, an accidental trip or books knocked out of my arms. One kid chewing a candy bar spit it at my face. I can't remember how many fights erupted during my sophomore year, but there were many. And, many were the visits to the principal's office.

The principal, Gary Kaminga, had told me to come to him anytime someone said or did anything to me. Because it was usually some different kid and me in each incident I was down to the office sometimes 5-6 times a day. He started to get frustrated with me and he would continually ask me what I did to provoke the fight this time. I was perceived as the outcast, the one that couldn't get along with others. Certainly I was a good share to blame for the fights, because I wouldn't back down from any situation.

Finally I tried to seek a solution with the principal. "I'm trying to not fight back anymore." "OK, you come see me when these types of things happen." That sounded good, however pretty soon he got tired of seeing me in the office. I think his initial solution of having me come down when an incident occurred was his way of trying to nip this harassment in the bud. But it didn't stop anything. I don't think he ever thought this would become a daily thorn in his side, which it was. I just wished he could have seen it from my side. My 10th grade year was a miserable experience.

My father and I decided that maybe things would be better if I transferred to Lansing Sexton High School. I really liked the change and even practiced with the Junior Varsity football team. Playing sports was something I always wanted to do, but I had never felt comfortable at Grand Ledge to try out for anything. Dramatics was another thing that somewhat interested me and that I had wanted to do at Grand Ledge, but how can you be on stage or on a field and depend on people that openly despise you? I was excited; maybe things could turn around for me at Sexton.

I also liked the idea of going to Sexton because my father had gone there too. Since my mother's death we had trouble hanging on to our traditions and I looked at this as a way of having a new kind of school heritage. Maybe the name, McCallum, could ring through the halls there again. It gave me something to smile about.

I wasn't driving yet so Dad had to drop me off and pick me up at Grandma's house. That resulted in too much running around for Dad and too much time at Grandma's. At first she liked having me over, but it quickly started to take its toll on her. My time at Sexton only lasted a few months. I didn't even get a chance to attend classes there just football practice. I was depressed about having to stop going to Sexton and dreaded a return to Grand Ledge.

After my brief time at Sexton I talked one day with Levertis and told him my school troubles. He suggested I go to Eastern High School with him. Again we decided that maybe any place other than Grand Ledge would give me a better shot at completing high school and maybe even a chance to enjoy it. I started my junior year at Eastern High School in Lansing. I was only there for a few months, but it was a breath of fresh air compared to Grand Ledge. Dad was still working for Senator Welborn at the Capitol so I was dropped off over an hour early each day at school. After school I went to the Crump's.

After finishing work at the Capitol Dad would pick me up at the Crump's, but sometimes it would be really late at night or when he did come he and Rubin would get into a political discussion for hours. The two of them really liked to visit with each other. This lasted several months, but as nice as these folks were it was obvious it was an imposition on the Crumps. Staying at their house for hours at a time made me feel that I was overextending my welcome. There was only one thing left to do now, that was return to Grand Ledge.

This time I decided to enter The Alternative Education program. Perhaps there, I could avoid my tormentors and continue my education. I thought going there would get me away from the environment of conflict. I mean, to my knowledge, most people there were drop-outs coming back to get a GED or guys who got into drugs and were way behind the normal level. Instead I found that the environment was the same: just a smaller group to contend with.

Some of the teachers at Alternative were very lax and the students could get away with almost anything. I was experienced at dealing with the racial element at Grand Ledge where I heard "Nigger Lover" yelled at me more than my own name, but now these guys at the Alternative school were wearing and drawing Nazi Swastikas. It was very unsettling and common to see that symbol on a book and on the chalkboard. The staff was very meek and felt that holding hands was a better tactic than disciplining.

My only friends at Alternative were Nicole, my girl friend at the time, and Jerrod. Jerrod lived two houses down from us and was also an outcast at Grand Ledge. His friendship with me put him in tough situations. Now that I was in Alternative Ed., he was going it alone at the High School and having a miserable time. I encouraged him to join me in the Alternative program. I explained to him how much easier it was and that there we could get our work done and actually achieve some better grades and improve our grade point average. What I said turned out to be true, but the stress and feeling of being an outcast remained the same. It really wasn't much better, but together I felt we could brave it.

The following summer was enjoyable and a relief from school, at least for a while. In July Jerrod and I were driving back to our house from Steve Russell's apartment in my 1967 Ambassador. It was beat up, but a joy to cruise around in. We stopped into the local Marathon station in Grand Ledge for gas. I was waiting to pump the gas while Jerrod went in to pay. Another car with some guys in it pulled out of the parking lot but saw me at the pump and did a quick u-turn back into the lot. With them was this girl, Brooke, who didn't like me. I heard Brooke yell to one of the guys in the car, "Randy why don't you kick that kid's ass?"

Randy Williams was a 11th grader who had been held back a year. His reputation reportedly included fights with the cops. He stood there glaring at me. We didn't like each other, but we weren't enemies either. At the time he was also attending Alternative with me. I didn't say a thing. Randy started swearing at me—moved over and was right in front of me. His face was getting red now; his verbal attack increased. He was much taller than I was and with me not looking to fight he leaned over pressing his head against mine. Randy was not afraid to be an aggressor.

I knew there was going to be a fight—I just couldn't avoid it. A little smart remark from me touched him off. His first swing missed; instantly I went for a headlock. With that accomplished I started whaling on him. "I'll let you go if you back off!" He just kept struggling, but I wouldn't let go and kept punching him.

"If you don't chill out someone's going to call the cops!" Now he stuck his fingers in my mouth and I bit him. About this time some more carloads of his friends pulled up. I knew now, that I was dead meat. I thought to myself, "I've avoided getting killed for four years, now I'm really going to get my ass kicked."

My friend Jerrod didn't help. He was pumping gas when the fight started and when the new adversaries arrived on the scene he said something to the affect of, "Look your friend's getting his ass kicked!" I really didn't need that. For some reason they didn't come to their friends rescue. I held him there like a hostage—maybe as an example of what they could get. I was about to let him go when he tried to trip me. Obviously he hadn't learned his lesson. I pushed him to the back of my car and rammed his head against the rear-end. He didn't look very good—it was time to leave. I told him again to relax and I'd let him go. In fear of the police I finally had to. Randy was still talking crap when they pulled away.

Nicole and I had been broken up for awhile, but we were together once again at an early fall football game in Grand Ledge. Because of her I would have my next encounter with Randy Williams.

We were walking with some of my friends in front of the stands and Nicole pointed out Randy in the stands and said that she had heard him talking about me. I decided it was time to take issue with

Randy's remarks. So, I stormed right up in the stands to confront him. It was a dumb thing to do. One friend followed me—the others stayed put. Now it was evident that Randy was surrounded by many of his friends. It was too late—I was committed and the fight in the stands erupted with the police arriving shortly to break it up. I kept my cool while Randy and David Parker struggled with the police, one of them spitting in the cops face. That only got them slammed into the side of the police car. I was released while they spent the night in jail. During the fight I had fallen against the stands and down the bleachers, badly bruising my back, so even though I wasn't in jail I was suffering.

I ended up limping to a local gas station to use a pay phone. As I was about to make the call, four carloads of Randy and David's friends pulled up. I didn't care anymore. I was at a breaking point. I talked back to all of them. They did nothing, only talked tough. I wanted it all to end and did my best to taunt them. But they just stood there. Finally, a big husky guy pumping gas saw this one lone guy being surrounded by 10 or so guys and came over to break it up.

I was now forced to recalculate my thinking. Yes, I felt like Mel Gibson in the movie Braveheart—the peaceful man forced to be the one-man army against the enemy. Practically speaking though, like it or not, I was no Charles Bronson. My reaction to what others did or said to me was not working. My reputation was established as that of a troublemaker. It was many different kids involved, but always me at the center. I decided to change and start to let things slide without confronting my tormentors. I was tired of fighting anyway. Williams and Parker now made regular trips over to the Alternative Ed. classroom during lunch to harass me. Word got around that I was now vulnerable.

Nate Barker was in Alternative Ed. and we were friends for about eight months or so. He quickly got involved in booze and drugs—we started not hanging out together. We were still acquaintances, but no longer as close as we once were.

The relationship between Nicole and I was like most high school romances, up and down, but far from perfect. There was a bad rumor going around about Nicole, that Nate got wind of. He called my Dad and told him about it. Dad said he'd tell me, but forgot to. The next day I was sick and stayed home. The following day I was back in class and heard Nate was busy continuing the spread of the rumor—even laughing about it. "Nate, it's not your place to tell everybody this kind of stuff. I'll deal with it." It really pissed him off because I wouldn't dump her. "Well, screw you!" he said. I never understood why he cared so much.

I was upset with him. I told him how pissed I was and that our friendship was dead. From then on Nate and another asshole, Ken Scribner, sat behind me in class and kept the pressure on. Ken was also one of the guys at Alternative that wrote Nazi symbols everywhere. Broken pencils would bounce off my back and my papers would get knocked off my desk. I'd say, "Hey! Cut it out." "Fuck you," was the response. "Don't pay any attention to them," my girl friend would say.

Nicole and I were in Subway one day at lunch break to get a sandwich, when in comes Nate with Ken. Laughingly he says, "Look who's with the bitch." He gives me a push, "Come on outside and fight asshole."

"No, just getting my food ladies," was my reply.

Nate proceeded outside and started kicking in the door to my car muttering, "Nigger loving asshole." He thought he knew all the buttons to push to get me to fight, but it didn't work. I kept my cool, didn't fight, and was proud of myself. There was one provoking button Nate could have pushed that would have done the trick. He knew it and I knew it. That was a buffer zone that he didn't step into. I know I had told my friend Jerrod and am sure word filtered around—say anything bad about my mother and that person will be dead. In my heart I meant every word of it and still do.

We took Nate to court for malicious destruction of property. On the court day he just didn't show up. He should have been in jail for numerous other things. I think he had been picked up for marijuana possession a couple of times too, but each time he just seemed to slip through the cracks. He was still in school, but with terrible grades. Sooner or later things would probably again come to a head with us.

The science teacher had given us an assignment and then left the classroom for a while. I thought that her departure was a mistake, considering this volatile setting. All the teachers and principal at Alternative knew the situation and really did nothing about it. Right away from the back of the room, Nate yelled, "Pussy, bitch!" Next Nate walked by and bumped me, then again. I made eye contact. "What the fuck you looking at?" I smiled at him, which only threw gas on the fire. "Let's go outside and fight!" Still sitting there, I laughingly said, "Okay bitch." This really pissed him off, "Don't call me that," he said. I replied with another, "Whatever bitch". That set him off and he started punching at the back of my head while I was still seated at the table. I put my hands up in defense and he pulled my chair backwards to the floor. He stood over me and continued to punch at me. I smiled and just blocked his assault. When the teacher finally came back in the room, she and some of the others teachers separated us and I stood up still smiling, knowing I hadn't thrown a punch back.

The result: in the principal's office, Norma Pryor said to me, "What did you do to provoke him?" I was floored with this question and argued back that he was the one that had made the first verbal and the first physical contact. It was to no avail as we both were kicked out for a week. I was blown away that they felt I was equally at fault.

After this incident my father and I thought it best to get a Peace-Bond against Nate. This meant he couldn't be anywhere near me. In return he filed one against me. When filing an order of protection against someone you have to give reasons as to why you need the order. I listed all the incidents with Nate and when he filed his order against me he and his parents listed nothing but lies.

Nate claimed in the order, that Levertis, I and another one of my black friends had assaulted him after he came out of a party store. He said that I ordered them to attack him and that I just sat back and watched. The only problem with that story was I was with my father and a family friend the night in question.

There was also an incident when Nate called the police on me. I had dropped off Nicole at her house which was on the opposite end of Nate's road. After dropping her off I stopped at a local grocery store and bought some milk and went home. About an hour later I was awakened by my father saying there was a Deputy at our door wanting to talk to me. Nate and his parents had called the police claiming that I had pulled into there private drive and threw a huge rock through this glass window above their front door and the rock had broken their oak banister leading upstairs. They also said I was yelling out of my window and peeling out as I left. It was a ridiculous claim. They had no proof that I did anything. They also had just called the police and said that I had just left their house. When the officer checked my car to see if it was warm, all he felt was a cold hood.

When we took Nate to court for the malicious destruction on my automobile, he and his parents in turn were suing me for the damage to their house. It amazed me that they would go to such lengths to make me look bad. In court I told my side of the story and then the judge heard Nate's version. The judge then ordered Nate to pay the restitution on my car. I went back and sat at the back of the courtroom and felt good that maybe for once, justice had been served. Nate and his parents then walked by us. He had a smirk on his face and when he passed me he said very loudly, "Bitch!" It echoed in the courtroom; people turned and looked. I shook my head and my father stood up and said something to the judge about it, but he didn't do anything. My faith in the system stayed perfectly intact.

I hated school. I mean I really hated school. Sometimes just thinking of going back in the morning made me sick. There were many times that I would get up and vomit into the sink. I'd look into the mirror and wonder why all of this was happening to me. If it hadn't been for my friends and the good times we had when I was out of school, I would have surely gone crazy. At 17 years of age I had actually developed an ulcer and it was on the verge of becoming a bleeding ulcer, so my doctor warned me.

For all of the years of fighting and harassment I should have flunked out. I only flunked second year Spanish. To make up for all the switching between schools I had to take some night classes and double up on credits, but I wanted to finish as quickly as possible and didn't mind the workload.

Shortly before graduation I found out that Nicole was cheating on me. Like my father in other instances, I did not handle it so well. I look back on that relationship and now laugh. We all learn from our mistakes and I definitely did from that. I learned you can't help someone that doesn't want to help themselves. I tried my hardest to help her get through school and to repair her relationship with her mother and step-father. But I was immature myself and was dealing with things that she couldn't even understand.

I didn't speak about my mother to people. I almost did with Nicole once, but I held back, and for good reason. No one else could understand what I was dealing with; even I couldn't. Levertis and Steve knew only because they were there, in my life, when it happened. Jerrod also knew. His mother was a corrections officer and what happened was no secret. I never ventured out to tell people about it. It was something that was personal and something I felt I had to deal with alone.

I was close to being finished with school and now that Nicole and I had broken up I had to go it alone. Jerrod had vandalized some cottages up north during Christmas break and was now looking at prison time. I mean kids do destructive things and I had also, just never to that magnitude and never had I gotten caught. With Jerrod gone, and only months before graduation, I really had to go it completely alone. To show what kind of friend Jerrod was, he called me when he was locked up just to see how I was handling the breakup with Nicole.

I didn't go to the prom or even the graduation ceremony for that matter. Why?

I would have been alone and surrounded by people that didn't like me at all. I tried desperately to have the Alternative Ed. Principal let me walk with the high school students because at least I had some friends that were graduating there. Of course she denied me from doing that, so I choose not to go at all. I went down and picked up my diploma like any other envelope. It had no significance to me.

High school was a complete hell for me, no exaggeration. For some it's the highlight of their life. For me it was anything but that. When school was over I was very relieved and said adios to Alternative Ed. and my hellish high school experience.

I have wanted to pursue acting ever since I was a kid and had taken a few courses at a local agency during my senior year of high school. That summer, after graduation, I enrolled at Lansing Community College. No one knew me there and I could finally do something for myself.

At LCC I learned that a lot of actors used the Method style of acting. This style incorporates the actors own like experiences into their work. With everything that I've had to endure in life, I thought that style might be appropriate for me.

Justo Hernandez, Steve Wright, Michael, Steve Russel, Levertis, Jerrod Root.

Levertis and Michael.

THE OMBUDSMAN

While Mike was experiencing his troubles in school, I was investigating his mother's death and focusing in on a rotten prison system. Was the reporter correct when he said I was consumed by this mission, "a fanatic"? Probably that was a good description—he might even have included the word obsessed.

Because the woman I loved had been taken away from me for what looked like more than accidental reasons—ranging from sexual harassment to extremely dangerous conditions that no one seemed willing to address, I had the incentive to get involved. When I looked at the results of task force investigations dating back twenty years and I heard the complaints of corrections officers on how bad things still were, like Senator Welborn, I thought the system needed fixing. And, hell or high water I was going to try.

The prison wardens and administrators probably would have been real happy to have never heard the name McCallum. In the lawsuits we had tried to prove that administrators had screwed up putting Jo in an isolated assignment, but for reasons I'll discuss later, each attempt failed. Now I had a new lawyer and we were going after them for sexual harassment.

Jo's sergeant had a history of harassing women, and one female corrections officer gave me even more of a low down on the guy that official reports didn't explain. Apparently the sergeant's girl friend at that time wanted to get rid of him so bad that she allowed herself to be witnessed by him having sex with another guy.

This lady said that info was in a psychologist's report. The breakup really stressed him out, but along came Jo, who even looked a little like his previous lady. He tried to latch on to her like a piranha. It wasn't just Jo though. This lady told me he tried to fondle any lady—good looking or not. She referred to him as a "slime bag".

Prison officials didn't have time or interest in talking with me, nor did the MCO Union leaders. Yes, the lawsuits probably caused all that to be the case, but I don't think they wanted any more poking around in their business than was necessary. It was bad enough having Welborn and the Feds to put up with, but they didn't have to tolerate me. Still I kept the pressure on.

Each year's anniversary of Jo's death gave me a new opportunity to talk with the news media. Each interview would bring more calls into my hot line and also give incentive to the reporters to ferret out any new dirt on the corrections system.

In 1993, at my suggestion, Senator Welborn gave me an official position within his office, that of "Constituent Ombudsman" (we invented the title). I think that Jack could see that I was going to be relentless in following up on what happened to Jo and seeing I was already going and coming from his office with information, he might just as well give me an office to work from. The position also netted me a coveted parking spot at the Capitol. That was as valuable as the office.

As Ombudsman I got involved in several administrative projects that Jack didn't have time to handle, but that official position also gave me more leverage to pry into the prison system. In addition it gave me even more notoriety, so people within corrections that couldn't trust their supervisor; that couldn't trust the Union, had someone to talk to. Granted, the majority of my informants didn't want to be named, for fear of reprisals. Their information was still valuable for me to pass along to Jack and also to help me put the pieces of this big puzzle together.

At first I thought that those who had something to cover up on Jo's death had created the threat environment Mike and I now lived in. Now, the trial was over, Hill was convicted and the threat still seemed to be there. There was just a lot of stuff in the Corrections Department that people didn't want uncovered. Probably a lot of that was a fear of political damage; a threat to prison job positions and of course the possibility of criminal investigations involving the route of drug money. As is the case in other parts of our society, drug money can find its way into high places.

There had been some incidents I haven't mentioned yet, that kept me very vigilant. One happened not too long after Jo was killed. As I recall it was around dusk and Mike and I were headed into Grand Ledge on M-43 to get some supper.

A white vehicle, like a Bronco, with overhead lights, passed going in the opposite direction. Abruptly after passing it made a U-turn and started following us. I didn't think much about it until it really started speeding up. I was watching the vehicle in the mirror and swore that I could see flashes coming from the drivers side, like you would expect to see from a gun's muzzle flash. I also thought I heard something hit the car. Mike had some earphones on and wasn't paying much attention. I pushed him down and floored the old '65 Impala. This car was souped up with a special built 454 engine and would really rock and roll.

I hit the first curve going about 80 mph, but the vehicle was still back there. I thought about heading towards the city police station, but knew it was after hours and I would have to push a door buzzer to get any attention. By then, our pursuers could nail us in the parking lot.

At the intersection of Saginaw and Highway 100 I blew through a red light at a high rate of speed. That could have caused a serious accident but I wanted to shake this guy. Cops usually hung out at the Shell station near the corner and I was hoping there was one there to see us run the red light. That was the first time I ever had such a thought.

As I passed under the I-96 expressway I could see the white vehicle was not in my mirror anymore. I pulled into the Delta Township Police Station.

Deputy Scribner was on duty at the station. At first he didn't want to open the door, but eventually he did. I told him what had happened. He couldn't understand why anyone would want to shoot at us. I couldn't either. As we looked over our car, I pointed to what looked like a bullet hole in the trunk. The deputy questioned how long the hole had been there. Eventually he made out the report, but I could tell it was a half-assed effort.

Another incident happened in the Meijer parking lot. I had a black full-size Chevrolet pickup then and I was sitting there when all of a sudden this guy in a blue jump suit rips off the opposite side mirror and with a pipe or rod smashes the passenger side window. By now I've got my Glock available and ready to fire. The guy sees this and exits between the other parked cars. I didn't pursue him but I did lay on my horn to get attention. In the distance I spotted an Eaton County Sheriff's car. It just slowly drifted out of the parking lot.

The counselor provided by the State, Ms. Salinas, said that as much as possible I should try and keep Mike from feeling threatened. I never told him about the above incident or a lot of the other things that happened. He was aware of the importance of being careful with strangers, but I wanted him to have as normal a life as possible. Whenever I turned him and his friends loose in a mall I gave him the standard, be careful briefing. On many occasions I would be shadowing them a respectable distance away.

One day I received a call on my hot line from a man that said he had information. He wanted to meet me at the Lansing River Front Park by the Lansing Center on the east side of the river at midnight. At that time I was willing to talk to anyone, anyplace and anytime. I had been distributing business cards everywhere, even had people handing them out within the prison.

Early before the scheduled meeting I went to the park and put a backup gun under a trash barrel, just in case I needed it. I carried my Glock in a back holster.

At around midnight I was at the park waiting for my informant. Soon this guy comes sauntering down the sidewalk. He spots me and says, "You want info, OK, I want some too." I felt his attitude was rather threatening. When he's about 12 feet away he kind of waves his arms and I see two big dudes behind him. When he gets close he turns around to see how close his buddies are behind him and when he faces me again he's staring into the business end of my Glock.

Now his attitude has changed. I ordered all of them to lay down on the sidewalk and put their hands behind them. The two guys that came along with my informant didn't have much to say so I concentrated my questioning on the main man—and he was scared. Come to find out, he identified himself as Corrections Officer Alfred Lee. He had used a different name when he called.

I was nervous and I didn't know whether Lee had any other friends out there in the shadows or not, but I talked tough to him, like I had all the confidence in the world. I already knew that a C/O named Lee had been pestering Jo to car pool with him—even had called her at home. Although earlier I hadn't been aware of this, Jo had told Tina about it—that she was sick of him following her around. I also knew that Lee had walked down to Jo's workstation in JCC the morning she was killed. He had removed her coat from the phone fixture, picked up the phone then replaced the phone and coat. Supposedly, he had also called in the auditorium for her and left.

Lee, lying there on his stomach had nothing new to offer. I said, "Why do you think Josephine would have gone out with you?" He said, "No man! I just was trying to see if she wanted to save some gas and car pool."

I let them all go, but should have fired a round in the air just for satisfaction. Lee would have probably shit his pants. I never saw him again. Piziali had interviewed Lee once, but no one ever questioned him as to why he visited Jo's workstation at the exact time he was supposed to be on duty at another cellblock several minutes away.

I heard later that Lee got into a fight at the trustee farm and punched somebody out. I don't know whether he's still in the prison system or not. If what I heard was true, that Lee was Director Bob Brown's nephew, he may still be there—shuffled around to another position.

The more I got to thinking about it, I decided it had been really stupid of me to agree to that river park meeting. In the future if someone wanted to talk it would be in daylight at a public facility, preferably a restaurant or coffee shop.

In June of 1987 Michael and I were invited to an outdoor ceremony for the second graduating class from DeMarse. Jo had been in the first class. I was told that there would be a presentation in honor of Josephine; the schedule was tight and I wasn't supposed to say anything. When Michael and I got up to accept the plaque and I opened my mouth, I could hear grumbling in the back. Like, "Oh shit he's gonna say something." I did, but it was brief and to the point.

"We were here not long ago for her graduation—now we're here for this."

"Be careful in there."

Calmly I walked over and dropped the award in Warden Foltz's lap. It was a nice plaque with a bronze likeness of Jo on the front. I gave it back because I felt like we were being used.

Finally I did get a meeting with Corrections Director Brown. Brown's brother, Gaylord, is a good friend of mine from way back. I thought with that association, perhaps Director Brown would listen to me. When I explained a lot of the stuff I'd heard about Jo's death, he basically just brushed it off as hearsay. Talking to him turned out to be a waste of time.

The year that I went to work for Welborn, something really bad happened. Commador Jack, our English bulldog, mysteriously died. When he was a puppy we took him to the vet to get his pallet trimmed. It's a common operation for English Bulldogs to allow them to breath easier. Other than that operation he was in fine health and we were really attached to him.

Commador loved to ride around in the back window of our car and one day I left him there while I was visiting my friend Charlie. The car windows were left cracked so there was plenty of ventilation for him, plus the car was parked in the shaded driveway. We were away for a few minutes to purchase a car part and when I returned there was really something wrong with him. At home Michael gently held Commador. He breathed heavily and erratic. I decided to take him to the vet. The veterinary examined him, but couldn't determine what the problem was. I decided to leave him overnight with the vet for observation. The next morning he was dead.

The vet performed an autopsy and found burned marks on Commador's body. He said that it looked like he had been subjected to electric trauma; his kidneys appeared to be cooked. I notified Welborn and a friend of his said a stun gun would do something like that. It's amazing how your mind connects things, but I remembered way back when Josie was talking to her brother Jim's wife on the phone. Jane was sobbing—something about Jim killing their beautiful dog Rex. From what Josie told me later, Jim came home after drinking and Rex snapped at him. That was the end of Rex. I talked with a neighbor of theirs and he too was aware of the incident.

After doing a little checking I found out that the Eaton County Sheriffs Department had about 9 stun guns. That seemed like a lot as Ingham County, which covered all of Lansing, only had two. That was all I ever found out, but I knew it would take a pretty mean person to electrocute a dog, especially Commador.

This seems to be a good time to tell you about my lawsuits against the State and my exposure to the attorney world.

As I said before my first attorney—the community designated "mover and shaker", made lots of headlines when he filed a $30 million lawsuit against the State. He didn't like me talking to the media. That was his job he said and he was making comments to the media regularly. I refused to be muzzled and did my thing anyway. The lawsuit ended up getting thrown out. The attorney got lots of media exposure and Blanchard appointed a member of his firm to a court judgeship. Later Jack Welborn introduced me to the judge in the case. He remembered me and said, "What do you want to know about that lawsuit you had?" I really didn't know what to say. He continued, "I told that pompous S.O.B. three times in my chambers that he had this suit in the wrong court. He should have filed for a loss of civil rights in federal court but he never did file and missed the deadline." Though I can't verify it, I've been told that in one of the state's law schools our lawsuit is often used as an example of a mishandled cause of death lawsuit.

Again, I tried to go for a name attorney and get some results. I sent a brief summary of the case to the famous attorney Melvin Belli and then I called him. To my amazement, he actually answered the phone. There was no mistake as to whom I was talking to; the voice was distinctive. He said he had reviewed the case and there was merit to the lawsuit, but he couldn't do it. Melvin recommended a Grand Rapids attorney he had some connections to. I was impressed and immediately got a hold of the attorney he recommended. I got the impression that this fellow had been on the winning side of many cases, which I guess was the truth, except on none of them had he ever been the lead attorney. I believe mine was the first.

Lots of time was spent in trial preparation with numerous depositions being taken and lots of money being spent. This lawsuit was specifically against the Department of Corrections, naming Director Robert Brown and Wardens Dale Foltz and John Whelan as defendants. The result of this lawsuit was a type of mock trial. I had never heard of such a thing and to this day I'm not real sure what happened as the records are sealed. My attorney and the state attorneys agreed to do this thing supposedly at the judge's request. It was a way of saving the cost of a normal jury trial by seeing if the case had merit. They selected two or three jurors from a jury pool and each side had a period of time to present their case with a 15 minute closing. It happened in Judge Houk's courtroom in Mason. The State really had their act together. Six of their attorneys presented lots of facts and precedents to defend their clients. My attorney relied on the sympathy approach. In his closing he pleaded for a settlement to compensate Michael and I for a great loss. It was a try at jerking tears from the jurors. My attorney ended his closing in exactly his allotted 15 minutes, but the state attorneys ran way over their time limit with lots of facts and rationalization.

The result was that the jury could only recommend a paltry sum of $15,000 as an award, so it would not be worth a full trial. I looked at my attorney, "You mean it's all over?" "Yep." Although I liked this attorney, after the 'mock' trial, he quickly backed away from really pushing the courts, as he had before.

The next attorney was at least successful in suing the state for the sexual harassment Jo experienced. That lawsuit netted us about $12,000 after the attorney took his share. Maybe in the end the big benefit of the lawsuits was exposing some of the problems in the system. The numerous depositions taken gave me more insight into what happened or didn't happen to Jo, though at this time I can still only speculate on the chain of events causing her death. I'm sure if he was willing Hill could tell us exactly what happened, but other than proclaiming that others were involved he has kept his mouth shut. Probably that's to his advantage.

There are two things that irritate the hell out of me about all of this. The first being the fact that the SMP administration would not admit that they screwed up by putting a probationary guard in an isolated assignment, especially an area like the JCC gate where so much drug and illegal activity had taken place in the past. Both Warden Foltz and ADW Whelan said that having a radio was protection enough. It may have been a Lieutenant or Captain that made the assignment for devious reasons, but to not acknowledge that error, smacks of the type of cover up that has existed in the prison for the last thirty years. Of all the information I have received from correction officers, they were unanimous in saying that she shouldn't have been assigned there. It was more than just not follow-ing the rules, it violated common sense and was a factor in her death.

The other thing that infuriates me is the effort by the State's defense team to paint Jo as being promiscuous. I think this may have originated as a little misinformation started within the prison. It was no secret that there had been sexual activity between male and female guards both on and off-duty as well as that same activity between female guards and inmates and male guards and inmates. In fact the state legislature finally passed a resolution forbidding sex between guards and inmates. Director Brown's comments were that it was not that big of a problem. It was also a fact that if a female guard didn't want to cooperate with her supervisors a little rumor could be started that she was playing with the inmates. That was bound to have an impact on her.

In Jo's case the rumor was started that Jack Budd and her had something going on. They were good friends and had studied together through school; that was no secret. I also know that Jo had asked Jack Budd to help her fend off Sergeant Rakowski's advances. After Jo's funeral, Budd and I had talked and we had agreed that the system was rotten. He also called on my hot line about problems he was having before he was killed.

I had made a big deal about not getting her wedding rings back before the funeral and it was insinuated by some that we were separating and that's why she didn't wear them at work. On several occasions she had told Pat and I that the less the inmates knew about your personal life the less problems one would have. What really torched me, was when someone started circulating a picture of Jo and Jack sitting together at a bar drinking and laughing. The picture had been taken at a graduation party and whoever cropped the picture forgot to cut out my elbow that was still in the picture beside Jo. Later I learned that state attorneys had even been questioning her old teacher about anything she knew of Jo's prior sexual activity.

My gun permit was about to expire so I went in to get it renewed. The clerk said that she was too busy to do it then; I would be contacted. I didn't think much about it, but because after a couple weeks I hadn't heard anything, I went back in. By this time the permit had expired. I was told that my permit would not be renewed. As far as I knew there was nothing that I had done that they could use to refuse reissuing a permit to me. It was pretty well known that we had been living in a threat environment for a long time. I felt it was necessary for me to carry a weapon for self-defense and equally important for my adversaries to know I was armed.

I filed a complaint about being refused a weapon's permit. From the gun hearing board I was informed I would never be issued a permit again. To circumvent the gun board's refusal, I got a federal license to be a gun dealer. Again they refused me a permit to carry the gun on my person. In fact any gun I transported had to be in the original box with the ammunition separately locked in the trunk.

There was a new sheriff now, who was real good friends with my brother-in-law Jim. Perhaps that was the problem. I tried to work through an attorney and the local prosecutor to find out more. Finally I got a copy of a report that had been written up during Hill's trial. It sounded like a good mystery writer had put it together. Supposedly, I had "modified my pistol" to hold 24 shots. My mental capability was questioned. I had been "stalking the prisoner" and I "might easily" be behind the TV reporter's light with a gun drawn. 'They had seen me sitting in my car two blocks away from the courthouse so they took evasive action in moving the prisoner.' It was all pure fiction, but it was enough for the gun board to use against me.

True. I had screwed up bringing the gun into the courtroom, but I'm not sure at that time it was illegal. The fact that at noontime I was sitting in my car two blocks away was also accurate, for that's where I ate my brown bag lunch each day. To pump some bullets into Hill was my absolute last intention. Through that trial I was learning more about what might have really happened, plus from what I had heard more than just Hill was involved.

My last association with the leaders of MCO and Corrections was several years ago in Kellogg Center at Michigan State University. The occasion was to honor the corrections officer of the year, with additional recognition given to Josephine. Mike and I were invited.

We were seated with a couple who were very pleasant to us. I believe the lady was coordinator of the event. Midway through the meal I started breaking out in a sweat. I couldn't get my breath and was bordering on real panic. I went outside to get some fresh air. There was a cement bench there, so I sat down to get my bearings.

In a few minutes I was feeling somewhat better. From around the corner of the building I heard a voice. He gave a name and said, "I know what you're going through. A lot of shit went on in your wife's death. People got away with murder." I guess the guy thought he couldn't be seen, but through the corner window, I saw him standing there smoking a cigarette.

"I live in Marquette. Give me a call sometime. By the way, watch what you eat." He tossed a business card down on a cement bench and walked off.

When I got back to our table the lady seemed really concerned about me. Other corrections officers came up after the program and were friendly. Frank Elo the Assistant Warden and Parks the union chief didn't even look at me, let alone say hello. I guess from all the lawsuits or whatever they hated my guts.

I tried to call the gentleman who had given me the business card. I left messages, but he did not return my calls. Finally, I ran into the guy and asked why he hadn't returned my calls. He said that he had nothing to tell me. I don't know whether he had just changed his mind about talking to me or was scared. It was typical for people not to want to get involved. His name was Robert "Bobby" Hill and I still have his card.

The doctor didn't know for sure what caused my attack at dinner, but said a certain flavor enhancer could cause that type of reaction in some people. For anyone to have intentionally spiked my meal didn't make any sense at the time, so I logged that off as a food reaction; now I have doubts.

One corrections officer stood out from all the rest as a man who recognized the problems at SMP and, as a union official, tried to do something about the situation there. I met with Robert Halmich several times, the first meeting being at Sparty's, where Mike and I had breakfast the morning that Josephine was killed. At first I didn't recognize the man, but finally I figured out that the big guy with the newly white bleached hair and beard wearing the 'Santa' t-shirt and smoking a cigarette must be him.

Halmich started out the conversation like this, "So you're the guy that's getting fucked. I knew someone was going to get killed down there."

Bob Halmich gave me a lot of information on the problems at SMP. He was very believable and had little to gain by talking to me, and a lot to lose. He really seemed to care, and wanted to see things improve. For a long time he had worked the JCC gate where Jo had been assigned. He knew first hand the dangers associated with the area and all the illegal activity that took place there. He fought with the wardens and supervisors to get things changed, but didn't get a lot of results. Halmich's efforts did bring him a lot of respect from corrections officers.

After his retirement Warden Dale Foltz received the Warden of the Year award from the American Corrections Association. I thought that was ironic, judging from the state of the prison during his tenure. Robert Halmich didn't receive any award, but in my mind he was the hero of the system. Here's what he had to say.

WILLIAM C. McCALLUM
CONSTITUENT OMBUDSMAN
SENATOR JACK WELBORN
13TH DISTRICT

OFFICE: (517) 373-0793
FAX: (517) 373-5607

P.O. BOX 30036
LANSING, MICHIGAN 48909-7536

THE REFORMER

Robert L. Halmich

Sparing you the morbid details, I'll just say as a neglected child I had a nasty, traumatic childhood. As a juvenile I was under the jurisdiction of the court since I was seven or eight years old. I've been placed in a couple of psychiatric hospitals, the first time for a year in the Ionia State Hospital at age 16 and later I was incarcerated in the Kalamazoo State Hospital. The diagnosis—schizophrenia personality with tendency for homicidal and suicidal acts.

Now it wasn't just my mental health background that kept me from being able to land a job, I also had racked up a criminal history of armed robbery and assault. That all happened before I turned the tender age of 22. Along with my tours in the mental hospitals, I was locked up in both the Jackson City and County Jails, Lansing City Jail, Ingham County Jail, and Eaton County Jail. I even had a couple tours as a temporary resident of Jackson in the Reception and Guidance Center (R&GC). That's where I first met Warden Scott, whom I told that I'd kick his ass. He never forgot that either. Unfortunately, I have trouble lying so when I entered the above information on my work applications it wasn't too surprising why I wasn't on anybody's short list for employment.

In the late 60's and early 70's my life started to turn around. Because I couldn't get a job I made a determined decision to get rehabilitated and get educated. Through adult education and

Lansing Community College (LCC), I finally achieved my high school diploma. Later on I received a completion certificate in social work from LCC and a large number of credits in psychology—enough to graduate if I'd returned.

During my years in school, I learned to read and write quite well. I became especially proficient in reading and understanding official policies, procedures and state legislation. Also, I started my volunteer work with juveniles. I used my criminal experience as a sounding board to identify with those young folks who were doing what I had done at the same age. I'd try to teach them that that's not going to work for them. And, then I'd try to encourage them to do something different.

After I gained some education I applied for work with the Department of Corrections. I certainly wasn't a shoo-in to get hired, but with the background of mental treatment and a felony record, I did qualify for what they referred to as handicapper status for employment. That status eventually allowed me to be appointed to a position before an interview ever took place. Finally, I was interviewed and passed, even by the doctor. I told him the truth, that I had mental problems as a child because my environment was pretty bad. Actually, I also had some health problems. For my height (5'10") I was pretty heavy (250) and I had phlebitis in one leg. They said, initially, that would be enough to keep me from getting hired, but thanks to the remedial action hiring program I made it through for a job appointment at Riverside Prison in Ionia. That was 1979.

When I reported for work in Ionia, the deputy warden said, "We are never going to hire you." So, I got a few tears in my eyes and left, made a few phone calls—one of which was to a circuit judge I knew. The judge called the deputy warden and told him if he didn't hire me he would be on the losing end of a lawsuit. Ten days later I was hired and went to work. Herb Grinage, who is a warden now, was my training officer. He said, "Bob, they're aiming to get your butt." I said, "They are going to have to work real hard."

I didn't work long at Riverside. For a while I was off on medical leave, then to get reinstated I had to file a grievance. When I returned to work it was in 1980 at the Michigan Dunes Correctional Facility in Saugatuck.

At Saugatuck I started being active in the MCO. In the Union I gained the reputation of being aggressive and forceful. I wrote memos and documented things that were wrong. As I said before, I was talented at reading and understanding regulations and with my aggressiveness I soon got under the skin of Warden Redman. In 1981 he terminated me. So, I filed a grievance and in 1983, after arbitration I returned to work and was awarded all my back pay and benefits. I was then assigned to the Central Complex at Jackson.

At Jackson I gained the reputation of always being in the thick of things. If there was a fight or major disturbance, on more than one occasion I was part of the goon squad the lieutenant sent in to quiet things down. When the cons saw my 250 to 300 pounds coming at them their first instinct was not to mess with me. That doesn't mean I wasn't assaulted, because I was, several times. Once, I was trying to close this door and a little guy hit me in the face about ten times. On another occasion there was a fight in front of 11 Block. I was in the south yard and the female dispatch called me on the radio and told me to send the yard crew in to break it up. I said, "I'm on my way." "Negative," she said, "Send the yard crew down." "Negative," I said, "I am the yard crew." I had been controlling 1,200 inmates in the south yard and now I was the lone ranger going to breakup a fight. Needless to say, we were really short staffed.

There also was the time when this short black female guard was trapped in a corner of the chow hall—surrounded by about 200 convicts. It was around Christmas time and I had dyed my hair to play Santa Claus for kids. The convicts were trying to get at her and the sergeant sent me in. Later, looking at the video film taken from the gun turret, you could see this white head wading through a sea of afros. Unfortunately, a lot of times I ended up getting hurt, punched, kicked and spit on.

After a while you get desensitized to working in this place. People have been stabbed and die right next to you—people bleeding to death, blood all over the floor.

One place that generated a significant amount of devious inmate activity was those areas associated with the JCC gate. I had a reputation of being a very conscientious correction officer so two of the assistant deputies requested that I volunteer for that assignment to straighten things out there. In fact, to make that happen, one of them, Richard Campbell, wrote a memo asking that I permanently be assigned to that post.

Supposedly, maintaining custody, security and control at the gate was the primary responsibility, however the duties really encompassed much more than that. The JCC gate controlled access to the entrance of special activities, the auditorium and Jackson Community College (JCC) area. Patrolling all these areas was part of the gate responsibility too, as I saw it. Some of the past gate officers had avoided doing this and that's really why they wanted me in there to bring things under control.

There were several areas inside the JCC gate that you had to keep an eye on, the hallways, the staircase leading up to the JCC and with the JCC gate locked behind you, it was necessary to check out the auditorium. Rounds in the auditorium involved checking the balcony, bathroom and stalls and 10 rooms underneath the auditorium. The auditorium was very dark and they didn't furnish us a flashlight. You had a hard time getting keys in the locks there, and sometimes the locks were just broken. Doors on the side of the auditorium were many times left unsecured. These doors needed to be checked as well as inside the JCC—the classrooms, etc.

Special activities held JCC, Vietnam vet and NAACP meetings. Next door to that was the prison legal service.

The JCC gate assignment had the potential to be a dangerous assignment. Especially, because of the number of prisoners usually in the areas, the many dark corners, the poor radio equipment the guard had and the fact that a lot of devious people were coming and going from prison legal services (PLS).

On more than one occasion drugs came through PLS and occasionally an inmate was arrested for that activity. Many were not. Frank Usher, known as Nitty, was up to that shit for years. He had a gold necklace worth about $5,000 and a diamond ring you could buy a car with. Another one was named Splash, both were either on call sheets or they had assignment cards for that area.

Then there was a homosexual inmate clerk down in NAACP. This "she" did sexual acts for money and carried dope. I know, not because I did her, but because someone else did. She got caught with $600 green money and it certainly wasn't from legal fees from convicts.

When I started on the JCC assignment Lieutenant McMurtie told me to stop all the sissy shit going on down there.

There were rumors of people from 4 Block having sex with 6 Blockers and eventually I got some information and busted three of them. Because I busted one of their sissies having oral sex with a 4 Blocker I heard there was a contract put out on me by one of their hit teams. I was told, "You get stuck next Mother Fucker!"

Not only was there a threat to me, Toormina, one of the inmates, was thought to be my snitch. He was stabbed 4 times in the throat. That really made me angry because he was a good inmate.

I knew that at least two of the prison clerks in PLS were homosexuals and doing their tricks on the premises. Stopping them was a problem. The trouble was that the hallway door adjacent to PLS was locked and I didn't have a key. It had a glass window in it that I could look through, but when one of the alleged perpetrators of homosexual acts and visitor to PLS came out of PLS into the hallway on their way to the restroom, there was no access to the hallway without going outside the building and coming up into the other end of the hallway. That would take some time and by then they would have left. What really irritated me was that there was one door in PLS that the inmates controlled electronically with a button from the inside. Another door to PLS I didn't even have a key to. To put it in a nutshell, the guards didn't have access to PLS if there was a lockdown. It was inmate controlled and stayed that way for years to come.

Curtailing the sexual activity in PLS was to be a real challenge. Trying to catch these guys was like being one of the old keystone cops. They go here; I go there. Sandy Girard who ran the PLS accused me of harassing and intimidating the people who worked there.

My main concern was not about the homosexual activity, but security in the whole area. I started to pick at it piece by piece and document things. Nobody had done that before. I was told not to do this, not to write it up because I would bring a bunch of shit on myself—which is exactly what happened.

Warden Scott told me to take any security issues up with Inspector Palmer. An Inspector was about the same level as a Captain in the prison structure. I sent a memo to Palmer with copies to ADW Roberts and Campbell. I detailed several security issues and the fact that guards didn't have access to the entrances to legal services. I mentioned the homosexual activity as an example of the need for access. Thanks to the prison grapevine my memo fell into the hands of Sandy Girard. She in turn sent a memo in response to mine accusing me of intimidating her staff and really not witnessing what I said was going on. A copy of her memo went directly to Warden Foltz and Deputy Warden Scott and worst of all it was circulated to about all of the prisoner staff in Central Complex. I was instantly enemy number one to the prisoners. I didn't like this because I had previously established a reputation of being fair with the cons and pretty easy going; take a lot of shit, give some slack, then draw the line.

There were other issues that added to my unpopularity. I started shaking down prisoner's briefcases that they brought through the JCC gate. Also, when I made my inspection tour of the auditorium I locked the JCC gate. After I finished my rounds and returned there were usually inmates banging on the gate waiting to get into PLS. If I would have left the gate open the inmates would have had free flow access to the area and invariably there would be a large number of skaters (inmates without authorization) hanging around. That's precisely what ADW Campbell wanted me to control.

The administrator of JCC wanted the gate closed when I wasn't at the station. She wanted me to run security tight. On the other hand Deputy Warden Scott wanted it left open like Sandy Girard.

I took my security concerns to Bob Hughes of the MCO and they were discussed with Deputy Warden Whelan and ADW Scott.

There were specific things I asked for to improve security but nothing happened. They'd say, "Just tell us what you need." Hell, I couldn't even get the God-damned area painted—or get a porter to clean up down there. If it got swept and mopped, I did it. Finally, I got a key to one of the PLS doors, but the cons could bolt it from the inside, so that didn't help.

The JCC area became a prime supply point for inmates and the Captain ordered us to stop the 'grocery flow'. Things would be dropped off by some inmates and picked up by others. Clearly this system kept a steady flow of contraband intact. I started confiscating the stuff and was told by Deputy Scott, "You won't do that, OK?"

As a Union representative I went to Scott and asked him to tighten up security in the chow hall. I also wanted to shakedown the lines of people going into the auditorium. The reason was, that the air in the auditorium was so saturated with marijuana smoke that I received a constant buzz when working in the area. If they had forced me to take a urine test I couldn't have passed, simply because of my work environment. I had a big discussion with Scott about that, and he more or less told me to go do something else.

In those years we had morale problems, staffing shortages, not enough radios, serious security concerns and no one seemed to care. I was union steward then and believe me, in our labor management meeting Deputy Warden Elton Scott and I fought like cats and dogs. There were too many problems around this institution and I was intent on solving some of them.

DW Scott and I did have a couple common interests that we could talk amicably about. He was a pilot; I wanted to be a pilot. Plus, we both had a genuine interest in helping kids. I played Santa Claus every year and I bleached my hair to play the part. Scott didn't think the hair bleaching was appropriate, until he got to reading about me. Finally, he was convinced about my sincerity in dealing with kids. I brought in a couple of magic tricks and showed him some tricks I do for them. However, when it came to the institution there was little we could agree on.

Warden Foltz was a man I respected. I can say that if other deputy wardens and wardens that I dealt with, had half the integri-

ty Dale Foltz had, they would make fine wardens. We had our dis-
agreements, but I always knew where Foltz was coming from and he
understood my positions. The problem was, that even though he was
the warden, sometimes he could get himself in farther than he should
have. He would agree to do something and sometimes he couldn't
always do it. Deputy Warden Scott and Robert Brown the Director
of Corrections had a close relationship. Need I say more? Eventually,
John Whelan came in to replace Elton Scott as Deputy Warden. I was
weary of all the fights with management, so I kind of backed off to
let Bob Hughes, the union president for Central Complex do it.

I was working in the Reception and Guidance Center (R&GC)
the day that Josephine was killed. I had met her husband, Bill, 20
to 25 years before that. Bill had an Austin Healy race car with a 327
engine in it. I was attending LCC classes and there was a gas
station over there where the car was. I admired Bill's car and we
met. I was back from the service and so was he; we kicked around
together a little.

When I found out Josephine was killed in JCC, I couldn't believe
that they had sent her down there.

I said, "Damn! That's stupid!" I felt bad for Bill. I called Senator
Welborn and told him that I considered that what had happened was
senseless to a point. That was my opinion at the time. I told
Welborn about the meetings with Foltz and all the memos I had sent
up about the security in the area. I considered the JCC gate assignment to be at least a job for two correction officers—certainly not
a one-month probationary officer with no experience. It was an
isolated assignment with the nearest supervisor 50 yards away and
out of sight. Quite honestly, if a corrections officer had been a
former guard, police officer or even in the FBI, I wouldn't put them
in that type of assignment with less than a month on the job. There
weren't even any post orders for that position.

I had met Josephine only once before and that was only in passing. I thought she was short and small to be working in a prison.
The problem was that not only was she probationary, but also she
was green. Possibly, if she had been there for several months and
established herself; the prisoners knew her, the guards knew her,

she could do the job, was quick on the radio and knew the orders and had basically established herself as a credible person who knows how to be a guard; if she fit that mold then possibly they could have given her one of the critical assignments.

Josephine was green. We referred to inexperienced guards like her as 'fish'. Common sense would tell you, you don't put fish in JCC. You don't put a fish in a single-officer isolated assignment. Those types of assignments required a degree of responsibility and knowledge a fish wouldn't have. You have to know what's happening or you don't go there.

To tell you the truth, I've worked with some female officers that I think are better than a lot of the male officers, and not because they are females, but because they are more dedicated and more intelligent. They pay attention to what's going on. But, to be in a custody assignment the personality must fit being able to walk up to 50 convicts and say, excuse me guys, you've got to go, and be able to say that with force and convince the convicts that they are going to have a handful of shit if they don't go where they got to or get tickets, or whatever and have the radio in hand. That type of authority doesn't come until that female has been there a while.

The first thing the inmates do with a new female guard is test them and see how close they can get. They also verbally abuse them. I don't know what they're told at the academy, but I've seen some new female guards turn white the first time an inmate tells them, "I'm gonna fuck your momma in the ass." This is common everyday language in the penitentiary. When it's directed toward a female it's more demeaning; cunt, slut, bush are common references. When they reach out and grab a female by the ass—they have nothing to lose. Personally, I've been threatened with violent sexual acts in 5 Block every time I walk through.

After Josephine's death a person that worked in the Control Center said don't tell—don't tell anybody I told you, but blah, blah, blah. I received a whole lot of that. Lots of people shared shit with me, because I tend to fight with everybody and as a union official I have aggressively supported several correction officers with grievances, including about 5 females.

There were a lot of rumors flying all over after Josephine's death, but the information I received seemed creditable enough to question whether or not her assignment was intentionally changed for some reason. In the Central Complex that was one of their favorite games. There were a couple cases that I know of where females got assigned at the Bakery gate because they weren't being friendly with the lieutenant. The Bakery gate was an isolated assignment with a lot of inmate traffic.

I have asked probably 50 to 100 people if they knew who made the assignments that day, who switched Josephine to the JCC from her original assignment and gave that to Ray McCormic. It was either Rakowski, McMurtrie or maybe Bitner—they were the kind to hit on new officers. Even if Rakowski wasn't actually responsible for assigning people a particular job, it is common knowledge around the penitentiary that pay backs are a bitch and a call to the assignment officer could make that happen. I tried to get the assignment sheet under the authority of the Union, so I could check it. Guess what was missing? I couldn't get that son-of-a-bitch so I firmly believe that somebody was covering somebody's ass for putting Josephine McCallum into that assignment. You just don't put a fish in JCC. It's not a matter of knowing policy, it's a matter of using common sense. You have to know what's happening or you don't go there. I know that just because I worked there.

If you asked me about instances where supervisors in a position to affect assignments have used the assignment as a mechanism to control female guards that don't cooperate, I can only tell you what I've seen. When one lady refused to continue a sexual relationship with her training supervisor, who was giving her passing grades, he beat her up, pulled her down the stairs and even blackmailed her. She filed charges. Soon it was rumored that she was playing with the inmates, which was false. But, when that word got out all kinds of shit happened to her. She was put on the Bakery gate and the turnstile down where the 4 Blockers go through. When she came around catcalls and verbal abuse were dished out routinely. The supervisor she reported her problems to actually was a friend of her perpetrator and this guy aided the other lieutenant in nailing her. I

was really angry at the lieutenant for getting involved with the
other lieutenant, because they are buddies, pals; but I definitely
know some phone calls were made and some information was
twisted and made to look like this lady was actually involved with
a convict, when she wasn't.

Another female officer I know of also ended her relationship
with a lieutenant and then he harassed the hell out of her. A couple
of other female officers questioned why they received particular
assignments and they received McMurtrie's famous reply, "Fuck
you, file a grievance."

When I was in R&GC a female C/O came there after being
routinely harassed in another section of the prison. I had discussed
the previous situation with her several times. In R&GC she and
another officer got written up for something completely ridiculous;
charged with arsonist behavior. She caught holy hell because she
didn't want to date and didn't want to play. I know that for a fact
because she complained to me.

There were a lot more grievances of that type, but I don't have
my notes any more. I got rid of most of that stuff when I transferred
out of R&GC.

During my employment with the Department of Corrections I
have held many positions with the MCO: steward, chief steward,
vice president and president of the local R&GC chapter for two
years. As much as my union activities meant to me, finally there
came a time when I wanted to get out of union work and try to be
one of the boys. I transferred to Transportation. When the prisoners
go from prison to prison or outside, for medical or court appear-
ances, that's my job to transport them. It was a plum assignment
that I wanted, but because of that work I am on a medical leave of
absence and in the process of receiving duty disability retirement.

What happened to cause my injury was that we had a gentleman
who was up for a sentencing court appearance in Jackson and he
became violent, and even though he was in restraints and chained,
he still hurt the county officer, my partner and myself. He rolled on
his back and when the county officer and I grabbed him, he
knocked my partner up against the bench on the corner and cracked

his back. I lunged for him, grabbing his feet. He rolled back and kicked me right below the knee with his chains, tearing ligaments and cartilage. That happened in January of '87 and it still hasn't healed. It cracks and pops and I have a limp, plus I have traumatic gout in the injury. I went back to work in the summer of '88, then went on medical leave again with surgery that fall. This spring it wasn't any better so I decided that my chances of going back to work are slim to none. Currently, I have been board approved for duty disability.

Robert Halmich and his admirers.

CLOSURE

In 1994 Senator Jack Welborn decided not to run for the Senate again. Probably the heart problems that had developed gave him a different perspective on life and he felt it was time to pursue something a little less stressful. He had his farm and family to enjoy and I couldn't blame him for the decision, but I did hate to see him go. Jack had done more to focus the public's attention on the problems in Michigan prisons than anyone I know. More than just pointing out the problems, he had been at the leading edge of those trying to improve the system, not only for the corrections officers, but also for the security of the inmates too.

There are probably those who would say that Senator Welborn would not have been so vocal on all the prison problems had there not been a governor and attorney general from the opposite political party in office. To those people, I would say that maybe with a different attorney general or governor, no matter which party they represented, he would have had their attention on the matter without resorting to the media and the Justice Department to get results. After all, I think there were scores of Democrats that wanted the system cleaned up too, it wasn't just Republicans.

My job as a Ombudsman came to an end when Jack left the Senate. Although we remain friends to this day, he distances himself from discussions of the prison chaos of the past. He probably figures he has paid his dues in that area, with it being time to move on. In retrospect, I think that perhaps I have burdened the Senator with my unceasing effort to find out more about Josephine's death. Maybe he's of the mindset, that sooner or later enough is enough and it is time for me to also get along with life and put it all behind me.

Many times I've read stories of people spending almost a lifetime trying to locate their lost children; about others pursuing the killer of their loved one long after both the public and law enforcement had lost interest. A good example of this was Muriel Kirby, a lady I had met with a victims rights group. After many years her persistence finally got her daughter's killer brought to justice. I wondered how these people kept motivated for the pursuit and I also questioned why they weren't willing to move on with life rather than dwelling on the past. It's been said that to understand you have to walk in their shoes. I think now, I can in part understand such feelings. At least I know how it is to be mentally driven to achieve some sort of rational ending to the disruption in my life that has caused so much grief.

From what I can tell, Michigan's prison system today isn't vastly improved over what it was in those years before and immediately after Josephine's death. There are new prisons with better security, a more adequate staffing level, and corrections officers with more education and experience walking the beat, but there are still some bad correction personnel who offset the positive. And, judging from the calls I receive, cover-ups still happen.

Some of the corrections officers, wardens, prison administrators and inmates that were there 16 years ago when it all happened are now not associated with the prison; many though still are. Certain wardens have been promoted, some corrections officers are now supervisors and others are just putting in their time for retirement. I am sure that whether they still work there now, have retired or found another line of work, that if they were involved with the day-to-day operation of the prison in the "old days," unpleasant memories still remain.

There is no doubt in my mind that there are those that know much more about what happened to Josephine than what they've told authorities. I also wonder if some of them were not directly involved in her death. Several who were active participants in the sexual harassment that was so widespread then, still are on duty today.

During my two years as Ombudsman for Senator Welborn, I was privy to much information that came through his office regarding problems at SMP. Also, as I have said so many times before, there was a wealth of information coming directly to me from corrections officers ever since Josephine's death. I was very active in trying to solicit this information, and eventually anyone there that was having work problems that they couldn't talk to their supervisor or the Union came to me.

Senator Welborn, with his sources, had a vast knowledge of the whole system. Some things he shared with me, other details he didn't fill me in on either unintentionally or maybe because he thought that I would go out on a limb I didn't need to be on if I knew.

Rumors and secondhand information may or may not be factual. However, when one hears things that fit a pattern or seem to support other rumors, such information seems quite creditable. Because so many people have been afraid to come forward with information, either because they fear for reprisals from their supervisors, co-workers or actually fear for their lives, it is not surprising why they do not want their name used. I can understand their reluctance, but I wonder how bad things have to be before more are brave enough to do so.

Without being too specific, I will try to recall a sampling of the things I have heard over the years that have kept rekindling my determination to discover what happened inside those walls.

Sexual Harassment

I still have detailed notes as to sexual harassment charges brought inside of SMP during the years shortly before and after Jo's employment there. The list contains the names of Lieutenants, Captains, a few Sergeants and other corrections officers. Judging from all the comments made to me I'm convinced that the list is only a minuscule fraction of the harassment that actually took place. Most went unreported.

Is it unusual that sexual harassment took place inside of a workplace that had previously been an all male environment? Of course not! Should the administrators of the prison been able to foresee the possibility of such harassment and conducted meaningful training for all employees? Yes. Should the administration have set up the type of reporting system that could deal with the problem without retribution to the person lodging the complaint? Yes again, however here was an administration that had been unable to deal with internal crime and corruption for 30 years plus. It would be highly optimistic to think they could handle sexual harassment.

Even the Union seemed ineffective in handling sexual harassment. It probably was because some of the Union officials were problems themselves. There was a lot of distrust of the Union and it's policies, however in other areas Union presence did a lot to improve things.

Snowbirds

The buses used to transport prisoners between prisons were rumored to be an excellent way to transport drugs. Another advantage was that at convenient times the prisoners on the road would temporarily relieve numbers, which reflected overcrowding of a particular state prison. That was very significant in the time frame when fines were being levied against the State for the overcrowding. This practice was documented and illegal.

Sex in the prison

Did certain female correction officers receive choice assignments, promotions and favoritism for providing sexual favors to supervisors? I heard this over and over from people inside. I'm sure this happened, but knowing how often misinformation was injected into the system it would be unfair to label specific individuals with this behavior without knowing for sure.

Did some female corrections officers have sex with male residents? Yes, but I doubt that it was widespread. If an unattractive female corrections officer was smooth talked by some handsome male resident, depending on her personality, she could become quite

vulnerable. If such a relationship was establis^
normally use it to maximum advantage. Doin^
inmate would usually lead to larger favors ar.
doing the favors wanted to stop that activity th^
mailed, personally threatened or even have their 1

Was there sex between male guards and male r̩   ̩ Several
told me there was. It wasn't a thing that was bragged about. Was
there sex between residents? Absolutely; that certainly was no secret.

Drugs in the prison

This was well established and reported as was the fact that corrections officers, other prison employees and resident visitors
brought in drugs and alcohol for inmates. There also were reports
of confiscated drugs disappearing. I learned there were even video-
tapes showing that certain employees were allowed to walk around
metal detectors in the prison. I heard many specifics—some of it
had to be quite creditable.

How high up did the drug money flow? Other than what I've
read in the papers I really don't know. Drugs bring in a lot of money
and it was well established that administrators were very tolerant of
its presence in the State's prisons. Were they tolerant because they
had something to gain, or was it because they for some reason
believed that inmates using drugs were less of a problem than they
would be without that influence.

I am completely convinced from what I have heard, that Jo's
reassignment to the JCC was because she rejected the advances of
a sergeant supervisor. Were C/O's directly involved in her murder?
I have heard it from enough different sources that I believe that to
be the case. Some suggested that correction officers had intentionally set up Jo so that a rescue situation could be initiated; this might
convince her to become a little more cooperative with her supervisors in the future. Supposedly, this had happened before, involving
the same group of people.

There was a lot of speculation as to how Jo's assailant or
assailants gained access to her area. Many people offered their
opinions, but really only those involved know for sure. If there are

who actually know they haven't stepped forward to tell their story. I can only say that from those that worked with Jo and knew her work habits, there was the opinion that she wouldn't easily be hoodwinked into opening the gate unless she was sure that person should have access to her area. My theory is that she opened the gate for Hill accompanied by a corrections officer. The coat on the phone box at her station was observed by everyone in the area and assumed to be hers, however Jo's coat had been found on the stage with her bloody blazer. Whose coat was on the phone box then? It was never mentioned as evidence or property in the official report and seemed to disappear. I believe it belonged to a corrections officer involved at the scene.

There was the possibility put forth that she could have walked in on a drug deal or sex act and killed and raped as a cover up. Everyone I've talked to seem to think that more than one person was involved, but that there was no premeditated plan to murder her, just the intent to scare or change her thinking.

It is very important for me to tell as much as I can about our lives before and after Josephine's death. I want others to see how this despicable act has affected our lives and how her work environment directly contributed to her death. I think that far beyond the presence of mind that we may gain from telling this story is the closure it may offer to the other men and women who have worked in corrections and know first hand the hideous nature of those years in the state prison system. In essence, this is also their story. There were then, and are now, a lot of dedicated, hard-working, caring people within Michigan's prisons. In no way do I want to tarnish their reputations.

With today's new techniques and technology I think a more thorough testing of all the evidence collected for Hill's trial should be conducted. If DNA, fingerprints or other fluid testing indicated the possible involvement of someone in addition to Hill, I think that a reinvestigation has to be conducted. I believe the first investigation was seriously flawed because they too quickly narrowed down their field of suspects to only Hill and that the possibility of correction officer involvement was never really addressed. With everyone's prints on file why weren't fingerprints taken at the crime scene? From so many sources I've heard about the sergeant that left work with deep scratches on his neck that day, and how the entrance from the quartermaster's area was used as a C/O exit route from the auditorium.

People have told me that MSP Investigator Piziali has stumbled more than once in his investigations and for my peace of mind we need to put some of the rumors associated with Jo's death to rest. If others were involved, they need to be brought to justice, no matter how long it takes.

There are other matters that leave a bitter taste in my mouth. One is the educational support promised by the MCO for Mike. Initially, the amount was $25,000. That was supposed to be the amount available for his college when the original contribution matured. The MCO paraded us around with a big oversized cardboard check indicating that amount. When the time came for him to receive the money it had "grown" to less than $8,000. That was a real surprise to us. To make up the difference Mike tried to get loans and a grant. It was very difficult because I didn't have much money to help. What hurt most over the years was the lack of any moral support from an organization that is supposed to exist for correction officers and their families.

We probably alienated a lot of folks with our lawsuit against the State and then the one against key Corrections Department officials. However, I believe the shabby, cold shoulder treatment Mike and I received from these people should be a real embarrassment to them. Maybe I just must realize that these folks have been covering their political asses for so long that it is difficult for them to show any compassion for their workers, let alone admit to the shoddy system they administered.

AUTHOR'S PERSPECTIVE

It is unfortunate that MSP detective Piziali didn't establish communications with Bill McCallum at the beginning of the investigation and at least keep him generally informed on the progress of the investigation.

Early on he met with Jo's brothers and informed them on the investigation, but the brothers never mentioned the meeting to Bill, and he wasn't invited. Bill thought that they probably told Piziali that he wasn't interested. Bill felt isolated from the official investigation and was suspicious of its integrity. I had the impression that for some reason, Piziali wanted to keep Bill isolated. In one report Piziali left instructions, 'If Mr. McCallum calls for his wife's watch (item #30) give it to him. Do not allow him to review this report.'

It seems to me that SPSM investigators and Piziali were fairly thorough in interviewing witnesses, both corrections officers and inmates involved in the case. When there was testimony that was questionable there seemed to be a concerted effort to cross check its accuracy and determine who was telling the truth and who was not. As far as I could discern through, there never was much thought to check for corrections officers involvement.

Bill had the newspaper reports and calls from correction officers inside the prison to formulate his theory of what had happened to Josephine. And, the fact that he had been threatened several times, added a new dimension to the picture he was seeing.

Different from the official investigator, Bill suspected officer involvement in Jo's death. He knew that Josephine had been harassed and threatened by co-workers and he knew from media accounts that the system was very corrupt. Without being privy to the official investigation to crosscheck what he was hearing, he was seeing only one side of the picture.

It became quite evident to me that a faction of the inmate population was trying to fabricate a story that corrections officers were directly involved in Josephine's rape and murder and Hill was the scapegoat. They tried to get this story to Bill's attorney and I imagine to Welborn. In the form of confiscated letters the story even made it's way to Bill. I would also guess, that it found it's way through the inmate population and to receptive corrections officers. Perhaps even some of the anonymous phone calls to Bill were tied into that effort.

One of the letters that reached Bill suggesting correction officer involvement was from an inmate on the investigators list that was in the JCC area on the 24th. However, when investigators checked out the letter the resident denied signing his name to it or having any knowledge of what the letter actually contained. In other letters, some of the facts within were so grossly inaccurate that it pretty much canceled out the rest of the message as far as I was concerned.

Much of the same information the inmates were supplying others eventually found its way to Piziali and was addressed in the official report. One letter was forwarded directly to Piziali from Welborn. It addressed the door leading from the quartermaster shoe repair room to the auditorium and how Jo had been beating on it and screaming as she was being attacked. This was the same door that other sources alluded to as the auditorium exit area for officers involved in Jo's attack. When the door was inspected it appeared not to have been used in years. In fact one lock had to be beat off because no key was available to unlock it. A table filled with repair equipment also blocked it. Sound tests were conducted and it was difficult to hear any noise on the other side at all. Finally when the supposed author of the letter was confronted he had no knowledge of what the letter contained and finally denied even writing it.

Key inmate testimony did place Hill in the JCC area at the same time that Josephine arrived for her assignment. Landon Mitchell was the inmate providing this information and it all started over a dollars worth of rice.

That morning one of the commissary workers was Michael James. James had been locked in one of the commissary food storage areas to inventory supplies. It was normal procedure to keep this area tightly controlled, otherwise many items would be slipped out to fuel a black market business within the general population of the prison.

James already had such an enterprise going and one transaction involved a quantity of rice for inmate Landon Mitchell. James had Mitchell's money, but Mitchell had not received the rice.

Mitchell worked in the JCC area and said that he intentionally arrived early, at 07:35, to confront James as to why he hadn't gotten his rice. He couldn't find James, but he talked to Mexico (Merryman) on the commissary dock. Mexico said that James was locked in the food storage cage doing inventory and he would talk with him. When Mexico returned, he said that James would see Mitchell in the afternoon and have his rice then.

Mitchell didn't believe that Mexico was telling the truth. A heated argument resulted which escalated into the exchange of loud, vulgar remarks. Food Service Supervisor Follick heard the argument and ordered Mexico off the dock and back inside the commissary. Mexico's friend Hill also heard the argument. He came from the front of the truck, where he had been talking with Sabrina Johnson, and confronted Mitchell.

"Mexico is my middle man, and I don't like the way you been talking to him. I think I should just stick you in the neck."

Hill had no more than made the threatening statement when C/O Josephine McCallum walked up beside them, opened the JCC door, and entered. According to Mitchell, Hill immediately followed McCallum through the door. It was as if he had been waiting for her.

Mitchell didn't know Hill, but he said that he took his threat seriously. He felt the need for some support on the matter. While Hill was absent Mitchell left the dock and woke up his friend, Lyles Bay, in 11 Block. Lyles Bay was serving life sentences for two different murders. He agreed to go down to the commissary with Mitchell to settle the rice dispute and deal with Hill.

When Mitchell and Lyles Bay went in the JCC area the gate was locked, an officer's coat was hanging on the phone box, but neither Hill nor the officer were present.

Mitchell and Lyles Bay then located Mexico. Mexico again explained why James could not now get Mexico his rice, because he was locked in the food storage area. Lyles Bay seemed to understand the situation and convinced Mitchell that everything was OK and that he was not being cheated out of his rice. Lyles Bay returned to his block and Mexico waited on the dock with some other inmates until JCC instructor Brian Ennis opened the gate, letting them in to work.

Piziali, ADW Grinage and I&I investigator Verlin witnessed Mitchell's written statement at 10:49 the morning of the murder and a few minutes later Piziali conducted a taped interview with Mitchell confirming the statement. Lyles Bay's statement was taken next and it supported what Mitchell had told them.

The only problem was that the truck driver, C/O Eddy, had reported seeing two big black residents follow McCallum into the JCC area with the door being closed behind them. To begin with Hill certainly wouldn't be considered a large man and Mitchell said only Hill followed her in. Also, another inmate, Arthur Blank, said that when he arrived at the outside JCC door Mitchell said, "You can't go in there." Lyles Bay, the inmate that initially confirmed Mitchell's statement, refused to testify when Hill's trial came up.

Later Piziali confirmed that Mitchell had entered the JCC with instructor Brian Ennis. It seems that C/O Eddy's observation of the two entering behind McCallum was disregarded by Piziali in favor of Mitchell's version. Obviously, one would question what really happened.

Sometime after the gate was open inmate Burke reported to Piziali that he saw Hill come out of the auditorium, look up the JCC stairwell and go back in the auditorium. A few minutes later Burke said Hill reemerged from the auditorium and exited the JCC through the gate that had been left open. He said that Hill's pants were spotted with something.

Piziali later threw out Burke's statement because Burke said that the only way he would testify in court is if they gave him a deal and pardoned him for the rest of his sentence. There were other facts that Burke was unaware of that made his statement look false to Piziali anyway.

Taking into consideration all the statements made to the investigators and the semen and blood evidence from Hill and McCallum's clothes, there seems to be little doubt that Hill was directly involved in Josephine's murder. Even Hill's defense attorney, conceded to that. Plus, on more than one occasion Hill made incriminating statements to a lot of people. To C/O Worley and Thorton at 09:40 on the morning of the murder he said, "I hope that bitch is dead. I hope she dies if she's not dead already!"

After Hill was briefed on a misconduct ticket given him by C/O Worley for grabbing Worley's shirt through the bars, Sgt. Garrison asked Hill if he wanted a hearing investigator on the matter. Hill responded, "Ask that bitch if she wants a hearing investigator."

The questions that remain in this case are:

1) Was Hill assisted in this assault on McCallum by others?
2) Was this a spur of the moment decision by Hill to follow McCallum into the JCC area or had Hill been waiting for her, being told ahead of time of her assignment there?
3) Had there been a conspiracy by McCallum's supervisors to reassign her to the JCC gate either as punishment for her not being receptive to their advances or to persuade her into becoming more cooperative?
4) Was Hill made part of the plot to make Josephine more cooperative?
5) Had other inmates been involved in planning an attack on Josephine or had she inadvertently entered into some situation within the auditorium that sealed her fate?
6) Finally, how did Hill get into the JCC area, behind a locked gate, to be a threat to McCallum?

At this point in time, 16 years after her death, I can only specu-
late on the chain of events that led to Josephine's death. There are
those that surely know more details as to what really happened on
that day. Whether or not they will ever come forward or be interviewed again on the matter is doubtful.

Hill has been unwilling to respond to my letters, which offered
him the opportunity to tell his side of the story. For an individual
that claimed to be innocent and said others were involved in front
of the TV cameras, to not want to speak up at this time either seals
his guilt or assures his protection within the system.

With Hill neatly packed away in prison for life, for many, that is
the end of the story. For others, particularly Bill McCallum, there
are many unanswered questions that should have been investigated
more thoroughly. Bill will need those areas to be addressed before
he can truly have any real peace of mind.

For instance, it should have been obvious to investigators that
Merryman (Mexico) knew or was more involved in what happened
than was ever indicated in their report. According to testimony by
C/O Jeanne Shappee both Hill and Merryman were running in and
out of the JCC before Follick spotted Hill and ordered him to go
back to his block. Even inmate Harris had seen Follick chasing both
Hill and Merryman out of the JCC area after Josephine's death.

When Merryman was initially interviewed he lied to protect Hill.
Later in the interview he demanded an attorney. Investigators never
did reinterview him, just kept him in administrator segregation. Also,
from Merryman's cell, C/O Edward Morris confiscated one pair of
Levi's still damp and one pair of prison blues still soaking in water
in a wastebasket. These were kept as evidence for testing, but no test
results were ever released. It is questionable that they were even tested. Added to this, the fact that C/O Halliwell had reported seeing
Merryman running down the sub-hall after the lockdown signal.

All this non-attention to Merryman was based on a statement by
Food Service Supervisor Follick, that Merryman had not been out
of his sight. That statement by Follick appeared to be inaccurate.

C/O Donna King was working in the dining room the day before
Josephine was killed. An inmate came up to her and said, "Officer

King, I like you so I'm going to tell you not to come in tomorrow."
Later, another inmate asked King, "Officer King, are you going
back to 4 Block?"

"Yes," she replied.

"Well keep your head up—they are going to get some more officers, OK? I don't know whether they are serious or not, but they
appear to be." King informed Lt. McMurtrie about what she had
been told.

No other information came to light to support the theory of an
inmate plot against correction officers, however Hill did seem to
have some reason for being in the JCC that morning before
Josephine arrived. Follick had actually gone inside the area behind
Hill and said, "You don't need to be in here!" One has to wonder
why Hill was in there. Did he know that McCallum would be on
duty? Was he in there to look for her?

Although inmates and spud juice were a common combination at
SMP, was there any reason that Hill would have been drinking on
this particular morning? Was it pure coincidence or had he received
information about a preplanned change in assignment for
McCallum and he was preparing himself for the assault. If Hill were
planning something, it probably would have been part of the discussion with Merryman as they sat drinking that morning in Hill's
cell. There was no indication from Follick that Hill had ever shown
up drunk previously and even Follick admitted that prior to this
incident he had been a good foreman and better than average work-
er. Then again, maybe it was just the spud juice alone that put
Hill in the frame of mind to attack Josephine. Follick did say that
on the 24th Hill was very aggressive. As was reported by the guard
in the previous chapter, liquor could make certain inmates very
violent.

As far as how Hill got behind the JCC gate; after Hill followed
Josephine through the JCC door, it probably would not have been
difficult for him to push his way through the gate before she
relocked it, or maybe he bull-shitted his way in and she thought he
was the porter that worked there. If she smelled the liquor on his
breath she was probably concerned.

There was no evidence of a struggle behind the gate. An officers state coat was hung on the phone box. It was never identified as being hers, so whose was it? Why was she on the stage in the auditorium? Did she follow Hill in to see what he was up to, or could he have lured her inside under the guise of showing her the facility. Possibly the coat on the phone box belonged to a correction officer already behind the gate.

Some have hinted that Hill forced Josephine into the auditorium, however unless he had a knife to her throat I think she would have struggled to keep herself in an area where there was a phone and possibly her screams could be heard by others. On his previous assaults Hill had used a weapon of some sort to threaten his victims. In this case, no weapon was found.

Maybe Hill was intent on getting into the auditorium to meet other inmates for drugs or sex. Previously, the auditorium had been notorious for such activity. If that was the case perhaps Josephine walked in surprising them and the assault and murder were the result. With as many as 80 prison passkeys unaccounted for, it wouldn't have been difficult for other parties to enter and exit the auditorium without being detected.

Hill was physically not much larger than Josephine, so almost everyone felt that Hill must have had help to subdue her. One thing was certain, Josephine received extensive facial blows. Hills right fist was freshly bruised and judging from scattered clothes and buttons a violent struggle took place. Had there been other assailants to help Hill she might have been more easily subdued. As it was, the struggle seemed to start left of the piano, then move around from in front of the stage to the east side behind a cabinet and a pillar.

From the autopsy it was evident that Josephine did her best to fight off her assailant (assailants), both her right and left knuckles showed bruising. Possibly early blows to her head provide Hill with time to start removing her clothes, but then because she fought him off so violently he was forced to struggle with her from the east side of the stage around to the pillar where her head was slammed against the cart or something very hard which incapacitated her. Probably that is where the belt was applied to her neck and the savage rape took place. From the blood smears on Hill's shirt it appeared that he then dragged her down the stairway. Possibly a voice from the open auditorium door interrupted his act forcing him to relocate her to the bottom of the stairway to continue the rape. Remember Leaphart heard noises there when he entered the auditorium and when he returned past the stairway to climb up on the stage.

I wonder if Leaphart, the inmate playing the piano that alerted Sgt. Hartsuff of the blood and radio on the stage, knew more than he admitted. Leaphart was really fearful of reprisals from Hill if he testified at Hill's trial. Why would Hill put out a hit warning on Leaphart unless Leaphart actually saw Hill in the area and knew of his involvement?

Now to address the possibility that Josephine was reassigned for her refusal to be involved sexually with other correction officers. All I can say is that it had been done in the past to others and that the notable absence of the assignment sheets for some period after the murder gave the scheduler plenty of opportunity to doctor the paper work and cover some tracks or at least create an envelope of suspicion that the records were being altered.

One might also wonder why Josephine's station wagon had been torn apart by those assigned merely to look for her ID. And, why prison officials were snooping around Bill and Jo's house shortly after her death. Although no one ever explained it to Bill, I am sure that they were looking for some evidence that might connect Josephine to illegal activity with the inmates, like transporting drugs into the prison. Guards had smuggled such material into the prison before so I think it was reasonable that they address the possibility, but it certainly was a clumsy effort at best. Judging from the fact that she had only been working there for 21 days, it seems like they would have realized that there just wasn't enough opportunity for her to get involved or even have knowledge of the drug trade inside.

Considering the threat environment surrounding Bill and Mike, I'm really not sure who was responsible. It could have been either employees or inmates that felt Bill's poking around in illegal prison affairs was a threat. It also might have been inmates trying to add creditability to the story that Hill was innocent and corrections officers were involved. Then again, Bill might have generated fear in certain corrections officers by allowing accusations against them to filter into the prison rumor mill.

Now if it appears that I have left more questions unanswered than answered, let me add some more loose ends to it.

No one ever explained or tested the blond hair on Hill's pants fly. It was reported not to be Josephine's. Also, many prints were found on different pieces of evidence, but those prints were compared only to Josephine, Hill, Leaphart and Archie Baker. These prints should have been run against more people, both employees and inmates. As far as I know it was never proven that the belt around Jo's neck was Hill's or were prints removed from it and checked.

Officer Alfred Lee at first told several people that he had walked into the auditorium to look for Josephine, but later he said that he didn't, that he just entered the cage, removed her coat from the phone box to check the extension number, and because he was worried about being late to his own assignment he left. Inmates Blank and Thompson were watching Lee that morning. They said that Lee asked where the officer on duty was. They said, 'back there' motioning to the auditorium door. In fact, inmate Blank said that he at that time heard the noise from a walkie-talkie radio coming from the partially open auditorium door. When Lee left the area Thompson said to Blank. "She's in the auditorium. Why didn't he go in there?"

Why didn't Lee go into the auditorium and look for Josephine? He had already been in the Control Center after his report time to 8 Block and then left to go down to the JCC to see her. If he were that concerned about being late why would he have gone down there to begin with? Did Lee know something was going on in the auditorium, and for his reasons did not want to get involved?

And finally, why was Sergeant Cotton, the south yard supervisor let off the hook so easily? That morning he was officially Jo's immediate supervisor. Cotton knew that Jo was a probationary officer who had never performed the JCC gate duty because that morning she had asked him directions on how to get there. Neither did he explain her duties or even check on her at that position. Cotton was neither reprimanded nor interviewed very extensively. In fact, not long after that he was actually promoted.

On the other hand, Food Service Supervisor Follick faced a disciplinary hearing on allegations against him arising out of the events of March 24th. Had his supervisor, Kenneth Martin, allowed him to send Hill back to his cell for being drunk, Josephine might still be alive. As it is now, Follick is also dead—shotgunned a couple years ago.

The Rest
of the
Story

Rod McLean

McLean has no intention of retiring from his auto repair shop even though he is crowding eighty years of age. Located just north of the Grand River on North Grand River Avenue in Lansing, for many this building and business holds as much historical significance as the well-known Dodge Estate down the road. That's because Rod McLean, the owner, has been elevated to celebrity status in the minds of many people.

In his youth Bill McCallum and many other car loving young boys hung around Rod's garage on a regular basis. As Rod put it, "The door was open and they just kept coming in." He helped them fix up their cars and they watched him at his craft, soaking up the basics of auto mechanics. Any schoolteacher would have been envious of his hold on their learning potential. Of course the fact that he had been associated with some of NASCAR'S most prestigious drivers did a lot to elevate his status with the boys, and I'm sure that they were fascinated when this guy did everything without using his legs. Most of all, I think what bound them to this man was his acceptance of them.

However minor Rod's part in this story is, I felt it wouldn't be complete without finding out a little more about him. Away from the tragedy of this books story, it seemed a much better conclusion to the whole thing.

Rod sat in his battery-operated cart on one side of his desk and I sat on the opposite side. I asked how his injury occurred.

"Football," he said, "A spinal injury. I had back trouble all winter after I was hit and the doctors couldn't figure out what was the matter." He continued, "Of course they didn't have all the things they have today to find out, but at that time I had the impression they didn't really care."

It was 1939 and he was 15 years old and on the freshman football team at Lansing Central High School when the accident happened. It wasn't long after that when he lost the use of his legs.

Rod's brother and he had an interest in automobiles long before he was injured. It all started when the two of them made a clever trade, of a washing machine motor for an old Model T Ford. They would drive it around the driveway of the Dodge Mansion and when no one was watching they'd be out on the road with it.

Yes, Rod's grandfather was the Dodge that built the house. He was an attorney from Ohio and his wife was a Turner. Rod's family moved into the mansion with the grandparents when he was 18 months old and he lived there until 1958.

The brothers progressed from a Model T to a Ford Model A and more advanced cars later. In high school they took auto mechanics classes, but a good share of their mechanical skills came the hard way, through trial and error. During the war Rod worked at Hill Diesel. They made large engines for generators and compressors, the bulk of the work for the navy.

After the war Rod and his brother ran a garage together until 1954, then they moved and built at the present location. His brother finally joined the faculty of a local college and Rod continued to run the garage and began to immerse himself into modified racing cars. He teamed up with a brother-in-law who owned a large company called Airlift, and together they entered their racecars into some of NASCARS most prestigious races with drivers that today are celebrities themselves. Their drivers included Lee Petty, Paul Goldsmith, Darrel Darenger, Buck Baker and Jim Paschal.

Rod's racecars were there when both the Dayton and Atlanta Super Tracks were opened. He also was in partnership on a car with John Demmer who owned an Oldsmobile dealership in Lansing. The racing participation lasted until the mid 60's when it got too costly to stay involved. For a couple of years Rod tried his hand at teaching mechanics at the Lansing Community College, but decided that what he wanted most was to continue running his own garage on North Grand River Avenue.

Rod's garage is painted maize and blue on the outside and with all the University of Michigan football paraphernalia inside there is no doubt that the owner is a very staunch U of M football fan. Rod's dog Bo, the Black Lab named after the famous Michigan coach has passed on, and Millie the Pit Bull who was named after the coach's wife has too, but the owner of the garage is going strong and living in the future not the past. And, Lord help any Spartan (like myself) who has the audacity to suggest that sometime in the future the U of M football team may not be great.

Rod McLean

Robert Halmich

from Deanna

My father, Robert Halmich, loved Christmas. He would sit in a beauty parlor for hours while they dyed his hair white for him to play, Santa Claus. Christmas was so important to him because more than anything else he loved kids and wanted to make life better for those that were having difficulty because of broken homes or poverty.

Dad didn't talk at all about his parents other than letting me know his childhood had been an unhappy one. For a while he had been an orphan, and then spent several years with his grandparents. Because his years as a kid had been so miserable he was driven to make life a little happier for those kids that might be in a similar situation.

Although Christmas was the highlight of his year, his generosity with money and time for kids was year-round.

Dad formed The Greater Lansing Children's Fund and through the years he would solicit money from local business' to help carry on his work. One of the local judges was treasurer of the fund. At Christmas time he would walk from business to business with his newly dyed hair and beard and ask for their help.

Dad purchased two busses from the city of Ann Arbor to haul kids around. He drove one and my husband drove the other. Every Wednesday he would fill the two busses with kids and take them roller-skating. He charged each one 50 cents, then after roller-skating he fed them all at a pizza parlor or someplace. Dad also took them to church. In fact, he was even kicked out of one church because he had brought in so many kids.

Another thing he would do during the holidays was to visit the jails. If an inmate didn't have any money in his account he would make sure that the inmate's children got gifts.

My Dad never mentioned to anyone that I was his adopted daughter. As far as he was concerned I had always been his daughter. When we first met I was nine years old and had been continually in trouble with the law. He was a voluntary probation officer and took me under his wing, then adopted me. He had two sons then, Jessie and Jordon.

I'm sure to a lot of people my father was a rather crude individual. Profanity was part of his demeanor with the F-word used regularly. At one time he was a hard drinker and even though he hadn't drank for a long time I think that the kidney and liver failure that eventually killed him could be traced back to the drinking years.

Dad had three wives. I think he lost the first one from his drinking, the second because she got tired of him bringing all these kids home all the time and when he died he had just been blessed with a son (Jacob) from his third wife. Jacob was born on Valentines Day and Dad died on March 4th in 1992.

My Dad was a big man (360 lbs. when he died) and a tough one too. One night he jumped into the middle of a fight to break it up and was shot in the stomach. He took the gun away from the guy and then went back into the bar with blood all over his shirt and continued dancing. The police came and tried to take him to the hospital, but he just gave them the gun and told them to leave him alone until he was ready to go.

I would always tell my Dad how much I loved him. I'd say, "Daddy I love ya."

He'd say, "Give me some money then." I'd always go get him a nickel and he would flip it in his ashtray. When he died the container was running over with nickels. On my son's gravestone we had the nickels all fixed in a row around the stone.

My son would probably be here today if my Dad had lived longer. Dad was the only male influence in his life and with Dad gone my boy got into trouble with the law. He finally committed suicide at the county jail.

Some of the kids Dad helped I still have contact with and they have done very well in life; others, Dad would have been disappointed, in how their lives turned out.

I really miss my Dad. Every time I see a nickel I think of him. Christmas will never be the same without him. I think that at Christmas time many others will think of him too, especially if they were one of those kids that rode his busses.

After my father died the Lansing Main Street Association presented a memorial plaque to us that was inscribed:

BOB HALMICH

~ ~ ~

SANTA CLAUS

Robert Halmich (Santa) and his new son Jacob.

Deanna at her fathers grave.

BILL McCALLUM

$\mathcal{Is}$ this the end of the journey? Not likely. My interest in what really happened on March 24, 1987, has never faded and unexpected things still happen to remind me. For instance, this last summer I stopped in Portland, Michigan to get a pizza to-go. My last name was called for pick-up, and as I started for the counter a large female in a corrections officer uniform blocked my passage. She demanded to know if I was Josephine McCallum's husband. I replied, "Yes, why?" She then proceeded to let me know that a bastard like me, trying to stir up all that shit was just making her union look bad. "Plus, all your poking around made it hell for all women in Corrections ~ just stop!"

This lady's attack on me really was a surprise as I hadn't been actively involved in this for years. She really got me riled though and I barked back, "The hell with you. This is what makes me do it more."

Now she turns to the waitress and loudly says, "Cancel my orders! I won't eat in a place that serves scum like him." Then, she storms out the door leaving both the waitress and myself rather stunned.

End of the journey?—No way. I'm here for the duration, until justice is satisfied. If the book encourages more people who were there to come forward, then I will listen to them and ask questions. I'm sure the circle of suspects will expand and with new DNA testing a conclusion quite different from that of the first investigation may evolve.

When Josie died, I set two goals for myself. First, I'd raise Michael in a stable, loving home. I think that's been accomplished and now he's an adult on his way to becoming a successful actor and film producer.

My second goal was to do my best to find out who additionally was involved in the horrible acts that were done to her, from sexual harassment by her superiors to her sadistic violent death at the hands of Hill and possibly others.

Hill or Mustafa Abullah Ali, as he is known now, is spending his days in solitary, far from the bustle and "freedom" of Jackson, while others are just quietly serving their time or have been paroled. Then we have the co-workers, who have been promoted and tucked away to work toward retirement and blessed anonymity.

And, for the Corrections Department and the State this whole thing has been a mere "bump in the road", that has been steam rolled and tucked away out of sight—too soon forgotten, Josephine McCallum.

Michael and Bill McCallum

"Josie, your tragic death leaves a gaping hole in my life and Michael's. The loss of your humor and love are missed every day. Justice will not bring you back or lessen the loss, but justice needs to run its honest course for us to be satisfied."

MICHAEL

J sit here trying to find a way to sum this all up; to neatly tie-up all my feelings and emotions. The truth is, this is impossible for me to do. It's taken me a long time just to write these last few pages. I think part of it is just the fact that it will actually be over with. It's been an emotionally draining and cathartic experience. This whole project has been years in the making and the more I initially pushed it away, and ignored it, the more I've gotten wrapped-up in it this last year.

It's difficult trying to put all my friendships and how I feel about things into a few pages, but I'll try.

To start off, during and after high school my small circle of friends eventually became unglued. People moved and I had some falling outs with Levertis and Steve over things that now seem somewhat trivial. A lot of things have been said here that chronicle the bad times while I was growing up, but there were so many good times with them that were shared when I wasn't in school. I look back on those times in my childhood, growing up with all of them, and I'm thankful and appreciate them so much.

In the 9th grade Justo moved to Wachington D.C. with his parents. When he returned the next year, he seemed a little different. We again were friends for a while. At the time I was skipping school a lot and he even gave me hell for smoking a few joints when we were sophomores. In our junior year I didn't touch the stuff and stopped hanging around the crowd that did. Later on in high school he got into pot and didn't even finish up. I heard he dropped out and later got his GED.

Jerrod was sent to prison our senior year of high school. He vandalized some property up north and received an extremely long prison sentence of three years. I think he more than paid his debt back to society. While he was in prison, I stayed in close contact with him. We wrote letters back and forth and I sent him books to help pass the time. He would call when he could and I also took periodic trips up to see him. I felt our contact was something we both needed.

While in prison Jerrod earned his GED and since he's been released he's gotten a very good job at GM, and also has become a father. He's probably one of the hardest working guys I know and considering everything he's been through he's also very resilient. Over the years he and I have continued to be very close. He's one of my best friends and one of a handful of people I know that would help me if I was in a bind.

Tina's son Steve and I had been very close growing up. Other than Levertis, there was no one I was closer to. My father would go pick up Steve and his younger brother Josh and bring them out to our house for long periods of time; sometimes weeks on end. I think it did all of us a lot of good to be around each other. Many times as kids, Steve and I would set up these elaborate military bases in our basement. It would take us days to put them together and we would use all my super heroes and G.I. Joes. My father would come down stairs to do laundry and enjoy the intricate battle laid out on the tiled floor.

I went through a lot of growing up and maturing with Steve. As Steve got older he had different jobs and worked to get himself clothes. When you're a kid fashion and fitting in, mean a lot. Steve and I didn't have a lot growing up, but we learned to make do with what we had. We both were always respectful of what little we did have and tried our best to take care of it. Tina didn't have much at that time but she did the best that she could.

After high school Steve and I had a falling out over something that seems pretty small now. I heard through Josh that Steve had some scrapes with the law. I think Steve had to be so responsible and grown up for his age for so long and take care of his younger brother that eventually, as he got older, he regressed back to acting like a kid.; kind of living his childhood in reverse. It had been years since he and I had talked, but I recently ran into him at a local bar. We talked a little bit and told each other how we were doing. It was kind of a distant conversation, but I'm hoping that he and I can one day be closer than we are now.

To this day Steve's younger brother Josh is still like family. We joke around all the time like brothers. When Steve and I were younger everyone would say that one day Josh would be big enough to push us both around. That day has arrived. Josh is at least 6'3" and weighs over 300 lbs. He just graduated high school and played almost every sport while he was there. He's a big guy, but very gentle and soft-spoken. Josh is one of the only people in my life that I know cares for me with no ulterior motives.

My best friend Levertis and I slowly drifted apart and took different paths in life. I started to pursue acting at Lansing Community College and he moved down to Mississippi for a while. He also had some trouble legally here and there. Levertis was always, in my eyes, too talented for his own good. He had many gifts that God had given to him and I always felt that he misused them. He was a talented athlete and very artistic. When we were young Levertis would draw pictures of Wolverine and other comic book characters that were good enough to be on a cover. It had been years since Levertis and I talked. The last time was after I graduated from high school.

I was down at LCC a few years ago rehearsing for a play I was in. I stepped outside for a cigarette during break and heard someone yell my name. I turned around and there was Levertis with a girlfriend. He and I hugged and he introduced me to her. We talked and he mentioned to me that he had a son. I was completely taken aback by that. To think that not so long ago we were children, and now one of us had a son. I still can't comprehend it sometimes, that both he and Jerrod have children. I look at myself and I'm far from being able to handle that responsibility. From that meeting on, we've tried to stay in touch. We've called each other occasionally, but it's hard when we are both so busy.

The very last time I talked with Levertis was only a few months ago. Gordon Galloway, the author of this book, was trying to get in touch with Levertis and his family to ask them some questions. Out of the blue I get this call from Levertis asking me if he needed to handle this guy who was coming around asking questions about my mom. It made me smile to know that after all this time he's still a loyal friend. That's one thing that I can always say about Levertis, is that he's loyal. He and I had a special friendship growing up, especially since my mother knew his family so well during her life.

This fall I'll be working on my first feature film. I called Levertis and asked him if he would like to play a small role in it. I actually wrote it with him in mind as it's a very personal story that has a lot of elements from my life and my growing up in it. Even the name, Fairview Street, is homage to my childhood. He agreed and expressed to me how much he wants to be involved in it. Even though we don't see each other as often as we used to, I know deep down he and I are still close and if worse came to worse we'd be there for each other.

The biggest thing to try to put in perspective is my mother. On March 24th, 1987 my life and my father's changed forever. I miss her in ways I can never even try to put into words. Language can't gauge and conquer my feelings when it comes to her.

Knowing everything that happened to her on that day, and the time she worked there leading up to her death, it's quite obvious that there's more then what is visible to the eye. Just the thought of all the harassment she went through makes me sick. I can't even fathom the day itself. It's too much for me. Just to know that somewhere the people that were responsible are thinking of other things, without a guilty conscious, kills me. I want justice.

I miss my mom and love her so much. There isn't a day that goes by when I don't think of her, and usually she crosses my mind many times everyday. The thing I miss most is the time that we didn't get to share together. The years and days are dead with no eyes. I miss seeing her grow and age into a sophisticated woman, for her to see her eight-year-old son become a man. It's a want that doesn't exist. It's a dream. Nothing and no one can bring her back, but maybe some questions can be answered. Maybe the people responsible for her harassment and murder can pay for what they did. They took a man's wife, the love of his life, and they took a young child's mother, his only hope of a soul. I want justice. For the time that has been lost, for her pain and ours.

I miss you Mom and the wasted moments in life that we can never share together. My life is full of moments that will never happen and memories that can never be born.

~ ~ ~

Michael McCallum has pursued acting since 1998. In that amount of time he has been a part of such plays as "Suburbia", "Spoon River Anthology", "Othello", "Romeo & Juliet" and many others.

He has also acted in over 26 films shot in mid-Michigan. These include, "Perception", "Money, Guns and Coffee", (which he also co-directed and co-wrote), "Under the Covers" (which he wrote, directed and edited) and "The Model Father". He is now working on his own first feature, titled "Fairview St." which will be shot later this year.

Michael writes and produces his own films under the company name of Rebel Pictures the name was derived from his admiration for Marlon Brando, James Dean and Paul Newman.

In addition to acting and filmmaking he also writes songs and poetry and puts together his own poetry chapbooks. Michael is planning to have his books published in the near future.

Josh Russel – not a little kid anymore.

Bill and Levertis clowning around.

GORDON GALLOWAY

Though I was born in Ionia, we moved to the farm south of town when I was four years old. I completed grades K thru 8 in the same one-room country school that my father and brother had attended.

As long as I can remember Ionia has been a prison town. I recall going with my father to boxing matches held inside of the Ionia Reformatory, which is Michigan's second largest walled prison. In those days I think the prison was pretty much self-supporting. There was a large prison farm where they grew their own food and maintained a large herd of Holstein dairy cattle. The prisoners provided the labor for all of this.

At the Ionia Free Fair the prison dairy cows were exhibited alongside all of the prize animals from other herds in the community and the inmate trustees were there to groom and show the animals. The inmates also exhibited a large collection of handicraft projects for the Fair crowd to see. I was always fascinated with their talent.

When I was growing up the local sheriff was a good friend of my fathers. He always had tales to tell of capturing escaped convicts. On more than one occasion I can remember law-enforcement officials with dogs spread across a farm field looking for a wandering trustee. I also can recall reading and hearing about the prison riots at Jackson and Ionia.

Ionia is now one of Michigan's fastest growing communities, in large part because the number of prisons there has increased to five.

Whether the economy is good or bad, a large work force is still an everyday necessity at the prisons.

One of those prisons in Ionia is the new Ionia Maximum Correctional Facility. It is called IMAX and that is where Edward Clay Hill now resides. It's a small world isn't it, that Clay now lives in my old home town. I would wager that his days there will not hold the fond memories that I had while living there.

There is still more to my association with the prison system than I have told you about. Back in the early '20's, or maybe just before, a man by the name of Bill Bannon saved my father from drowning in Woodard Lake. Dad had developed cramps and wouldn't have made it if Bannon hadn't rescued him. Bannon would later become Warden of Jackson Prison. So, I'm here to tell you this story because a future warden at Jackson kept Dad alive to meet my mother and hence forth, allow for my existence.

EDWARD CLAY HILL

At Ionia's IMAX Facility Edward Clay Hill (alias Mustafa Abdullah Ali) is in Level VI Administrative Segregation, the highest security level. He is in his cell 23 hours a day.

Five days a week he is permitted one hour per day in an outdoor cell. That cell is a fenced 12x12x12 cage. Hill is fed in his cell. A food cart is secured to his door. A food tray is placed in the cart and the cart is closed and locked. Then, the window area to his cell is opened and he can remove the food tray. The window is again secured before the food cart is removed. He has no direct contact with, nor access to the corrections officer.

Hill is allowed three showers per week. He has access to a barber once a month. Anytime he is out of his cell for any purpose, he is in full restraints (leg irons and belly chains). Restraints are applied before he leaves his cell. He is then pat searched and is escorted directly to his destination by two escorting officers. One officer holds his chains at all times.

Hill has access to the law library by requesting books that are delivered to his cell. He is allowed four non contact visits per month. He has access to a telephone to contact his attorney or for family emergencies. All mail, incoming and outgoing is screened for contraband. He has in-cell study via a TV monitor that receives internal broadcasts, including educational programming, religious services and the Warden's forum.

Hill's personal property is restricted.

As you might guess the cost of keeping Hill would probably alarm most taxpayers, but then how costly was it for the freedom and lack of security provided before at SPSM and other Michigan prisons? In terms of inmates murdered by other inmates, drugs, corruption, and the price of a corrections officer's life—maybe someone should have listened to Jack Welborn, Bill McCallum, Robert Halmich and all the others that were brave enough to press for change.

"Words Can't Express"

by Michael J. McCallum

I'm suppose to try and come up with
a poem for this book about my mother.

How can one take the task
of writing in one paragraph
        the sum of a lifetime of loss?

Growing up without a mother
and only the memory of her touch
        is a curse.
A bed of hellfire that never ceases.

It has formed
not only my personality
        but my way of interacting with people,
especially women.

I watch a family together
as I write this
        knowing I'll never experience that.
That togetherness.

That sense of family.

Growing as an adult
and having her see me
        in love for the first time,
graduate,
discover acting and the arts,
rise only to fall.
        That wish falls on deaf ears.

A wickedness I wish I could cut from my heart.
I walk
        and breathe pain.

And this is no exaggeration
no hyperbole.

I move about the world in a trance
wearing a thick mask of humor and laughs.

My mother was 28
when she was murdered.

As I near that age,
I feel
A mountain of guilt.

For not knowing her,
for not cherishing her when my 8 yr. old eyes should have.
Most of all for not saving her.

My little fists,
looking back,
wished they could have done anything.

Punch,
maul,
or even hold her pant leg back from the abyss
she was about to enter.

And so with that,
that mound of guilt
I'm now and forever
unrelenting on myself.

Too hard, too soon
and unremorseful
in the worst way.

Never near perfect
even if *perfect* was the air I breathed.

I stand motionless and motherless
in the shadows of my heroes.

Maybe that's why I feel such a close connection to
James Dean
(who lost his mother at a young age, 8 years old to be
exact)

and all the "Who-Ha's" and "Sorry's" and such
don't mean shit
when you have your mother stripped from you
and I too stripped from her.

In her dying moments,
after being brutally raped and defouled in every way
I wonder

If she felt that too
knowing she was in over her head
and not going to see her husband
or her son
Ever again.

Most likely.

The savages that killed her and took her
innocence

Raped,
and stained their own souls
with the blood of a man's wife
and an 8 yr. olds only sense of self.

I have no sense of that.

No grounding
No color
No earth

Nothing solid to put my faith in.

Seeing all too well
first hand the true harsh nature of men.
I see things through the eyes of a young man
with a bruised and battered
extremely old soul.

And my poor father did all he could
my Grandmother too
(God bless them).

He tried to pull me out of a black hole void
with no hands
no power to change what already happened.

For some
my mother's best friend,
my father,
and myself
The three that hurt the most in the aftermath.

It is easier to not talk
and open new wings on one's bleeding
pained self.

If memories are in a locked room,
Burn the house down.

The worst part is
knowing that the doers of the deed
are alive and well.

Without pity
without remorse.
A set-up of the worst kind
"If there's a hell below"...I think.

While I hope and pray to Jesus
for retribution
and maybe one day inner peace.

So the question was:
How can one take the task
        and sum up a lifetime of pain
in one paragraph?

        One can't
it's taken me a full page to scratch
        the surface of my sad,
trying to smile,
        sleeping on razors,
swallowing broken glass pills daily,
        tormented self.

        I'll never stop asking for answers.

        This rebel has a cause that drives his soul.

        I love and miss you Mom
with more misery and undying love
than all the angels in heaven could ever convey to you …

Michael Joseph McCallum

On the shores of Drummond Island.

BOOKS BY
GORDON GALLOWAY

with a 2003 Update to Each Story

SCARS OF A SOLDIER
VERNON HEPPE'S TRUE STORY

A Michigan farm boy with an eighth grade education is drafted into the Army during WWII, and becomes a man on the Pacific battlefields of Kwajalein, Leyte and Okinawa. Wounded four times, he received both the Silver and Bronze Star. With a keen sense of humor, Vernon Heppe tells about growing up on the farm and his adjustment to becoming a soldier. He describes combat in vivid detail and the memories that remain.

— 2003 UPDATE —

Vernon Heppe is experiencing the subtle realization that the number of his fellow veterans from WWII is quickly shrinking. Like many other veterans from that era, Vernon feels that Americans need to remember the sacrifices that were made in that war and perhaps his book has given him peace of mind in that respect. He is aware that his story will now be available to enlighten future generations.

Vernon still has contact with a few of the soldiers from his Unit. Arthur Nebe was Vernon's First Sergeant in combat and he felt that the story was very accurate. Although he wasn't mentioned by name Nebe distributed many copies of the book to his relatives so that they too could really know how it was for them.

Another old Army buddy, Don Viani, said, "I don't know if people of today will truly understand what the foot soldier went through or would even care. I can look in a mirror and know what our thoughts and agony were then and still remain today. Your story should be part of America's history. God Bless You."

Since Vernon's book was published he has had two hip replacements and a pacemaker installed. His wife, Kathleen, had a slight stroke a few years ago that limited some of her activities, but together they still live by themselves on the farm and enjoy life and their grandkids.

Vernon maintains a keen interest in current events around the world and has followed the various conflicts and wars America has participated in, since the big one that he served in. He notes that the common thread for the combat soldier through all these wars is that survival is based on doing what is necessary to keep you and your buddies alive and that patriotism and love of country are important, but far removed from your thoughts when a combat environment is your world.

Vernon and Kay Heppe

HILLBILLY POET

The boy was half Cherokee. He was raised by his blind grandmother until he was sent to an Episcopal boy's home. Ambitious and rebellious, he knew what he wanted out of life, and when the system wouldn't react to his needs, he simply bypassed it.

The mountains and rivers were his refuge and constructing power lines across this country became his vocation. This is a story filled with love, laughter and tears. The last chapter contains Ted Aldridge's poetry. Each poem remembers a special part of his life.

— 2003 UPDATE —

The autopsy revealed that it was a peanut lodged in his intestine that had started the infection in Ted's body; that was long after the fight with the infection had started. After some time in the Big Rapids hospital, he was transferred and spent many excruciating days in the intensive care unit at Spectrum Hospital in Grand Rapids.

I last saw my old friend hooked to a multitude of monitoring machines with tubes running to needles in his arms and an oxygen mask on his face. I knew that it was an existence Ted would have rejected if allowed a choice.

Mary was as dedicated and loyal as ever. She drove the 50 miles each day to be at Ted's bedside even as chances for recovery seemed futile. During the last days it was doubtful whether Ted was aware of anyone's presence. His life finally came to a peaceful end.

The funeral service was conducted by an old friend by the name of Charlie Tolliver. It wasn't a large gathering; mostly relatives, and a few friends and neighbors. One Amish couple sat in the back. At the end of the service the black pastor asked for anyone who wished to come forward with comments about Ted. One grandson got up and read one of Ted's poems. That stirred even more emotion from those that were already crying. Although I was mentally grasping for the right words to offer I sat silent and said nothing. I felt guilty afterwards for not being able to offer some words of kindness about such a fine friend, but I just was not mentally prepared to do that.

It was not long after Ted's death that Mary's sister moved in with her. Her sister's health problems were extensive, requiring kidney dialysis trips regularly and exhaustive care from Mary. Again Mary was as dedicated to caring for her sister as she was for Ted. Finally her sister also passed away.

For the last 6 years Mary has been a foster grandparent for the 1st grade at the local elementary school. She loves the children and has been very successful in aiding them in their reading and for those from broken families, she has brought some brightness and love.

We consider Mary a part of our family. She regularly is a guest at our family dinners and remains a cherished friend. For me, Ted will always be there with his devilish grin and his take on the state of the world. One reader put it right when he said, "This story is a diamond in the rough."

Mary Aldridge. Foster grandmother with her class.

THE BULLDOG

He was half Chippewa and left in a Grand Rapids orphanage. He also would become one of Michigan's most successful Sheriffs.

This is a true story of a Michigan Sheriff who uncovered corruption in his county that caused him to be a threat to some of the biggest names in Michigan politics. Trying to expose this wrongdoing cost him his career in law enforcement, his reputation and almost cost him his life. If you care about the truth, or if you just like a fascinating true story, you should read THE BULLDOG.

This book was enthusiastically endorsed by Michigan's longest serving Governor, William G. Milliken. Ted Nugent has also made a personal effort to promote it.

— 2003 UPDATE —

For Bob and Dee Blevins life is now good, but in the years following the publication of THE BULLDOG there were a series of personal difficulties that, using an understatement, made life challenging.

The meteorologists called it a straight-line wind, but the results looked more like the handiwork of a tornado. Although Bob and Dee's home was spared, the beautiful forest surrounding it was devastated from the storm. With chain saw in hand, Bob began the long-term process of cleaning up the fallen trees. Some could be used for lumber and others dismantled to be burned. On the north side of his beaver pond a large maple that branched into three large limbs had fallen victim to the wind. Bob was standing on the trunk as he finished cutting through the last limb. As the weight from the main trunk was removed with this final cut, the tree roots still in the ground, acting like a compressed spring, abruptly brought the trunk towards the vertical position. Bob was shot like an arrow through the air. He wasn't sure how long he lay unconscious, but when he came to he had an excruciating pain in his side. He lay there for a few moments, trying to access his injuries. The pain in his side was the result of falling on a small beaver sharpened sapling. Once that was removed he felt a little better. He noticed that his protective headgear was broken. As it was obvious he had hit his head on something, that hard hat had probably saved his life.

Bob knew he couldn't walk to the house, so he crawled over to the borrowed bulldozer that had its engine still running, and pulled himself up to the drivers seat. Once in the seat he felt a little relief from the pain and decided as long as he was up there he might as well do a little more bulldozing before going home. When he finally did stop working and go back to the house the extent of his injuries became more evident to him and Dee's critical eye. She questioned his judgment for continuing to work after it happened and as she had so many times in the past, pointed to the pitfalls of working in the woods by himself.

Medical tests revealed a concussion, 4 fractured vertebra and slight kidney injury from the stick in his side.

Although he made a reasonable recovery from his injuries in the woods, reoccurring fever and headaches that he attributed to the 'Gulf War' inoculations continued to plague him. He seemed extremely vulnerable to various ailments and when he picked up the flu bug late in the year, it just about destroyed his will to do anything. He spent the whole winter in the house being sick and miserable.

Dee had her own tragedy to deal with. An errant truck driver crossed the center lane hitting her parent's car head on. Her father was killed instantly and her mother's injuries made recovery questionable.

Adding to all of the above was the fact that both of their children were having marital problems.

Though Bob eventually went back to work at his job for the State, because physicians would not rate his back 100% healed with no limitation he was medically retired. Not long after the entire left side of Bob's body went numb. Mecosta General Hospital admitted him for a slight stroke and kept him hospitalized for 8 days while he continued to experience a series of mini strokes. Shortly thereafter it was discovered he had a heart blockage, and a stint was put in. After all this he still didn't feel well.

Making a long story shorter we will slip to the present day. Through intensive study on his own and through contact with a Doctor expert on the subject, for the past year Bob has been dedicated to a mineral and supplement program. His heart seems to have healed itself; he no longer takes blood pressure medicine or has headaches and he feels great. He is back in the woods chain sawing logs and plans an elk bow hunting trip to Colorado this fall. He and Dee are presently at the forefront of making others aware of the benefits of how this health care program has changed their lives.

Dee's mother has also made a miraculous recovery from her injuries and their children's lives seem to have become more stable.

Probably the highlight of the last years was when Bob's old Marine unit invited him and Dee to there formal military ball and honored him as the Marine of the Year, an honor normally reserved for the high ranking officers, not enlisted folks.

Of course there were other bright moments that came as a result of the book. The Michigan State Trooper that unexpectedly showed up at Bob's doorstep to shake his hand admiringly. There was the letter from the Lake County lady that said how proud she was of him for his work as Lake County Sheriff, and that now she knew the whole story after previously thinking he had left the county in disgrace.

It wouldn't be fair not to mention in this update that Count Fisher, who is now 80, and his lovely wife, Eve Renee are still making great music. Their latest gig was at the Grand Rapids Hilton Hotel where for several days of the week they provide the finest of jazz. It was there that my wife, Mary Ann, and I together with The Blevins' had the rare privilege of bringing in 2003 at a New Years Eve party with the Fishers'. The hotel chef provided a special meal for just the six of us. Dancing to the Count's music was great, but the highlight of the evening was when Bob reached over the dinner table and handed his old friend and former deputy his last Lake County Sheriff badge. Count had tears in his eyes and couldn't speak. After all these years I could see that their bond of friendship was as strong as ever.

Front left: Bob and Dee Blevins
In back: 'Count' and Eve Renee Fisher
Right side: Mary Ann and Gordon Galloway
Celebrating the arrival of 2003 at the Hilton.

RIVERS CHANGING
A SOLO CANOEING ADVENTURE

For 2400 miles from Billings Montana, to St. Louis, Missouri, Scott followed the rivers, the Yellowstone, the Missouri and the Mississippi. This solo canoe trip was the fulfillment of a young man's dream; however, on so many occasions its hazards created a nightmare. This solo journey was unique enough to generate widespread public interest along Scott's route. He was interviewed by at least six newspapers and featured on the nightly TV news in Omaha, Nebraska. He was also asked to make presentations to Boy Scout Troops in Yankton, S.D. and Lexington, MO.

— 2003 UPDATE —

In the years following the Missouri River trek Scott continued to pursue his solo adventures.

In 1998 we dropped him off in Toronto Canada and from there he traveled by train to Cape Gaspe in Quebec Province where the new International section of the Appalachian Trail was to be dedicated. Scott was the first hiker to cover that 600-mile stretch of trail southbound to Maine. From Maine he walked on the U.S. Appalachian Trail to Georgia.

In Atlanta he bought a canoe and paddled down the Chattahoochee River to Northern Florida. There he sold the canoe and continued his walk all the way to Key West Florida. Our family was there to meet Scott and watch the mayor present him the key to the city.

The following fall we left Scott and his canoe in northern Minnesota at the headwaters of the Mississippi. In December we met him at its end in New Orleans.

Scott's last excursion was a bit farther away. In New Zealand he back packed on some of that country's trails and made three breathtaking bungee jumps. Watching the videos of those awesome plunges was definitely an eye-opener for his family.

Scott next planned to canoe the Yukon River in Alaska with a fellow he met on the Mississippi River trip. It was in early summer however when he said, "Dad my priorities have changed." We found out what he was talking about shortly thereafter, the evening we were attending a Circle Theatre performance in Grand Rapids. His girl friend Jennifer was in the play and as the performers took there final bow Scott was up on the stage with an armful of roses and in the presence of a full house made his proposal of marriage. This October their first child was born.

With all the spirit and enthusiasm of a new adventure, Scott has tackled his role as a husband and a father. His enthusiasm for adventure has not dampened though, it's just not the center of his life now.

Scott and Jennifer Galloway.

Granddaughter Claire.

ABOUT THE AUTHOR

In 2004 Gordon Galloway celebrates 44 years flying airplanes, over 50 years raising sheep and the 10th anniversary of his endeavor to write true stories about Michigan people. His stead-fast partner in all of this is his wife Mary Ann.

Gordon Galloway with Col. Ray Even in front of one of the fighters they flew together in the Michigan Air National Guard.

Gordon's present flying assignment.

ORDERING
ADDITIONAL COPIES
OF

SCAR OF A SOLDIER

HILLBILLY POET

THE BULLDOG

RIVERS CHANGING

JOSEPHINE McCALLUM

SEND $10.00 *plus* $1.75 FOR SHIPPING AND HANDLING
(CHECK OR MONEY ORDER)
TO

DEERFIELD PUBLISHING
BOX 146
MORLEY, MI 49336